Best Hikes of the

TRINITY ALPS

and Yolla Bolly-Middle Eel, Castle Crags, and Snow Mountain Wilderness Areas.

by Art Bernstein

**Published by
Mountain N'Air**

This is a Mountain N'Air Book
Copyright in 1993 © by Art Bernstein

First Edition 1993
All rights reserved

Published in the United States of America by Mountain
N'Air Books, P.O.Box 12540, La Crescenta, CA 91224.
Phone (818) 951-4150

Cover photo: View of Sawtooth Ridge from Morris Meadows, by Art Bernstein.
Cover and book lay-out designed by Gilberto d'Urso

Library of Congress Cataloguing-in-publication data:
Bernstein, Art.
      Best hikes of the Trinity Alps / by Art Bernstein. –
1st ed. p. cm.
ISBN 1-879415-05-4
1. Hiking– California– Trinity Alps Wilderness– Guidebooks.
2. Trinity Alps Wilderness (Calif.)– Guidebooks. I. Title.
GV199.42.C22T752 1993
917.94'21– dc20   93-22446
CIP

ISBN:1-879415-05-4

Table of Contents

Yolla Bolly - Middle Eel Wilderness Area:

Castle Crags and Snow Mountain Wilderness Areas:

I. The Trinity Alps.

I first heard of the Trinity Alps back in 1968, at the University of Michigan. At the time, I was a total city boy, fresh from the backwoods of Detroit. My enrollment as a Forestry student traced to interests aroused during a 7 month stay in San Francisco in 1966, during the fabled "Summer of Love."

I had fallen in love, that long ago California summer. It was not with a person or ideology but with places like Yosemite, Lake Tahoe and Big Sur. In my little Plymouth convertible, I explored the Golden State as far south as Death Valley, and as far north as the Avenue of the Giants, up in the redwoods.

My principal professor and main mentor at the University of Michigan was a colorful gentleman by the name of S. Ross Tocher. Ross had grown up in the California wine country and earned his PhD in Recreation Resource Management at the age of 48. He's now 71 and we remain in fairly close touch.

Ross was a nationally recognized expert on America's loveliest places– places hardly anybody knew about. In 1968, he was convinced that California's most spectacular mountain scenery lay not in Yosemite or Sequoia but in a place called the Trinity Alps– or as it was known back then, the Salmon-Trinity Primitive Area.

Dr. Tocher enthralled us with stories about the Trinity Alps and it became one of those exotic places his students dreamed of visiting –or "achieving"– along with Montana's Bob Marshall

Wilderness, Alaska's Glacier Bay and Minnesota's Boundary Waters Canoe Area.

I not only achieved the Trinity Alps, I've spent the better part of 20 years exploring them. By coincidence, I ended up living less than two hours from my old professor's favorite mountains. I obtained work as a Forester, first in Yreka, California, then Grants Pass, Oregon, near the California line.

Back in 1970, far fewer people sought out back country trails and there were fewer roads on which reach them. Today's 3 mile hike often entailed 7 or 8 miles. Also, many trailheads weren't marked. You drove back and forth— or parked and beat the bushes on foot— until the trail appeared (which it sometimes didn't).

Old Ross Tocher, it turned out, spoke true and well. I do not mean to denigrate Yosemite or Sequoia, which I dearly love, but like those places, portions of the Trinity Alps compare favorably to any scenic locale on Earth.

The Trinity Alps; despite its size, beauty and national reputation; and despite having been a designated Primitive Area since 1932; did not enter the federal Wilderness system until 1984, 17 years after the system's creation. At 525,000 acres, it ranks as California's largest Wilderness and as the third largest in the lower 48 United States. Should the more popular Trinity Alps trails prove inadequate to elevate visitors to Hiker Heaven, 708 miles of pathway riddle the area, exploring an incredible variety of terrain.

A few Trinity Alps pathways crowd up during the height of the season— after all, it is California. On most, however, you'll likely have the place to yourself (Except, of course, during hunting season when even such remote routes as Jim-Jam Ridge and Fish Lake Creek fill to overflowing).

II. The Yolla Bolly-Middle Eel.

Not once did Dr. Tocher mention the Yolla Bolly-Middle Eel Wilderness. Despite its proximity to the stomping grounds of his youth, it was one place he somehow overlooked. Either that or he slyly left it for me to discover this wonderful area on my own.

As noted, the Trinity Alps were not yet a designated Wilderness when I first moved to the region. Northern California's only Wilderness Areas then included the Marble Mountains, west of Yreka; the South Warners, near the Nevada line; and

4

a place called the Yolla Bolly-Middle Eel. These days, the back country north of Sacramento boasts a dozen federal Wilderness Areas.

At 100,000 acres, the Yolla Bolly-Middle Eel ranked as California's smallest wilderness in 1970. Wilderness bills in 1977 and 1984 have since created areas with as few as 5,000 acres. The Yolla Bolly-Middle Eel, meanwhile, has grown to a respectable 154,000 acres. Its moderate size is offset by the longest name of any California Wilderness.

The Yolla Bollys differ markedly from the Trinity Alps, one range north, lacking its granite peaks and spectacular glacial lakes. Still, they claim their own special beauty which should not be overlooked by wilderness enthusiasts. The 7 Yolla Bolly-Middle Eel trails included herein, all rank confidently among the best hiking experience to be had anywhere.

III. Castle Crags and Snow Mtn. Wildernesses

The Wilderness bill of 1984 created a number of small Wilderness areas— and several huge ones (including Northern California's Trinity Alps and the Siskiyou). Two of the nicest and most interesting of the smaller Wilderness Areas are Castle Crags and Snow Mountain.

Once I made the decision to tack the under-reported and highly scenic Yolla Bolly-Middle Eel onto my book on the Trinity Alps, it seemed logical to include the two small Wilderness Areas peripheral and integral to these larger ones.

IV. On writing hiking guides.

Somebody once wrote a book on the trails near my home, up in southern Oregon. One path the author elected to describe was a particular favorite of mine. It wound dizzyingly up a mountain amid groves of the rare and beautiful Brewer spruce and the highest elevation knobcone pines I've ever seen. Its upper reaches peered down on a gorgeous glacial valley and across to a 2000 foot cliff with waterfalls fanning over its flank.

Here's what the writer said about it: "It climbs up one side of a ridge and comes down the other."

While most hiking guides— and I've read hundreds— do not take quite such a limited view, my quest for the perfect trail book has been frustrating. All too often, writers describe every rock, tree, wildflower and bend in the path while failing to capture an overall sense of the place or to concern themselves with the poetry it inspires or why one should bother to go there.

I have, over the years, drawn a few conclusions about trail guide writing. First, last, sideways, upside-down, always and above all, descriptions should make enjoyable and interesting reading. Enumerating every rock and tree puts readers to sleep faster than a chloral hydrate cocktail.

The majority of guide book users — even the most active outdoors enthusiasts — will not visit most trails they read about. When they do venture onto the beaten path, they're unlikely to walk with their nose buried a book. Most read the descriptions before starting out, at home, to decide which trails they'd like to try. And they may read it again, on returning, to compare notes.

The purpose of this book, is to screen out the worst of the area's trails, to provide a solid reference if you do hit the dirt promenade and to capture each locale's essence (although, admittedly, there are only so many ways to describe a lake or an uphill climb). Even if you never leave home, you'll know what it feels like to trod these magnificent pathways.

V. On selecting trails.

I hasten to forewarn the reader that my hiking habits, like other aspects of my personality, tend to be compulsive and quirky. I collect alpine lakes the way some people collect stamps. Although hiking may be the most important thing in my life —after my wife and children— once I've reached an objective, the challenge ceases and I feel no urge to hang around, except to catch my breath before starting back.

Thus, my marathon, 46 mile trek up the Stuart Fork, to Alpine Lake, Sapphire Lake and Stonewall Pass (Chapters 17 & 18), took only 3 days and 2 nights. This flabbergasted the Wilderness Ranger at the Weaverville Ranger District. Most *"normal"* people, he informed me, would spend a week on such a journey.

I've learned that visitors bring to the wilderness a diverse and enthralling array of personal styles, needs, interests and motivations. Mine aren't any more bizarre— or any more or less valid— than anybody else's.

I am reminded of a gentleman I met atop California's Mt. Whitney, in 1967. Wearing sandals, dress slacks and a white shirt with— yes— a bow tie, he'd hiked the exhausting, 10 mile trail carrying his lunch in a picnic basket. His reason for undertaking the climb up America's highest mountain outside Alaska? He was observing butterflies.

Despite their splendor, the Trinity Alps, Yolla Bolly-Middle Eel, Snow Mountain and Castle Crags Wilderness Areas contain many miles of trail best described as "klunkers." A klunker is a secondary or connecting route which is extremely long, traverses low elevation areas which boil in the summer, and/or does not lead to a significant destination. While many are perfectly dandy if you seek only solitude, a walk in the woods or a place to hunt, they hardly measure up to the best of this region.

Thus, I've exercised a certain amount of selectivity in preparing this book. It makes no sense to go to the trouble of writing about a trail if I can't come up with a good reason to visit it.

I've tried to organize this book in an orderly manner, grouping the trails into neatly tied, comprehensible clusters. Bear in mind that this merely reflects my personal style. The number of possible routes are infinite. One could, theoretically, enter the Trinity Alps at Tangle Blue Lake, hike every inch of its 708 mile trail system and come out at the Salmon Summit trailhead — without ever crossing a road.

VI. How to use this book.

The *"nuts and bolts"* information on each hike is condensed at the head of each chapter. It includes:

Maps. Maps include the trails themselves, surrounding features and the last connecting road or two. All are oriented with north up and the scale varies with the trail length.

Supplementary material is recommended. National Forest Wilderness maps cost a few bucks and show contour lines, associated features, connecting trails and roads. U.S. Geological Survey maps further detail steepness and minute twists and turns.

Many book and outdoors shops sell Forest Service and USGS maps. Forest Service maps can also be obtained at any Forest Service office. Their West Coast headquarters is at 630 Sansome, San Francisco, CA 95814. Phone (415) 556-0122.

The fact that I borrowed liberally from various Forest Service maps– some not generally available –in preparing this book, is herewith gratefully acknowledged.

Destinations. Each chapter head lists the important destinations visited by the main trail(s) described in the chapter– usually lakes, summits, meadows and creeks. They do not describe all possible destinations.

Trailhead location. This gives the township, range and section of the trailhead. A township contains 36 sections while a section consists of one square mile or 640 acres. Range designations refer to the Mt. Diablo Meridian, except for the western third of the Trinity Alps, which is based on the Humboldt Meridian. If the range says "East," it's the Humboldt Meridian.

On the Forest Service Trinity Alps map, you'll notice many unsquare sections– even a couple triangular sections. This is because (1) there was some very shoddy surveying done at the turn of the century and (2) the tidy grid lines of the more populated areas –the earliest areas surveyed– contained minute errors. By the time the survey worked its way to the wilderness– as late as the mid-1970's in places– some of the errors had become massive and the middle of nowhere seemed the least obtrusive place to correct them.

USGS 7.5" Topo: This refers to the appropriate USGS quadrangle map on which the trail appears, as described under "Maps", above. Such maps are more luxury than necessity since Forest Service Wilderness maps, available for all areas herein, contain contour lines and excellent detail. General National Forest maps do not. USGS maps have the best topographic detail but often aren't as up to date on trail or road locations.

Trail length. Each chapter head gives length as distance from the trailhead to the farthest objective or turnaround point. For loop trails, both the distance to the farthest point and the loop distance is given. For branching spur trails, the distance is given to the end of each. Distances are rounded to the nearest 1/2 mile.

Since flat maps show only horizontal distance, that is the length given in most cases. Bear in mind that a trail which rises 1000 feet over a horizontal mile (5280 feet), actually spans 5373 feet. Total distance is calculated with the old high school snoozer, "The square of the hypotenuse (total distance) equals the sum of the squares of the other two sides (horizontal and vertical distances). Don't forget to square root your answer.

Hiking time, being highly variable, is not given. A level mile, without pack, takes me 20 minutes while a fully loaded uphill mile can require an hour or more. While I leave many people in the dust, others leave me in the dust.

Access. Since life doesn't begin when you step out of the car, the trailhead drive is treated as part of the experience. The two word chapter head description of the access road is backed up, when necessary, by comments in the text.

Difficulty. In general, an "easy" rating means the path rises at a grade of less than 5% (5 feet vertical per 100 feet horizontal). The "difficult" ratings begin at 12%, or 12 vertical feet per 100 horizontal. It may not seem like much of a difference but a 5% grade translates to a rise of 265 feet per mile while a 12% grade gains 636 feet in a mile.

The very steepest trail pitches herein rise 1000 to 1500 feet per mile. A section of the Grizzly Lake Trail gains 600 feet in 1/4 mile, which comes to 2400 feet per mile or a 45% grade. The grade of the hillside which that trail climbs exceeds 100% (one foot vertical for every horizontal foot, or a 45 degree angle). In places, it approaches infinity (one foot vertical for every zero feet horizontal– or straight up and down).

Everything between 5% and 12% is considered "moderate." This is sometimes modified by the trail's overall length and the amount of level trail contained between upgrades. A 2 mile trail with a rise of 500 feet per mile obviously takes less out of you than a 5 mile trail with the same average rise.

Water. If a trail is less than 2 or 3 miles long, it's below 70 degrees out and the path is rated "easy," you probably needn't worry about water. Consider leaving a canteen or cooler in the car.

As for drinking from creeks, my personal rule is not to if there's habitation, cattle or heavy horse use between me and the stream source. Cattle grazing and horses are common in Northern California Wilderness Areas so never assume anything. Also, if I can't cross a creek in a step or two, or the water is stagnant, I won't drink from it. Icy springs in the deep woods or near a mountaintop are probably safe.

I tend to be a little reckless, however. Any water can make you sick and the means through which disease is spread are numerous. So except in an emergency, it's never wise to drink unpurified water.

Season. Since northwest California weather varies greatly, the seasons indicated are based almost entirely on elevation (modified somewhat if the entire trail climbs an exposed south or sheltered north slope), and should be considered extremely general. If it snowed down to 1000 feet a few days earlier, inquire before setting out on a 3000 foot elevation trail. Look for mud and high water in the wet season.

On the other hand, California winters can be marvelous, with clear, sunny days and temperatures which keep you cool yet invigorated. While most Trinity Alps trails don't open until June or July, areas of some trails— such as Lower Canyon Creek or the North Fork of the Trinity, may remain opened year round. The low elevation canyons of the Middle Eel resemble the surface of Hell in mid-summer and are best undertaken in spring or fall.

The high country offers a wonderful respite from mid-summer valley heat. Be prepared, however, for an occasional cold night. Also, summer thunderstorms, frequently born in these mountains, can be terrifying. Avoid ridgetops, open areas and standing under the highest trees if caught in a lightning storm.

To avoid hypothermia (the loss of body heat— which can be deceptive and fatal), always wear a jacket or sweater in cool, breezy weather and in the rain. You may work up a drenching sweat underneath the clothing but your body heat will stay where it belongs.

Elevation. Elevations are given in feet and most are rounded to the nearest 100. The figures in the chapter head represent the trail's highest and lowest points, not necessarily its beginning and ending elevations. If a trail rises 1500 feet, loses 100 feet, then rises another 1000 feet, the loss would be mentioned only in the text. If it rises 1500 feet, loses 500 feet, then rises 1000 feet, the loss would be mentioned here.

Ownership. The proprietary agencies have devoted much time, money and expertise designing, building and maintaining the routes under their jurisdiction. They are justifiably proud of their efforts and I am pleased to acknowledge them. I might add that the folks at the Forest Service have been uniformly patient, gracious and helpful in responding to my incessant barrage of questions.

Their kind assistance is available to you, as well. Pertinent Forest Service addresses are:

KLAMATH NATIONAL FOREST

Supervisor's Office
1312 Fairlane Road
Yreka, CA 96097   *(916) 842-6131*

Salmon River Ranger District (Tr. Alps)
PO Box 280
Etna, CA 96027   *(916) 467-5757*

MENDOCINO NATIONAL FOREST

Supervisor's Office
420 East Laurel St.
(Willows, CA 95988   *(916) 934-3316*

Corning Ranger District (Snow Mtn.)
1120 Solano St.
Corning, CA 96021

Covelo Ranger District (Yolla Bolly)
78510 Covelo Road
Covelo, CA 95428   *(707) 983-6118*

SHASTA TRINITY NATIONAL FOREST

Supervisor's Office
2400 Washington Ave.
Redding, CA 96001   *(916) 246-5222*

Big Bar Ranger District (Tr. Alps)
Star Rte. 1, Box 10
Big Bar, CA 96010   *(916) 623-6106*

Mt. Shasta Ranger District (Castle Crags)
204 W. Alma St.
Mt. Shasta, CA 96067   *(916) 926-4511*

Weaverville Ranger District (Tr. Alps)
PO Box T
Weaverville, CA 96093   *(916) 623-2121*

Yolla Bolla Ranger District (Yolla Bolly)
Platina, CA 96077   *(916) 352-4211*

SIX RIVERS NATIONAL FOREST

Supervisor's Office
507 F Street
Eureka, CA 95501   *(707) 442-1721*

Mad River Ranger District (Yolla Bolly)
Star Route, Box 300
Bridgeville, CA 95526   *(707) 574-6233*

Orleans Ranger District (Tr. Alps)
Drawer B
Orleans, CA 95556   *(916) 627-3291*

Phone. The number given in the chapter head will reach the nearest Forest Service Ranger Station rather than the Supervisor's office. Phone ahead if you plan to bring a horse, dog or large group. They are not permitted in all areas.

Directions. My goal, as noted, is to make each chapter interesting and readable, not bore the reader with minute details. The purpose of the "Directions" paragraph is to cram all such detail into as small a space as possible. Read it only if you actually plan to hike the trail. In most cases, only rough mileage estimates are provided, or none at all, unless an exact figure is crucial to locating the trailhead.

I might add that among the trailheads in this book, I failed to find only two using my trusty Forest Service Wilderness map. The Devils Canyon trailhead (Chapter 22) had been deactivated while road markings for the Tangle Blue Lake trailhead (Chapter 5), have greatly improved since my initial abortive foray.

VII. About hiking.

Before getting to the standard list of hiking do's and don'ts required in all books of this nature, I'd like to offer a few observations on a variety of subjects.

A free permit is required for entry to some areas of the Trinity Alps. Technically, it's required for all areas, except the Forest Service realizes this is not always feasible. Ranger stations near the most popular trailheads are open weekends in summer. Or phone ahead.

Since hiking offers a means of getting in shape, lack of conditioning shouldn't dissuade you. Start on easy or moderately easy paths and take your time. If you have a heart condition or other limitation, consult your physician first.

In my experience, weight control (and avoiding cigarettes) contributes more to success on the trail than does leg conditioning, although a winter jogging program can help immeasurably. I say this having hiked in all combinations of obesity, slimness, in shape-ness and out of shape-ness.

Physical stress is not confined to uphill tracks. The overweight or out of shape person is likely to notice upgrades more because they stress the cardiovascular system. Steep downgrades stress the knees, ankles and feet. That's when most blisters occur.

As I settle into middle age, I've developed a paranoia about dehydration. Back in my 20's, when nothing much tired me out, it didn't bother me if my mouth got a little dry. These days, I worry about fatigue, blood pressure, respiration and pulse rates, the color of my urine (dark yellow indicates dehydration), electrolytes, etc. I sip water constantly as I hike and have been known to slip a little Gatorade in my canteen.

Fluid retention, I've learned, can be enhanced by eating (and avoiding) certain foods. Grains (particularly wheat), milk and carbonated drinks should be kept to a minimum. Foods with high water content, such as celery or fruit, are the most beneficial. Also beneficial are foods rich in unsaturated oil, carbohydrates, acid and salt.

The objective is to get the nourishment into your blood as quickly as possible. Difficult to digest meals should be avoided and several small, nibbly snacks are far better than a Bacchanalian binge. Since foods cut into bite sized portions tend to get chewed more thoroughly, bring apple slices rather than a whole apple.

Peanut butter and jelly sandwiches, cookies, cheese sticks and the redoubtable trail mix are dandy, provided you keep the portions down. Liquefied foods are marvelous.

I'm pretty much of a minimalist when it comes to hiking and camping. On day hikes, I eat cold– and extremely light– meals. And I never, ever build a campfire, even when camping overnight.

The once popular heavy hiking boots with non-skid, Vibram soles are somewhat out of vogue. They may be environmentally damaging and need be worn only when rock climbing, in snow, or off the trail in wet weather. I find a lightweight running shoe infinitely more comfortable. I have extremely tough feet, however.

Lightweight hiking shoes of construction similar to running shoes, with stiffer, heavy-duty soles are available. They are generally good shoes that may get wet, but have the advantage of drying faster than the conventional leather boots.

I've always carried a few Band-Aids and gauze pads on my treks but have yet to use them. I also never had a blister until the third day of my Stuart Fork/Deer Creek excursion. Luckily, my companion brought a package of mole skin. It worked great– until I got home and tried to get the stuff off.

They no longer call it "mole skin," by the way. Now it's "blister adhesive" or some such euphemism. I guess the manufacturer ran into trouble with the mole rights lobby.

No hiking book is complete without a sanctimonious list of Boy Scout aphorisms: Never hike alone. Always bring matches. Inform someone of your destination. Never drink unpurified water. Get a doctor's OK. Carry toilet paper. Never leave home without a map, canteen, whistle, compass, rope for hanging bear bags, etc.

All these advices are wonderful, but I rarely follow them, and occasionally, as a result, I get in to trouble. I once got lost and spent the night at 8000 feet (not in the Trinity Alps), with no food, jacket, water or matches. After that, I vowed never to leave home without a basic survival kit. I haven't forgotten my lunch since.

The Forest Service offers a list of camping guidelines far more important than mine. As part of "no trace" camping, they ask the following:

1. Pack out all litter.

2. For human waste, select a spot at least 200 feet from open water and dig a hole six to eight inches deep. Cover it with dirt when done.

3. If a fire is absolutely necessary, build it in a safe, pre-viously used spot– preferably a fire ring at an established campsite. Wood collection can be environmentally damaging and portable stoves are recommended.

4. Pitch tents so no drainage ditch is required and replace rocks and other material removed from sleeping areas. Camp sites should be at least 100 feet from open water and animals should be pastured at least 200 feet from open water.

Finally, I love hearing from readers, and while I do my best to present up to date, accurate and clear information, I am not responsible for the outcome of other people's journeys. Part of the charm and adventure of these mountains is that things change. Roads may be gated without notice or become washed out or blocked, forests burn, boundaries get moved, things dry up or get muddy, bridges deteriorate or disappear, trails become overgrown, trees fall, trailhead and road markers vanish, new roads and trail get built.

These uncertainties, to me, enhance the experience. If I'm unable to reach an objective, which happens from time to time, I simply go somewhere else or go home.

VIII About the land.

The descriptions herein include a trove of natural history. Since several trails may penetrate the same area, and since each description is written to stand on its own, some repetition was unavoidable. The following concepts failed to find their way into the chapters or are spread thinly among many:

Geology. Three major Northwest California geological provinces are represented in this book: The Cascade Mountains, the Klamath Mountains and the Mendocino Mountains. Of these, the most spectacular and best known are the Cascades, capped by 14,161 foot Mt. Shasta, Northern California's highest peak; and by Mt. Lassen, the state's most recently active volcano.

The Cascades are characterized by extremely young volcanic peaks. Lassen National Park and Lava Beds National Monument superbly interpret the range's California portion. While no areas in this book overlap the Cascades, they are never far away and tend to make their presence felt. Sudden views of Mt. Shasta invariably surprise and delight.

The Klamath Mountains rank as northern California's oldest, remotest and most rugged geological formation. Dating from the Mesozoic Era (200 million years ago, when dinosaurs and my grandmother walked the Earth), they consist of an immense granite intrusion (granite is molten rock which hardened before working its way to the surface), possibly formed as part of the Sierra Nevada range. Other Klamath rocks include an ancient, metamorphosed lava known as greenstone, various schists and marbles and an occasional chunk of limestone.

Several theories attempt to explain the Klamath Mountains. The "Klamath Island" theory postulates that the range broke loose from the Sierra a zillion years ago and drifted out to sea, spending eons as a 20,000 square mile offshore island. Other theories suggest a subterranean connection between the Sierra, the Klamaths and Oregon's Blue and Wallowa Mountains. Or these systems may be totally unrelated.

Renowned for their rugged beauty and hundreds of alpine lakes, the Klamaths include such ranges as the Trinity Alps, Marble Mountains, Siskiyous and North Yolla Bollys. They do not include the South Yolla Bollys. The Klamath system's highest peak is Mt. Eddy, opposite Mount Shasta on I-5. Eddy reaches 9045 feet and makes a wonderful, non-wilderness hike, via the Deadfall Lakes and Pacific Crest Trails. The second highest summit is 9002 foot Thompson Peak (Chapter 1), keystone of the Trinity Alps range.

Northwest California's dominant system is the Coast Range, also called the Mendocino Mountains. Geologically, it is known as the Franciscan Formation, a region dominated largely by steeply folded and faulted sandstone. Extending from San Francisco Bay to Eureka, the range attains 8000 feet elevation in the South Yolla Bolly Mountains (Chapter 26), and 7000 feet at Snow Mountain (Chapter 34). Few summits exceed 5000 feet, however.

Unlike the Klamaths, the Coast Range forms a series of lineal ridges, cut by deep river valleys, parallel to the coast. The highest peaks line up along the system's eastern edge, rising abruptly from the Sacramento Valley.

Serpentinite is a granitic rock lacking in calcium and rich in heavy metals. The Klamath and Mendocino Mountains contain more of this rock than any other region of the United States (the largest single serpentinite formation occurs in Alaska's Brooks Range).

Both serpentinite, and the closely related peridotite, are the basement rock of the ocean floor. On land, they appear as elongated dikes and sills parallel to the coast. Such formations are believed to have been bulldozed from the sea by the advancing continental plate.

Douglas-fir, ponderosa pine, madrone and other common species won't grow on serpentinite or are stunted by it. Other species love it, however, including knobcone pine, western white pine, incense cedar and Brewer spruce. In the Klamath Mountains, Jeffrey pine occurs only on serpentinite. Numerous endangered shrubs and wildflowers grow nowhere else.

Many northwest California peaks over 5000 feet elevation have experienced glaciation. Glaciers form when annual snowfall exceeds melt and ice starts oozing down the mountain. The only glaciers these days are on Shasta, plus a few tiny ones in the Trinity Alps around Thompson Peak. Gouged out scars from former glaciers abound.

Glaciers not only carve out round-bottomed valleys as they move downward, they chisel sharply backward into the peak. This headward cutting creates cirque basins with steep, ampitheater headwalls rising above a bowl. Almost all the Klamath Mountains' alpine lakes occupy glacial cirques.

Botany. More important than memorizing long species lists, in understanding the botany of Northern California, is the concept of "association." This refers to plant species which consistently grow together in similar kinds of places. For example, while you'll never find black oak and mountain hemlock in the same stand, Douglas-fir and black oak hang out together all the time.

Associations range from the broadly geographic to the highly site specific. Several major geographic associations cross Northwest California:

The Pacific Northwest (Douglas-fir, mountain hemlock, whitebark pine, Western white pine, Oregon white oak, Pacific madrone).

The Sierra Nevada (Douglas-fir, sugar pine, incense cedar, white fir, foxtail pine).

The North Coastal (Pacific yew, tanoak, canyon live oak).

The California Coastal (California black oak, bay laurel).

The region also boasts several unique species, including Brewer spruce, Sadler oak and Shasta red fir. Knobcone pine and tanoak don't extend far outside the region.

Northern California mainstays as blue oak, toyon, redwood, Bishop pine and digger pine grow either at too low an elevation or too near the coast to turn up in the areas covered by this book. Should you run across a cypress, Alaska cedar, Pacific silver fir or subalpine fir, give me a call. While I've never seen these species in the Trinity Alps or Yolla Bollys, I suspect they're lurking there somewhere.

The chapter descriptions devote the most time to elevational associations. It's fascinating to observe the transition as a trail begins down in the oaks, madrones and Douglas-firs; works its way through the Shasta red firs, white pines and mountain hemlocks; and ends up in the foxtail pines and whitebark pines adorning the highest ridgetops.

The chapters devote more space to trees and shrubs than wildflowers. Because there are so many species of the latter, they're difficult to list without lapsing into a boring recitation. Also, I hiked many trails in August and September or later, when many wildflower species were no longer in bloom.

While I would love to include a complete, illustrated botanical key to every tree, shrub and herbaceous species, that would be impractical. If you are unfamiliar with the local botanical denizens, try looking up some of the following before taking to the trails:

CONIFERS

Cypress Family

Incense cedar, ground juniper, Western juniper

Pine Family

2 and 3 needle pines: Jeffrey pine, knobcone pine, lodgepole pine, Ponderosa pine.
5 needle pines: Sugar pine, western white pine, whitebark pine, foxtail pine.
White fir/grand fir, Shasta red fir, Brewer spruce, Douglas-fir, mountain hemlock.

Yew Family

Pacific yew.

HARDWOODS

Barberry Family

Oregongrape (dwarf)

Beech Family

Golden chinkapin, evergreen chinkapin, tanoak, scrub tanoak.
California black oak, canyon liveoak, interior liveoak, Oregon white oak, sadler oak, valley oak

Birch Family

Mountain alder, red alder, hazel

Buckthorn Family

Deerbrush/buckbrush, California coffeeberry, snowbrush, squaw carpet, whitethorn

Cashew Family

Poison oak

Currant Family

Red flowering currant, prickly gooseberry

Dogwood Family

Pacific dogwood, Western dogwood

Grape Family

Wild grape

Heath Family

Western azalea , California heather, evergreen huckleberry, Pacific madrone. green manzanita, pinemat manzanita, white manzanita , pacific rhododendron, salal

Honeysuckle Family

Blue elderberry, honeysuckle

Laurel Family

California bay laurel (Oregon myrtlewood)

Maple Family

Bigleaf maple, Douglas maple, vine maple

Olive family.

Oregon ash

Pea Family

Red Bud.

Rose Family

Cutleaf blackberry, Himalayan blackberry, wild blackberry, blackcap raspberry, thimbleberry.
Bittercherry, chokecherry, mountain mahogany,oceanspray, sweetbrier rose, little wood rose, Pacific serviceberry, Douglas spirea

Sunflower Family

Rabbitbrush, sagebrush

Willow Family

Quaking aspen, black cottonwood, willow

HERBACEOUS PLANTS

Barberry Family

Vanillaleaf

Bedstraw Family

Bedstraw

Birthwort Family

Wild ginger

Bleeding Heart Family

Bleeding heart

Broomrape Family

Ground cone flower

Buckwheat Family

Naked stem buckwheat

Buttercup Family

Buttercup, columbine, delphinium, marsh marigold, monkshood, pasque flower

Carrot Family

Angelica, cow parsnip, yampah

Forget-Me-Not Family

Hound's tongue, stickseed

Honeysuckle Family

Snowberry

Iris Family

Wild iris

Lily Family

Bear grass, cat's ear, fairy bell, fritillary, corn lily, fawn lily, glacier lily, tiger lily, Washington lily, wild onion, ookow/brodiaea, queen's cup, soap root, hairy star tulip, trillium

Milkweed Family

Milkweed

Mint Family

Mint, pennyroyal, skullcap, verbena

Mistletoe Family

Douglas-fir dwarfmistletoe

Morning Glory Family

Wild morning glory

Mustard Family

Milkmaid, Douglas wallflower

Orchid Family

Coral root, calypso orchid, rein orchid, lady's slipper

Pea Family

Clover, lupine

Phlox Family

Gilia, phlox

Pink Family

Indian pink

Pitcher Plant Family

Darlingtonia

Primrose Family

Shooting star

Purslane Family

Miner's lettuce, pussy paw

Rose Family
Cinquefoil

Saxifrage Family
Saxifrage, woodland star, umbrella plant

Sedge Family
Bulrush

Sedum Family
Stonecrop

Snapdragon Family
Brooklime, Indian paintbrush, monkey flower, great mullein, pentstemon

Sunflower Family
Arnica, aster, wandering daisy, mule ears, star thistle, bull thistle, yarrow

Violet Family
Western dog violet, violet

Waterleaf Family
Waterleaf

Water Lily Family
Pond lily

Wintergreen Family
Pine drop, prince's pine, white veined shinleaf

MAMMALS.

Observation of wildlife is a prime reasons people take to the Wilderness. While most mammals— except for deer and chipmunks— tend to be quite elusive, a sharp eye frequently pays off. The following is an abbreviated list of Northwest California's most common mammals. It presumes you already know what the species looks like.

Opossum. This sluggish marsupial, which has a terrible problem steering clear of cars, does well in a surprising variety of environments. It nests in hollow trees and rock crevices and can use its tail for swinging. The species was introduced to Western North America— for some inexplicable reason— at the turn of the century.

Deer. The Columbian blacktail, North America's second smallest deer, belongs to the same family as domestic cattle. Since it has a cloven hoof and chews its cud, it is the Trinity Alps' only kosher wildlife species (there are no mountain goats or bighorn sheep).

This highly adaptable species turns up in many low and middle elevation environments— especially open areas with forest cover nearby. They actually benefit from logging clearcuts.

In the Trinity Alps and Yolla Bollys, deer can get extremely pesky, prowling the edge of campsites in quest of salt and food handouts. Fortunately, most campers are more intrigued than annoyed by their presence. Do not feed them.

Elk. Yes, there are elk in the areas covered by this book, but they're extremely scarce. These majestic creatures claim to be California's largest land mammal. In contrast to the diminutive blacktail, a bull elk can stand seven feet tall at the shoulder, with antlers 5 feet long. They have a much stronger herding tendency than deer.

Cattle. These are the bane of the Trinity Alps, turning up in nearly every basin with open meadows. Aside from destroying the natural ecosystem and poisoning the water, they're pretty much harmless. Sharing a campsite with a herd of cattle can be annoying. They moo loudly and often at dusk and in the morning, although a loud yell usually runs them off.

Bear. The story of how the last grizzly was eradicated from California is well known. Suffice to say, any bear you meet will be a black bear— a much less aggressive species.

I've seen only a single bear on the trail (plus two from the car), in my years of wilderness hiking. Bear sign turns up often, however— usually in the form of seed laden droppings.

While I've never had a bear enter my camp, or heard of anybody being menaced or injured by one in California (they usually hightail it if they see a human), they are not to be trifled with. They frequently rummage through camps in quest of food and have been known to damage parked cars if they see something edible through the window. The Forest Service recommends you hang all food at night, well out of reach.

Cougar. These may be the most beautiful— and most elusive— of all Northern California's large mammals. I've been lucky enough to see cougar three times over the years. Many veteran hikers have never been so honored.

The cougar is North America's largest cat. Despite its secretive behavior, it is found in virtually every state.

Bobcat. Bobcats are much smaller than cougars and have stubby tails and pointed ears. You're far more likely to encounter one.

Coyote. These relatives of the dog are extremely common in Northern California, although they prefer open range and desert to high mountains. They're much more solitary than wolves and eat mostly small rodents.

Fox. I've seen only one fox in the wild but it was well worth the wait– it's huge, fluffy tail would put even the showiest squirrel to shame. This canine species is more cat-like than dog-like in its behavior. Although lacking retractable claws, it stalks, pounces and climbs trees.

Raccoon. This common, adorable animal can be a pest, raiding camps and chewing through and rifling packs. It's another good reason to hang your food at night. Unless you sneak up on one of these nocturnal critters with a flashlight, you're not likely to meet once face to face. Raccoons belong to the same mammalian order as dogs and cats (Carnivera), and are quite compatible with human populations.

Ringtail cat. This racoon relative is even more nocturnal and secretive than its masked cousin. I've not only never seen one, I'm not convinced they exist. I suspect it's a massive hoax by a gang of zoological pranksters.

Otter. This fish eating member of the weasel family lives in low and middle elevation river areas. If you're lucky enough to see one, usually early in the morning, you'll find it among the most entertaining and charming of all mammals.

Rats and mice. These are by far the most abundant mammals. They hold the unenviable distinction of occupying the bottom of the food chain (although their populations are so enormous, the likelihood of any given mouse getting eaten is not that great).

Despite their numbers, you're unlikely to run across one since they are nocturnal and extremely wary. Don't look for the familiar European house mouse or Norway rat in the wilderness. More likely, you'll find an All-American furry tail variety such as a kangaroo rat, harvest mouse or meadow vole.

Tree squirrel/ground squirrel/chipmunk. 98% of the mammals seen from the trail will fall into one of these categories of day feeding nut munchers. Tree squirrels have big bushy tails (except for flying squirrels), and climb trees. Ground squirrels can have bushy tails or not and come either plain or in stripes. Some climb trees. All chipmunks are striped but unlike striped ground squirrels, the stripe extends to the head.

Beaver. You're more likely to notice the work of beavers than the animal itself. Beaver dams, impoundments and lodges are a unique treat even if their creators never poke their noses out of the water.

Muskrat. This aquatic mammal hangs out in still waters along riverbanks. It is trapped for its fur and secretes a musk scent used in perfume.

Porcupine. Porkies became my favorite mammal following a zoo demonstration. The slow, wary beasts can reach up to 40 pounds. Despite their infamous defense mechanism, they can be quite friendly under the right circumstances. They adore young growth forests, much to the chagrin of foresters.

Rabbits. Bunnies are smaller than hares and behave differently. The former nests in underground dens while the latter nests above ground in shallow depressions. You're more likely to see a cottontail while hiking, except in the lower areas of the Yolla Bolly, since hares prefer more open county.

Bigfoot. I love the idea of bigfoot and am convinced that a large, intelligent, herbivorian primate could exist undetected in the wilderness back country of the Northwest. Especially when you consider that the 708 miles of trail in the Trinity Alps barely scratches the surface.

I've never seen a bigfoot but know a couple people who have. Don't try to tell them it was their imagination or a bear.

Mosses, ferns, lichens, fungi, insects, arachnids, mollusks, reptiles, amphibians, birds, protozoa.

While these are all fascinating subjects, I had to cut this section short somewhere. I'd especially love to have included a litany of bird species observed on my back country rambles. The trouble is, there are even more bird than plant species and birds tend not to hang around. Were I to report, for example, that I spotted a spotted owl or saw a saw-whet owl, the reader would be unlikely to repeat the experience.

Rattlesnakes. While the average reader can live without detailed information on the rough skinned newt or blue tailed skink, the western rattlesnake is another matter. Only our friend the black bear evokes more curiosity, rumor and apprehension.

Trust me on this— there's little to worry about. In my 1/2 dozen or so rattlesnake encounters, they've been even more anxious than I to avoid confrontation. Keep an eye out for them in grass, brush, near bridges or when stepping over logs or rocks. Should you spot (or hear) one, walk a wide berth around it. They're pretty slow and have a striking range of only a couple feet.

The recommended snake bite treatment is to apply ice and get to a doctor within two hours. Neither is very feasible at a place like Morris Meadows (Chapter 18), which is crawling with rattlers. Keep in mind that they don't always get the venom out, and that a healthy adult can usually shake off a snake chomp. Victims should avoid walking and either be carried out and/or or have help summoned. If a small child or someone with asthsma or a heart condition gets bitten, it should be taken extremely seriously.

The practice of killing rattlesnakes is, to me, unconscionable. Bear in mind that you're the intruder, not the snake.

IX. LAKE SUMMARY/ANGLING INFORMATION.

Since I couldn't catch a fish to save my life, any assessment I might make on fishing in the Trinity Alps and Yolla Bollys would be useless. I hasten to add that to most anglers, the high lakes of the Trinity Alps, and wilderness streams such as the New River and the North Fork of the Trinity, offer some of the premiere fishing anywhere.

The vast majority of California's alpine lakes contain Eastern brook and/or rainbow trout. A few turn up an occasional brown, cutthroat or golden trout. A couple lakes were stocked with Arctic grayling years ago, on an experimental basis, but you're not likely to run across one.

In the major streams and rivers, look for brook, rainbow and brown trout higher up; with steelhead, king and silver salmon, a few minnows and the inevitable suckers and eels lower down. Bass and sunfish sometimes turn up in low elevation, warm waters. Lucky anglers may land a coastal cutthroat trout or green sturgeon in the main rivers, outside the Wilderness Areas near the coast.

Most high (and low) lakes in Northern California are stocked annually, or nearly annually, by the California Department of Fish and Game. You'd be amazed at the remote pools they visit regularly on their aerial drops of finny fingerlings.

Virtually no high lakes boast honest to gosh native fish populations. There's no way a trout could find its way to a place like Grizzly Lake without ropes and carabiners. Furthermore, there is little natural reproduction in most lakes, either by planted or native stock.

The present 6 year drought (as of 1992) has caused lake levels to drop, water temperatures to rise and slowed the replacement of stagnant water. This has impacted fish survival and angling success in the smaller, shallower lakes. I encountered only one lake which had dried up altogether (Little Castle Lake– Chapter 33).

As of 1992, much of the Yolla Bolly-Middle Eel Wilderness had been closed to fishing since the notorious 1964 flood washed away its spawning gravels. By the early 1980's, the gravels– and the summer steelhead for which the Middle Eel was famous– appeared to be making a comeback. Since the drought, however, steelhead runs have declined alarmingly. It's difficult (but not impossible), to spawn in a river with no water.

The Middle Eel is closed to fishing below Uhl Creek, the North Fork Middle Eel is closed below Willow Creek, and Balm of Gilead Creek, a major Eel tributary, is closed. There are other closures as well so phone ahead before undertaking a fishing trip to the Yolla Bolly.

Most material on Trinity Alps fishing relies heavily on a pamphlet called "Angler's Guide to the Trinity Alps," put out by the California Department of Fish and Game. It hasn't been available in years and hasn't been revised since 1969 (I stashed away a few copies when I worked for the Department in 1970). The 1969 guide did not include the area west of Limestone Ridge while much of the present Wilderness was covered in a companion pamphlet called "Angler's Guide to the Salmon and Scott Mountains."

The following table includes only lakes mentioned in the text– some 95% of the lakes in the Trinity Alps, Yolla Bollys, etc. Where lakes mentioned in the text are omitted, it is because they contain no fish. In a few instances, as with Adams Lake, I made the subjective judgment– with which you are free to take exception– that they were not worth writing about.

Lakes	Chap.	Acres	Depth	Elev.
1. Alpine	18	14	26	6150
Steep, rocky shore, good brook & rainbow.				
2. Anna	17	4	56	7500
Barren, steep shore, good brook trout.				
3. Big Bear	6	28	73	5800
Brushy outlet, deep end. Lots of brook, rainbow.				
4. Li. Bear	6	6	74	6200
Deep cirque. Good brook & rainbow.				
5. Wee Bear	6	5	14	6150
Brook trout.				
6. Black Rock	25	2		6200
Brook trout. Much drought mortality.				

Lakes	Chap.	Acres	Depth	Elev.
7. Boulder	13	8	27	6100

Brushy, lily pads. Good Brook, rainbow.

| 8. Boulder Cr. | 20 | 5 | 17 | 5750 |

Rocky. Fair rainbow, brook.

| 9. E. Boulder | 4 | 32 | 60 | 6700 |

Barren, grassy shore. Rainbow,brook, brown. Natural reproduction.

| 10. High Boulder | 4 | 1 | 11 | 6850 |

Grassy. Natural brook reproduction.

| 11. L. Boulder | 13 | 4.5 | 19 | 6100 |

Brushy, lily pads. Good brook & rainbow.

| 12. M. Boulder | 4 | 6.5 | 12 | 6500 |

Private. Grassy shore, natural brook reproduction.

| 13. U. Boulder | 4 | 7 | 11 | 6850 |

Open, grassy shore. Natural brook reprod.

| 14. W. Boulder | 4 | 7 | 29 | 7000 |

Rainbow, brook.

| 15. L. Canyon Cr. | 20 | 14 | 56 | 5600 |

Rocky shore. Popular. Good brook, rainbow, brown. Excellent fishing in creek.

| 16. U. Canyon Cr. | 20 | 25 | 86 | 5690 |

Very rocky. Good brook, rainbow, brown, golden trout.

| 17. Caribou | 11 | 72 | 72 | 6850 |

Rocky, meadowy shore. Lots of brook, rainbow and brown.

| 18. Li. Caribou | 11 | 3 | 16 | 7150 |

Brook trout.

| 19. L. Caribou | 22 | 8 | 3 | 6500 |

Steep shore, brushy outlet. Rainbow, brook.

| 20. M. Caribou | 11 | 5 | 10 | 6600 |

A few brook trout.

| 21. Castle | 32 | 47 | 120 | 5400 |

Brushy. Excellent rainbow and brook. Little Lake Castle was dry.

| 22. Conway | 10 | 1 | 3 | 6850 |

Brush, lily pads. Brook trout.

| 23. Deer | 17 | 4.5 | 19 | 7150 |

Grassy, open basin. Large brook trout.

| 24. Diamond | 17 | 2.5 | 13 | 7200 |

Rocky shore. Good brook trout.

| 25. Doe | 7 | 4.5 | 15 | 7000 |

Deep, brushy basin. Good, small brook.

| 26. Echo | 17 | 2.5 | 17 | 7250 |

Open shore, steep headwall. Brook.

Lakes	Chap.	Acres	Depth	Elev.
27. East Fork	19	2	11	5850

Brook & rainbow.

| 28. Emerald | 18 | 21 | 68 | 5500 |

Rocky shore. Brook,rainbow. Excellent fishing in Stuart Fork.

| 29. Fish | 2 | 3 | 4 | 6050 |

Brook, Arctic grayling.

| 30. Forbidden | 20 | 1.5 | 18 | 6250 |

Steep, rocky shore. Small brook.

| 31. Foster | 10 | 5.5 | 20 | 7250 |

Deep, rocky basin. Good brook.

| 32. Found | 13 | 2.5 | 9 | 7250 |

Rocky, grassy shore. Brook trout.

| 33. Fox Creek | 4 | 9.5 | 38 | 6600 |

Open, meadowy shore. Good brook, brown, rainbow. Natives.

| 34. Granite | 15 | 18 | 64 | 6000 |

Very brushy shore.

| 35. Granite | 7 | 6.3 | 12 | 6400 |

Mucky, brushy. Brook and rainbow trout.

| 36. Grey Rock | 2 | 11 | 20 | 5950 |

Brook trout.

| 37. U. Gr. Rock | 32 | 4.5 | 20 | 6300 |

Brook trout.

| 38. Grizzly | 1 | 42 | 173 | 7100 |

Rocky shore. Popular. Large rainbow. Good fishing in creek.

| 39. Heart | 32 | 1 | 11 | 6050 |

Rocky shore. A few brook.

| 40. Hidden | 3 | 3 | 15 | 6700 |

Brushy, wooded shore.Brook trout.

| 41. Horseshoe | 1 | 2 | 22 | 6850 |

Rocky, brushy shore. Brook trout.

| 42. Josephine | 12 | 17 | 47 | 5800 |

Private.

| 43. Kalmia | 20 | 1 | 13 | 7500 |

Brook Trout. Very remote.

| 44.'L' Lake | 20 | 2 | 17 | 6350 |

Rocky, meadowy shore. Excellent, small brook.

| 45. Landers | 10 | 6 | 17 | 7100 |

Rocky, open shore. Fluctuates. Fair brook and rainbow.

| 46. LilyPad | 14 | 2 | 8 | 6300 |

Marshy, lily pads. Brook trout.

Lakes	Chap.	Acres	Depth	Elev.
47. Lion	10	3	37	7000

Rocky basin. Large rainbow and brook.

| 48. Lois | 1 | 2.5 | 40 | 7650 |

Very rocky basin. Brook trout.

| 49. Long | 2 | 6 | 2 | 7100 |

Marshy. Brook trout.

| 50. Long Gulch | 2 | 14 | 21 | 6450 |

Much shoreline vegetation. Fair to good brook.

| 51. Luella | 17 | 2.5 | 13 | 6950 |

Brush, willow. Good brook.

| 52. Big Marshy | 4 | 5.5 | 15 | 6400 |

Wide, marshy basin. Brook trout.

| 53. Little Marshy | 4 | 1.5 | 6 | 6100 |

Marshy. Brook trout.

| 54. Mavis | 4 | 3.5 | 16 | 6700 |

Green water, meadowy. Brook, brown trout.

| 55. McDonald | 7 | 4 | 15 | 6000 |

Meadowy. Good brook and rainbow.

| 56. Mill Cr. | 4 | 3 | 16 | 6600 |

Open, barren shore. Good brook trout.

| 57. Mirror | 18 | 14 | 25 | 6600 |

Steep, Rocky shore. Large brook, rainbow.

| 58. Morris | 18 | 3.5 | 31 | 7350 |

Brook trout.

| 59. Papoose | 21 | 28 | 70 | 6660 |

Grassy, rocky shore. Submerged bench. Excellent large rainbow.

| 60. Red Cap | 23 | 5 | 20 | 5200 |

Muddy, weeds. Big brook trout.

| 61. Rock Lake | 23 | 2 | | 6200 |

Steep shore, brushy outlet. Brook trout.

| 62. Md. Rush Cr. | 19 | 1 | 12 | 6540 |

Meadowy pond. Brook, rainbow trout.

| 63. Up. Rush Cr. | 19 | 2 | 44 | 6950 |

Very rocky shore. Thaws very late. Good brook, rainbow.

| 64. Salmon | 11 | 1.5 | 13 | 7150 |

Brook trout.

| 65. Sapphire | 18 | 43 | 200 | 6100 |

Very steep, rocky shore. Brook, rainbow, brown.

| 66. Shimmy | 14 | 1.5 | 10 | 6400 |

Grassy, weedy shore. A few brook trout.

Lakes	Chap.	Acres	Depth	Elev.
67. Section Line	4	2.5		7100

Steep, rocky shore. Small rainbow, brook trout.

| 68 Smith | 18 | 24 | 167 | 6950 |

Steep, rocky shore. Good brook, rainbow.

| 69. Snowslide | 11 | 10 | 42 | 6700 |

Steep, rocky shore. Brushy at lower end. Good brook, rainbow.

| 70. Li. S. Fork | 21 | 9 | 21 | 5950 |

Rainbow trout.

| 71. L. So Fork | 3 | 4.5 | 23 | 6700 |

Grassy shore. Rainbow, brook.

| 72. U. So Fork | 3 | 6.5 | 34 | 6720 |

In woods. Steep headwall. Many brook and rainbow.

| 73. Square | 26 | 1 | | 7000 |

Open, grassy shore. Brook trout.

| 74. Stoddard | 7 | 25 | 84 | 5900 |

Brushy, meadowy shore. Good brook and rainbow.

| 75. U. Stoddard | 7 | 1 | 14 | 6400 |

Brook trout.

| 76. Sugar pine | 9 | 9 | 43 | 6600 |

Brushy, rocky shore. Good brook and rainbow.

| 77. Summit | 17 | 13 | 24 | 7350 |

Open, rocky, steep basin. Fair to good brook and rainbow.

| 78. Tangle Blue | 5 | 12 | 17 | 5700 |

Brushy shore, green water. Excellent large, brook & rainbow.

| 79. Tapie | 13 | 1.5 | 15 | 6500 |

Brushy shore. Good brook trout.

| 80. Telephone | 4 | 3.5 | 30 | 6900 |

Fluctuates. No outlet. Rainbow.

| 81. Timber | 33 | 2 | 15 | 6000 |

Good brook trout.

| 82. Trail Gul. | 2 | 10 | 47 | 6400 |

Meadow and brushy shore. Popular. Large rainbow, brook. Natural reproduction.

| 83. Union | 10 | 3.5 | 14 | 6050 |

Brushy shore, green water. Brook trout.Good fishing in creek.

| 84. Virginia | 4 | 3 | 16 | 6900 |

Meadowy, open shore.Good brook, rainbow, brown trout.

| 85. Ward | 12 | 5.5 | 23 | 7100 |

Rocky, grassy shore. Good brook trout.

| 86. Washbasin | 4 | 11 | 85 | 7000 |

In woods. Brook trout.

87. E. Weaver ....19 ....1 ....12 6350
Brook and rainbow.

88. N. Yolla Bolly ....25 ....1.5 6400
Deep basin. Brook trout. Much drought mortality.

Acknowledgments and bibliography. This book would not be nearly as thorough or interesting without the considerable assistance of a number of individuals and resources. Above all, let me again acknowledge the patience and helpfulness of the staff of the USDA Forest Service. Among their many employees I've pestered over the years, a few stand out: John Sanstrom at the Weaverville Ranger District, my friend Chuck Smith at the Scott River Ranger District, Al Molitor at the Salmon River Ranger District and Vaughn Hutchins and Mike Van Dame at the Covelo Ranger District.

I would also like to thank Brian Boothby, an enthusiastic companion on a number of these excursions; Glenn McNeil, a perceptive and articulate friend who spent many years living in and exploring the Trinity country; and Gilberto d'Urso who put me up to all this.

Finally, I confess to having consulted a number of references in finalizing the material herein, including the works of those who preceded me in writing about the Trinity Alps and Yolla Bollys. I cite the following:

Bailey, E.H., *"Geology of Northern California,"* (California Division of Mines and Geology– Bulletin 190, 1966).

Bernstein, Art, *"Best Day-Hikes of the California Northwest,"* (Mountain N'Air Books, 1991).

Bernstein, Art, *"Native Trees of the Northwest," (Magnifica Books, 1988).*

Linkhart, Luther, *"The Trinity Alps," (Wilderness Press, 1983).*

Lorentzen, Bob, *"The Hikers Hip-Pocket Guide to the Mendocino Highlands,"* (Bored Feet Publications, 1992).

Lowe, Don and Roberta, *"41 Northwest California Hiking Trails,"* (Touchstone Press, 1981).

Niehaus, T.F., and Ripper, C.L., *"Peterson's Field Guide to Pacific States Wildflowers,"* (Houghton-Mifflin).

The Trinity Alps
Wilderness Area

Trinity Alps Wilderness Area

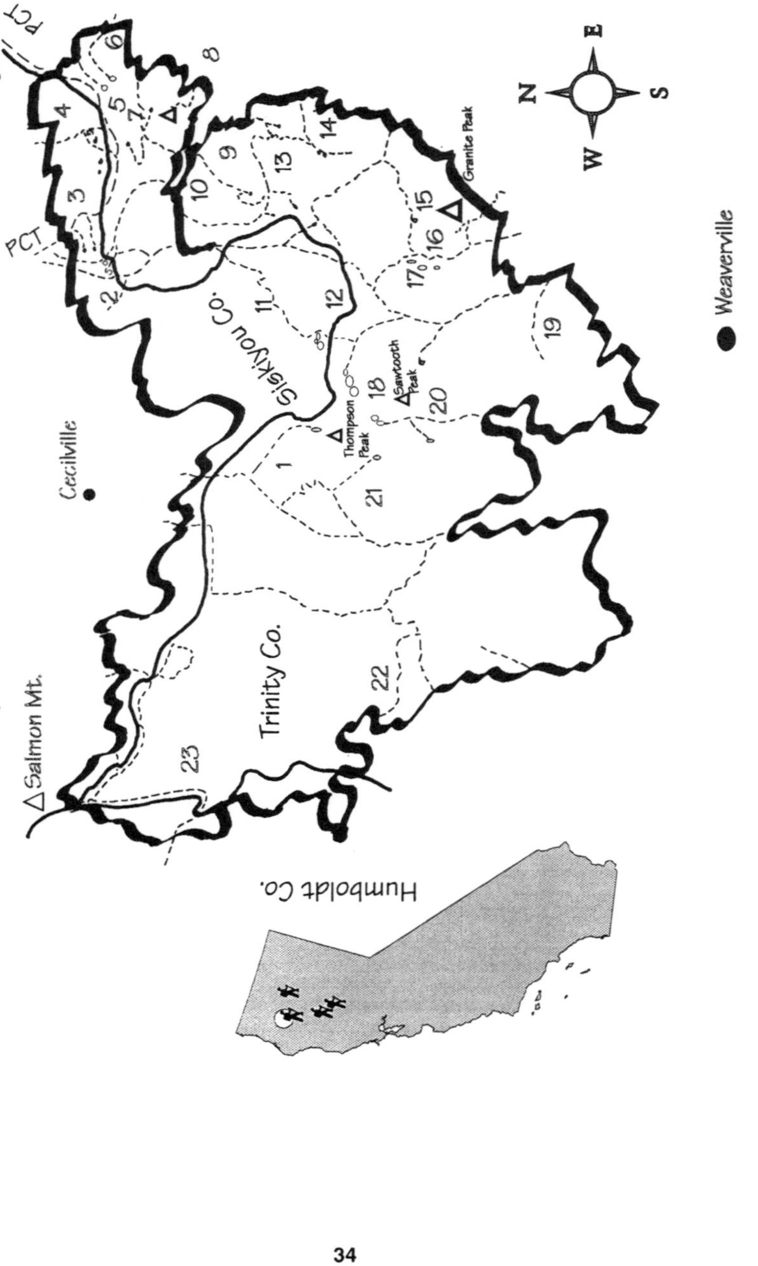

Callahan •

PCT

△ Salmon Mt.

Cecilville •

Siskiyou Co.

Trinity Co.

Thompson Peak

Sawtooth Peak

Granite Peak △

1 2 3 4 5 6 7 8 9 10 11 12 13 14 15 16 17 18 19 20 21 22 23

N
W — E
S

• Weaverville

Humboldt Co.

Destination: Grizzly, Louis, Little South Fork Lakes
Location: R37N-T11W-Sec. 23
USGS 7.5" Topo: Thompson Peak
Length: 6 miles
Water: OK
Access: Good paved and gravel roads
Season: June through October
Difficulty: Difficult
Elevation: 4400 to 7100 (with an 1100 foot drop)
Ownership: Klamath NF
Phone: (916) 467-5757

Directions: *Take Highway 3 from Yreka or Weaverville, to the town of Callahan. There, turn onto the South Fork Salmon Road to Cecilville. The South Fork Road may also be reached by taking 299 from Eureka, turning onto Highway 96 at Willow Creek, picking up the Salmon River Road at Somesbar and bearing south (right) at Forks of Salmon.*

Three miles east of Cecilville (27 miles from Callahan), turn up road 37N24. After 4 miles, just over the bridge and at the end of the pavement, you'll come to the signed turnoff to the China Gulch trailhead (right, onto 37N07). It's 6 winding miles to the trailhead, past several signed intersections. The trailhead area has infinite parking along the wide shoulders.

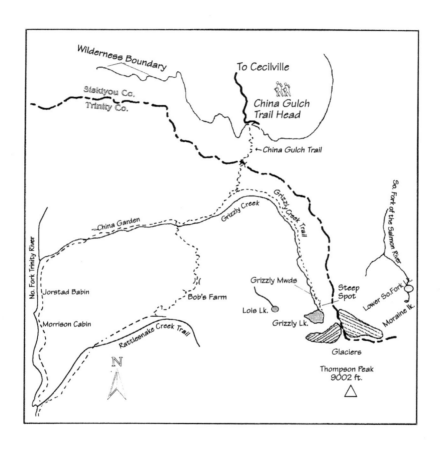

Wilderness Boundary

To Cecilville

Siskiyou Co.
Trinity Co.

China Gulch
Trail Head

←China Gulch Trail

Grizzly Creek

Grizzly Creek Trail

So. Fork of the Salmon River

China Garden

No. Fork Trinity River

Grizzly Mdws

Steep
Spot

Lower So.Fork Lk.

Jorstad Babin

Bob's Farm

Lois Lk.

Grizzly Lk.

Moraine lk.

Morrison Cabin

Rattlesnake Creek Trail

Glaciers

N

Thompson Peak
9002 ft.

Something my grandfather used to say best sums up this popular, fantastic and difficult hike: "Oy gevalt!" Before I get to the good stuff— like the fact that Grizzly Lake may be the most spectacular single location in the entire Trinity Alps— let me hurl some numbers at you. They may explain why I put off visiting this sublime chunk of real estate for over 20 years.

From the trailhead, the path rises 1500 feet in its first mile. The second mile drops 1100 feet while the next 3 miles gain "only" 1500 feet. The final mile rises 8 million— oops, make that 800 feet, most of it concentrated into a dangerous, nearly perpendicular goat slope up a cliff.

Despite its only 6 mile length (one reference claims 7 1/2), this is not a good day-hike prospect. It took me 5 1/2 exhausting hours to reach the lake and another 5 1/2 to return. I was glad for a night's sleep in the middle.

The best place to begin the trail description is back on 37N24, near the turnoff from the Cecilville-Callahan Road. This may be the only spot from a paved (or unpaved) road where Thompson Peak, highest summit in the Trinity Alps (9002 feet), can be seen. According to every available map of Thompson Peak, two two-mile long glaciers adorn its north face.

Aside from a few much smaller ice fields on the back side of Thompson Peak and neighboring Sawtooth Mountain and Mt. Hilton, these are the only glaciers west of the Sierra-Cascade system and south of Washington's Olympic Mountains. While they hardly compare with Mt. Shasta's Whitney Glacier, Alaska's Muir Glacier or Canada's Columbia Icefields, they're part of what gives the Trinity Alps its special magic.

Grizzly Lake, third largest in the Alps, sits at the base of the right-hand (west) glacier. The one on the left (east) feeds the much smaller Little South Fork Lake (9 acres) which, alas, has no trail access. The Little South Fork Trail, from the end of 37N24, climbs to within 2 miles of LSF Lake, then veers towards Caribou Lake. Run-off from the left-hand glacier flows into the Salmon (and, ultimately, the Klamath) River while that from the Grizzly Lake glacier ends up in the Trinity.

The relentless uphill rise of the trail's first mile starts the hike off on a discouraging note. Most of this section runs though a dense but fairly young, north slope woods of Douglas-fir, gradating to white fir as the 5900 foot saddle is approached.

Beyond the wooded summit– which I was never so happy to see in my life– the down side is much like the up side, except being a south slope, it's brushier, with extensive patches of evergreen chinkapin and snowbrush.

These first 2 miles would be much easier were they at least a little bit scenic– of if you could see the summit for more than the last 500 feet. The prospect of having to reclimb this on the way back, loomed heavily for me.

Halfway down the second mile (which some references claim is the 3rd mile), the first good view up Grizzly Creek canyon emerges, enclosed by craggy black peaks on either side. Thompson Peak cannot be seen yet because the canyon curves. The most striking thing about the canyon, from this vantage point, is the steep, rocky rise of it's floor. It is not as steep or difficult as it looks, however. The Grizzly Creek Trail is far easier than the China Gulch Trail you just came over.

As I struggled up, then down the China Gulch Trail, I couldn't help wondering why it didn't contour across from the saddle instead of dropping 1100 feet. A ranger at the Salmon River Ranger District confided that he wondered the same thing. He speculates that jurisdictional problems between Klamath and Shasta-Trinity National Forests have been known to stand in the way of logic.

I hasten to add that the China Gulch Trail was originally much more difficult. Before logging roads pushed into China Gulch, it began down at the South Fork Road, at 2700 feet elevation instead of it's present 4400 feet.

The path finally meets the Grizzly Creek Trail a few hundred feet uphill from Grizzly Creek, in a dense woods of giant Douglas-fir and ponderosa pine. One of the few side creeks with drinkable water lies near the junction. The only other water I encountered in my late August visit– and you will need water– was Grizzly Creek itself, beginning a mile from the junction. Bring some sort of purification system.

After turning left, towards Grizzly Lake, at the China Gulch/Grizzly Creek junction, the path wanders through a deep woods for a mile, along a blessedly level segment. It then ascends the first of many rock outcroppings, offering a commanding view of the canyon below.

The trail meets Grizzly Creek for the first time at the top of this initial series of rock ledges, near a little waterfall. You'll find some fine campsites here, from which to witness superb sunsets through the west facing canyon. Established campsites may also be found back at the junction, as well as at Lower and Upper Grizzly Meadows and at the lake.

Miles 2 and 3 from the junction steepen significantly from the first mile, as the path alternates between rock ledges and woods. The forest transitions from Douglas-fir and ponderosa pine to white pine, white fir and Shasta red fir. Brewer Spruce and mountain hemlock begin to dominate as Grizzly Meadows is approached.

Grizzly Creek, meanwhile, has its moments in this section, with several impressive waterfalls. The rock is mostly green-stone, a crumbly material not nearly as striking as the Thompson Peak's white granite. Grizzly Creek is supposed to be a fine trout stream.

Thompson Peak takes its first bow 1 1/2 miles from the China Gulch junction. I approached the spot at 7:00 AM, after camping on the rock ledge by the waterfall, just as the sun broke over the high peaks. What more can I say?

Grizzly Meadows, between miles 2 and 3 from the junction (miles 4 and 5 from the trailhead), aren't very big. They stretch in a narrow ribbon along the creek and consist mostly of brush (alder, willow, serviceberry), with a few patches of grass and corn lily.

Somewhere between the lower and upper meadow, one of the most incredible mountain vistas I've ever witnessed comes into view. Thompson Peak, with its glacier, scree fields, white granite slopes and radiating ridges, dominates the head of the Grizzly Creek canyon. Moving away from Thompson Peak, on either side of the gorge, knife-edged slabs of jagged greenstone thrust relentlessly skyward.

Below the summit and glacier moraines, Thompson Peak drops off to a high bench, then to a sheer, absolutely perpendicular cliff, 800 feet high, which blocks the canyon head like a giant door. The cliff sits at the end of a narrow horseshoe alcove of white granite. An immense, snowy boulder field litters the base, ending at the upper end of Grizzly Meadows.

As you draw closer, a waterfall can be seen, tumbling the cliff's entire length and broken only by a couple short cascades. The waterfall is the outlet from Grizzly Lake, perched atop the ledge, 800 feet overhead.

On witnessing this for the first time, most people– after catching their breath and saying "wow"– conclude that there's no way a trail could possibly scale all that.

According to the lake chart on the Forest Service map of the Trinity Alps, "the last portion of the Grizzly Creek Trail is extremely steep, slippery and unmarked." Most of what I've read about Grizzly Lake, in fact, insist there is no trail up this impossible barrier— or if there is, it is an unmarked or poorly marked way-trail.

While the path is indeed steep (occasionally requiring hand holds), and slippery (in spots), I found it extremely well marked. There's no way most people could find their way up otherwise.

The Forest Service admits that the next logical trail classification, after "use at your own risk," is refusal to acknowledge that a trail exists. Thus, should someone say to them, "you call that a trail?," they can honestly answer, "no, we don't call that a trail."

Officially, therefore, the Grizzly Creek Trail ends at the beginning of the boulder field above Grizzly Meadows. In fact, the first 1/3 mile, across the boulders, is quite well constructed, with elaborate stone steps.

Things quickly deteriorate when the path bends to the left, away from the boulders, and heads up the nearly vertical canyon wall. The trail's slope occasionally exceeds 100% and approaches infinity in a couple spots— rising straight up in zero feet horizontal distance. The worst of this segment, fortunately, isn't very long. It gains 600 feet elevation in 1/4 mile on a route well marked by rock ducks.

Look for clumps of the rare and beautiful Mendocino gentian growing among the rocks here. The brilliant blue tubular flower closes up at night and reopens when the sun hits it.

This is one of the few trails where cleated, Vibram-type shoe soles may prove helpful. On the other hand, I made it up easily in ragged sneakers with a hole in the bottom. Nowhere, if you stay on the path, is the going so steep that you'll do more than skid a few feet on your behind if you fall. You're unlikely to hurl off into space.

This steep, loose segment features a narrow, nearly vertical rock chute, requiring careful selection of foot and hand holds. Immediately above, the going improves markedly and you soon find yourself atop the ledge, looking down on the meadows and across to the Russian and Marble Mountains as you hike the final 1/8 mile to the lake, through a fairlyland of rounded boulders and windswept, stunted whitebark pines.

Grizzly Lake far exceeds any possible expectation. At 42 acres, it's the third largest in the Trinity Alps after Caribou (72 acres) and Sapphire (43 acres) Lakes. Its 172 foot depth ranks second to Sapphire Lake. The water in Grizzly Lake is a clear, sapphire blue, with little vegetation and a solid rock bottom. A bouldery headwall rises sharply from 2/3's of the shore, 1900 upward feet to Thompson Peak.

A smooth, narrow bench separates the lake from the perpendicular drop-off above Grizzly Meadows. While most cliffs are eroded and rounded at the edge, this one's lip is absolutely square, as though the entire structure– from the valley up– was built of giant sugar cubes. The lake comes right up to the rim, with the water abruptly hurling into space. In the distance of a few feet, Grizzly Lake is transformed from a placid alpine jewel to a freefalling torrent hundreds of feet high (although the longest drop is only 70 feet).

A short, difficult, off-trail hike from Grizzly Lake, over a ridge to the right (west– two ridges if you don't hit it high enough), leads to tiny Lois Lake. The 2 1/2 acre brook trout pond is generally shallow but has an exceedingly deep spot. The preferred route to the top of Thompson Peak, up the mountain's least steep flank, begins at the crest above Lois Lake.

It's also possible– if not advisable– to hike to the glacier. Like most glaciers and ice falls, it is riddled with ice caves and crevices. It tends to spit out rocks as it melts, often with rifle-like retorts. The terminal moraine is very unstable.

***

A right turn, instead of a left, onto the Grizzly Creek Trail from the China Gulch Trail, will take you to the North Fork of the Trinity River, and a path which emerges at the Hobo Gulch trailhead west of Weaverville. Before they built the China Gulch Trail, determined hikers trekked 19 miles from Hobo Gulch to Grizzly Lake, which was a very lonely spot back then.

For fishermen with time on their hands, the Hobo Gulch route to Grizzly Lake offers much, with angling in the North Fork and lots of deep woods, riverside camps and historic sites. Above Rattlesnake Camp junction, where you decide whether to go to Papoose Lake (Chapter 21), or Grizzly Lake, the trail passes Morrison Cabin, Jorstad Cabin and China Gardens, all idyllic spots. China Gardens boasts a fine campsite near a now obliterated mining claim, where an observant eye might spot a few surviving domestic flowers.

Papoose Lake, via the China Gulch trailhead, is two miles closer (12 vs. 14 miles), than via Hobo Gulch. Unfortunately, it uses the horrific Bob's Farm cutoff, which is nearly as steep as the China Gulch Trail and much brushier and more exposed. Bob's Farm can be avoided by following Grizzly Creek to the North Fork, and then taking the Rattlesnake Creek Trail to Papoose Lake. But it's 16 miles that way.

Bob, by the way, used to grow produce, which he sold to gold miners along Rattlesnake Creek. It's hard to imagine a working farm on that rocky, high elevation site. All that remains now is the remnant of an old mill.

GONE GLACIERS

It struck me, on viewing the glacier above Grizzly Lake in 1992, that it was not nearly as large as indicated on the map. While it's possible that I could not see it all from the lake, it's also possible that the recent extended drought has severely diminished it. On a photo I took of Thompson Peak in 1970, the South Fork and Grizzly Lake glaciers pretty much corresponded with the National Forest map. Each measured about 1/2 by 1 1/4 miles.

The map drawing of the glaciers has not been revised in years. The glaciers my 1984 map are identical to those on the 1978 map, and probably identical to the 1943 map.

While the Forest Service could not reply precisely to my inquiry about glacial meltback, they did sell me a copy of an aerial photo taken in 1991 (which took 6 weeks to obtain from a government office in Salt Lake City).

On superimposing the photo over my 1984 Wilderness map, I found— to my horror— that the Grizzly Lake and Little South Fork glaciers have shrunk by a good 90%.

If the recent drought, as some allege, is a result of the greenhouse effect and therefore man-caused, the Thompson Peak glaciers may end up as yet another casualty in the relentless march of civilization. It would be tragic if these relics of the last ice age, possibly dating back a million years, were to vanish forever in our lifetime.

TRAIL GULCH/LONG GULCH/FISH LAKES

Destinations: Trail Gulch, Long Gulch Lakes; North Fork, South Fork Coffee Creek; Fish Lake.
USGS 7.5" Topo: Deadman Peak,CA
Location: T39N-R9W-Sec. 29
Length: 3 1/2 miles to Trail Gulch, 8 miles on the Trail Gulch Loop, 5 miles via the South Fork, or 9 miles via the North Fork.
Water: Lots
Access: Good paved and gravel roads
Season: June through October
Difficulty: Moderate
Elevation: 5400 to 6400 feet
Use: Non-motorized only
Ownership: Klamath NF
Phone: (916) 468-5351

Directions: Take I-5 to the south Yreka (Highway 3) exit. Turn right at the town of Callahan and follow the paved, two lane road towards Cecilville. Just beyond the summit, take the first turnoff left to Carter Meadows/Horse Camp. This leads to a gravel loop paralleling the main road, which is rejoined after 7 miles. Follow the gravel road 2 miles to the Long Gulch trailhead, 3 to the Trail Gulch trailhead and 6 to the Fish Lake turnoff.

The Long Gulch trailhead contains several campsites and infinite parking. The Trail Gulch trailhead can accommodate a dozen or so cars along the shoulder.

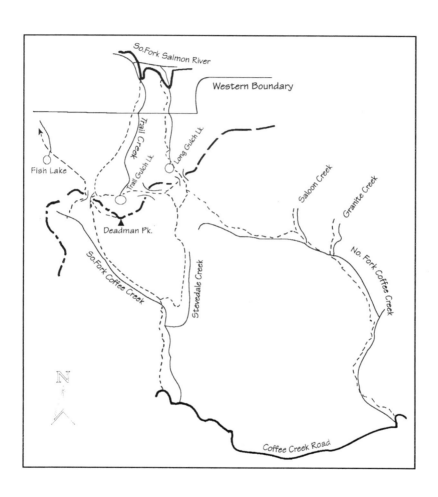

So.Fork Salmon River

Western Boundary

Trail Creek

Trail Gulch Lk.

Long Gulch Lk.

Fish Lake

Saloon Creek

Granite Creek

Deadman Pk.

No. Fork Coffee Creek

So.Fork Coffee Creek

Stevedale Creek

N

Coffee Creek Road

Trailheads for the North Fork, and the South Fork Coffee Creek Trails are located 9 and 15 miles up Coffee Creek Road, which leaves Highway 3 at the village of Coffee Creek, between Weaverville and Scott Valley. Both trails are well marked, with ample parking.

It used to baffle me how bodies of water as exquisite as Trail Gulch and Long Gulch Lakes ended up with such unaesthetic names. When I first encountered these magnificent examples of glacial architecture, in 1970, they lay outside the Wilderness boundary, with unmarked trailheads. Only local fishermen ever heard of them or deemed them worth visiting. From this, I theorized that the names were meant to discourage the swarms of humanity who converged on places with more poetic names like Emerald and Sapphire Lake.

The secret of Trail and Long Gulch Lakes is now out as both are firmly and deservedly ensconced within the Trinity Alps Wilderness Area.

The glacial cirques forming Trail and Long Gulch are among the most noticeable in a cluster of extremely deep basins visible from the paved road near the Callahan/Cecilville summit. It's a beautiful drive offering an excellent lesson in glacial geology.

The gravel loop road to the trailheads boast several campgrounds. The best lies at Carter Meadows, 1/2 mile from the turnoff. Carter Meadows contains a horse corral and paths connecting to the Long Gulch Trail, 1 1/2 miles distant, and to the Pacific Crest and Hidden Lake Trails, 1/2 mile away (Chapter 3). Neither the Carter Meadows Campground nor any of its emanating pathways are shown on the Wilderness map.

Other campgrounds in the vicinity include a small, pretty campground at the Long Gulch trailhead and the Trail Creek Campground, where the loop rejoins the Callahan/Cecilville Road.

Trail Gulch Lake features a 3 1/2 mile hike from the roomy trailhead. The route contains some steep pitches but rises only 1000 feet as it wanders from woods to meadows along the creek. A side trail left, three miles up, leads to the lake.

If you continue straight, it's less than 1/2 mile to the ridge top. There, one can peer into an area much like the Yosemite high country, with glacially polished granite domes. Look for the 9002 foot summit of Thompson Peak, the one with glaciers, to the southwest. From the ridge top, trails lead to Fish Lake, Taylor Creek and the South Fork of Coffee Creek. A short walk along the crest, to the top of Deadman Peak (7600 feet), affords a dizzying view down to Trail Gulch Lake.

The 10 acre lake, as noted, rests at the base of a sheer headwall. Its aqua water is surrounded by woods on the downhill side but boasts a large corn lily meadow above the creek inlet just east of the headwall. For the best swimming, follow the trail through the meadow, past lingering snowfields, to the gap between the headwall and a little island.

One of only two quaking aspen stands I've observed in the Trinity Alps, decorates the area around the meadow. The other lies at the upper end of the Stuart Fork Trail (Chapter 18).

From Trail Gulch Lake, it's a steep, spectacular, 1 1/2 miles up the rock face to the east and back down to Long Gulch Lake. After the rocky climb-out from the Trail Gulch, the path drops several hundred feet into Stevedale Creek. A half mile beyond the crest, look for a faint, extremely rocky trail marked by rock ducks, leading uphill to the left. It leads to the ridge above Long Gulch Lake. At this second crest, trails branch southward, down Stevedale Creek and the North Fork of Coffee Creek, and northward into Long Gulch.

Long Gulch Lake is virtually identical to Trail Gulch Lake but covers 14 acres. The trail from the Long Gulch trailhead is shorter, steeper and rockier than the one up Trail Gulch. Given a choice, I'd use it as a way out, not in (or double back and not use it at all), although it's perfectly good. Both lakes are popular these days and offer good brook trout fishing.

***

Personally, I can't imagine taking a 5 or 9 mile path to Trail and Long Gulch Lakes with an excellent 3 mile route so readily available. Still, hikers and riders come with a variety of agendas. For those seeking long trails beside shaded trout streams, the routes up the South and North Forks of Coffee Creek offer extremely popular alternatives.

My main problem with these trails is the name "South Fork." Never before in my life, including 20 years as a forester and travel through all 50 states, have I encountered a south fork entirely north of a stream's main channel. The South, North and East Forks of Coffee Creek all run parallel to one another, north of Coffee Creek. It would make far more sense to call them the East, Middle and West Forks.

The roomy North Fork trailhead is located on Coffee Creek Road, a mile past the East Fork trailhead, just before the road crosses Coffee Creek. The South Fork trailhead comes up 6 miles beyond. It is also well marked, with plenty of parking.

The North Fork Trail hugs a wooded canyon for a mile, then crosses the creek via a metal and concrete bridge. After making its way up a wide valley, past Hodges Cabin, it comes to another bridge 5 miles up, where the Granite Creek Trail takes off. The Granite Creek Trail ends up at Granite Lake (Chapter 7) and ties into pathways to Wolford Cabin, Eagle Creek, and the Pacific Crest Trail. It hits the latter at the Mavis Lake junction (Chapter 4).

But never mind all that. A mile past the Granite Lake turnoff, the Saloon Creek Trail branches off, tying into the South Fork Lakes Trail (Chapter 3), after a steep 3 1/2 miles.

Above Saloon Creek, fishing in the North Fork improves markedly, with rainbow and golden trout luring fishermen, and they, in turn, luring the fish. Finally, 9 miles from the trailhead, the path zig-zags up to the granite crest above Long Gulch Lake.

The South Fork route to Trail Gulch Lake is shorter, easier and much more scenic than the North Fork. It hits lake in a mere 5 miles. The first mile climbs steeply, high above the creek, up a closed road ending at a cabin site. Turning into trail, the path descends gradually for a second mile, through Douglas-fir forest and meadow, to the South Fork crossing.

Here, the valley opens spectacularly as the route continues past the Stevedale Creek junction, through floral meadows, towards the cirque basin's granite head. At the Stevedale Creek junction, take the trail labeled "Taylor Creek."

It's a steep, beautiful climb up the valley's broad slopes, to the Deadman Peak ridge. The Taylor Creek Trail takes off to the west from there, while the Trail Gulch Trail trails off into — yes— Trail Gulch.

***

For some reason, I've never seen Fish Lake mentioned in anything written about the Trinity Alps. Nor is it listed in the lake guide on the Forest Service map of the Trinity Alps. Too bad.

The 3 acre pond lies within 1 1/2 miles of the summit above Trail Gulch Lake. In fact, you can look down into its basin from the summit. To hike there from the ridge top, take the Taylor Creek Trail briefly, then hang a right.

The Fish Lake trailhead is located on the same road as the Trail Gulch/Long Gulch trailheads. A spur road (39N05) takes you to within 1 1/2 miles of the lake. From the trailhead, the path rises 1200 feet, to a pretty little glacial basin. You can see it from the road if you look carefully.

Exceedingly shallow Fish Lake is one of the few in the Trinity Alps where introduced brook trout do so well, it is not necessary to stock the lake. If you're really lucky, you might land one of the Arctic graylings planted there in the mid-70's.

HIDDEN LAKE/SOUTH FORK LAKES

Destination: Hidden, Upper So. Fork, L. So. Fork Lakes
USGS 7.5" Topo: Deadman Peak,CA
Location: T39N-R9W-Sec. 21
Length: 1 1/2 miles (Hidden); 3 miles (S. Fork)
Water: OK
Access: Paved highway
Season: June through October
Difficulty: Easy (Hidden); Difficult (S. Fork)
Elevation: 6200 to 6700 feet
Use: Non-motorized only
Ownership: Klamath NF
Phone: (916) 468-5351

*Directions: Take the south Yreka (Highway 3) exit off I-5 and pro-
ceed 30 miles to Callahan. Turn right at Callahan onto the paved, two
lane road to Cecilville. Park at the summit, on the left, in the parking
area.*

This lovely brace of short trails explores the deeply gouged glacial cirques visible from the highway near the Callahan-Cecilville summit. The South Fork Lakes Trail penetrates the deepest and most impressive of these cirques. Surprisingly, no lakes occupy the cirque in question, only a small marsh.

The two pathways begin at the same trailhead and both can be knocked off in a couple hours. The South Fork Lakes Trail

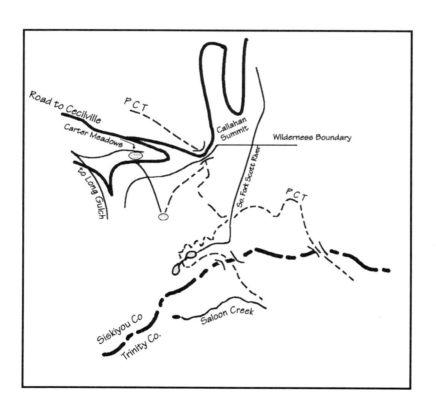

is twice as long and infinitely more difficult, however. Unlike the Hidden Lake Trail, it drops several hundred feet before ascending into the high cirque containing the lakes.

Hidden Lake was the objective of my very first hike in northern California. The memorable event occurred in 1970 with my wife, seven children (including one of ours), and a suitcase full of fried chicken. Everybody had a wonderful time swimming, fishing and chowing down.

It was a splendid introduction to my favorite real estate on Earth. The road is paved, the trail flat and short, the lake picturesque and the surrounding scenery breathtaking.

Approaching the pass between Callahan and Cecilville, a maze of rocky peaks, gouged by huge glacial cirques, appears on the left. The cluster lies within the Trinity Alps Wilderness but technically belongs to the Scott Mountains.

The cirques are extremely deep and there are dozens of them. From the trail, the South Fork cirque (which does not contain South Fork Lake), is most obvious. Less obvious is the Hidden Lake cirque.

From the highway, you'll see a little hillock with a helipad on top. A short, dirt driveway to the left leads to a parking area. Trailheads, sign-in boxes and signs clutter the area. The main trailhead, for the Pacific Crest Trail, leads to South Fork Lake and points south. Only a tiny oak plaque, tacked to a tree, marks the Hidden Lake Trail. If you jump aboard the PCT too near the end of the parking area, you'll miss it.

The Hidden Lake Trail winds through high elevation woods of Shasta fir and mountain hemlock for a while, then comes out on a brushy ridge. The South Fork of the Scott River lies far below; with the Scott Mountains' steep, craggy flanks rising beyond. The orange rock is serpentine while the jagged gray stuff is schist. It's an amazing vista.

Finally, the trail re-enters the woods and crosses a series of low, rolling glacial moraines. Then the 3 acre lake appears, gentle and shaded, with the usual cliff rising from the far end. The area near the outlet is relatively flat, with open woods and easy lake access. The lake has clear water, a solid bottom and little shoreline brush. It's a marvelous place to eat chicken out of a suitcase.

**

To reach the two South Fork Lakes, follow the Pacific Crest Trail south from the parking area. The route descends gradually through a forest of Shasta fir, mountain hemlock and western white pine, to a crossing of the South Fork of the Scott River. It's a little muddy and mosquitoey at the crossing, an open area of moisture loving shrubs, willows and wildflowers. The turnoff to the lakes lies just beyond, uphill to the right.

The path soon enters the immense, tan cirque seen from the highway. Alas, it contains only a swampy meadow, surrounded by thousand-foot cliffs. Admiration of the basin is tempered by the thought that your objective lies near the top of the headwall.

Now the fun begins. The really steep push, up rockfalls and cliffs, only lasts a mile but can be a challenge. Before starting up, I spoke with a man with an 8 year old daughter in tow. He warned me that the trail was so steep, he was forced to let the child rest once.

With vertical rock faces on all sides, the trail suddenly disappears over the top into a piney woods on a gentle plateau. The shallow, 3 1/2 acre lower lake soon appears in the middle of a field.

A five minute stroll through the woods from the lower lake leads to the 4 1/2 acre upper lake. You can't miss it, although one could miss the trail to it. The upper lake is nestled at the base of a low cliff, in a tiny cirque even more hidden than that containing Hidden Lake.

Fishing is outstanding, I hear, and the entire experience is worth the effort. Even if you are forced to rest once. Or even twice.

Creek just below East Boulder Lake

The BOULDERS, MAVIS, MILL CREEK LAKES

Destinations: East Boulder, Upper Boulder, High Boulder, Middle Boulder, Mill Creek, Washbasin, Telephone, Mavis, Fox Creek, Virginia, Section Line Lakes; Pacific Crest Trail.
Location: T39N-R8W-Sec. 9
USGS 7.5" topo: Billys Peak,CA
Length: 2 to 8 miles
Water: Lots (don't drink!)
Access: Good gravel and dirt roads
Season: June through October
Difficulty: East Boulder - Moderate; Mill Creek/Washbasin - Difficult; Middle Boulder - Moderate; Mavis - Difficult, then easy
Elevation: 5850 to 7300 feet
Use: Non-motorized only
Ownership: Klamath NF and private
Phone: (916) 468-5351

Directions: Take I-5 to Highway 3 south of Yreka. Follow it to the town of Callahan. Turn right just past the Callahan Emporium (40N16, which becomes 40N17). Follow signs to the McKeen Divide and East Boulder Lake. It's 3 miles to the divide, 3 more to the trailhead. Roads are well signed. A mile before the trailhead, bear left, uphill, at the signed fork (by bearing right, you'll end up at the Middle Boulder trailhead, with its cow corral, after 1/4 mile). Both trailheads are roomy and well marked.

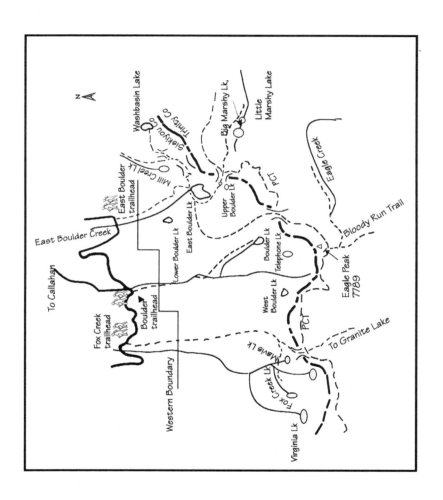

East Boulder Lake, among the largest in the Trinity Alps Wilderness, adorns the upper reaches of a grossly underrated range between the Scott and Trinity Rivers, called the Scott Mountains. The Scotts are notable, among other things, for their high number of private inholdings, which accounts for the teeming cow population. They also contain the Wilderness Area's only Pacific Crest Trail segment– 16 miles between the South Fork Lakes Trailhead (Chapter 3) and Scott Mountain Summit.

Hundreds of lakes adorn the Trinity, Scott and Marble Mountains of northwest California. And a superficial description of East Boulder Lake would differ only slightly from that of dozens of others. For the record, it covers 32 acres inside a glacial cirque, at an elevation of 6700 feet.

The last thing one would expect at that elevation, amid some of California's lushest forests, is a high desert plant community. Why this particular area, and no other, abounds with desert sage, one can only speculate.

It may have to do with the proximity to Scott Valley, 6 miles away and 3500 feet down. Such vegetation is common to the upper valley, a rainshadow where moisture is blocked by high mountains. Poor, porous soils and logged off, south slope sites lend themselves to high desert invasion.

The desert brush may have been helped by cattle. The cows winter in the valley, where they consume, among other delicacies, large quantities of sage brush– seeds and all. Of course, the serpentine crags and ridges around East Boulder Lake support little plant life of any stripe, even where cattle couldn't possibly find their way. The wide basin is nearly barren of trees.

From the wooded ravine at the trailhead, by East Boulder Creek, the path takes off through white fir, Jeffrey pine, western white pine and incense cedar. A little steep at first, it soon levels off in a series of grassy openings.

Since the trail crosses private property, visitors should respect it accordingly. They should also respect public property. Because of the cattle, I'd avoid drinking from the numerous creeks and springs along the trail.

Beyond the woods and fields, the trail passes a sizable waterfall on East Boulder Creek, 1/4 mile below the lake. There, the path shoots sharply but briefly upward as it enters the wide, barren lake basin.

Despite the basin's desolate appearance, it hosts a surprising variety of trees. In addition to those mentioned earlier, I noted Shasta red fir, lodgepole pine, whitebark pine and, on the ridge tops, foxtail pine. Brush species include sage and rabbit brush, manzanita and mountain mahogany.

East Boulder Lake's designer decorated it with brown, rocky shores; wide, flat banks; clear water; a vast meadow at the upper end; picturesque, widely scattered clumps of trees and an encircling ring of jagged peaks. The surrounding marshy grasslands make the lake so productive, the introduced brook trout are thriving. East Boulder (and Middle and Upper Boulder) Lake is among the few in the region where annual restocking is unnecessary.

A stroll along the trail, around the lake's west shore, will land you at 7 acre Upper Boulder Lake and a pair of secluded 1 to 2 acre ponds. One pond is High Boulder Lake while the other is unnamed.

The trail petered out at Upper Boulder Lake when I visited in 1990. The Forest Service assures me that it has since been maintained and now connects readily (if steeply), with the Pacific Crest Trail, just over the ridge top. A faint side trail at the PCT junction leads to Big and Little Marshy Lakes after 1 1/2 miles.

East Boulder Lake is nowhere near Boulder Lake, just south of Coffee Creek, or Boulder Creek Lake, off Canyon Creek. I guess any place with boulders is fair game for the name. In my experience, Duck Lake, in the nearby Russian Wilderness, has the most boulders. I didn't see any ducks there, though. Go figure.

***

Two other trails, aside from the PCT/Marshy Lakes link, take off from East Boulder Lake. When you first hit the lake, a sign on a tree says, "Little Mill Creek Trail," with an arrow pointing left. This well constructed, easily followed path begins, strangely, at a random point on the hillside, 500 feet away. To locate it, follow the lakeshore to the left, around the peninsula, then head uphill through the sagebrush until you cross the trail.

The reach Mill Creek Lake, 2 miles distant, one must first climb out of the East Boulder cirque's walled fortress. The trail accomplishes this in a bazillion switchbacks, each offering an improved panorama of East Boulder Lake and Scott Valley.

Look for a view of Lower Boulder Lake in the woods below the East Boulder cirque.

The cinnamon brown basin around Mill Creek Lake offers a miniature version of the East Boulder cirque. The shallow lake covers only 3 acres, on a bench above Little Mill Creek canyon. Once over the East Boulder/Mill Creek summit, the trail dispenses with switchbacks, plunging 500 feet in 1/4 mile. A gated but unlocked drift fence blocks the trail just before the lake. The fence looked to be electrified but I didn't test it.

Reaching Washbasin Lake, 2 miles past Mill Creek Lake, is a challenge. Not only must one climb back out of the Mill Creek basin, the trail is mostly non-existent. There's just enough visible path to get you there and no more.

Beyond the meadow above Mill Creek Lake, the route climbs to a small terrace, then shoots up an extremely steep pitch to a saddle. There, things level off briefly before gradually descending the densely wooded (wash)basin. For a look at 11 acre Washbasin Lake from the saddle, make your way a short distance out onto the rocks to the left.

***

Back at East Boulder Lake, the spectacular Middle Boulder Lake Trail takes off from its west shore. The sign at the junction says "Marshy Lakes (left), Eagle Creek Benches (right)." Go in the Eagle Creek Benches direction.

From East Boulder Lake, the path climbs up and over a low ridge, past granite outcroppings and a small meadow, leveling off in the woods high above Middle Boulder Creek. Eventually, the forest fades away, replaced by an endless sea of sagebrush.

The 6 1/2 acre Middle Boulder Lake appears in the distance after 1 1/2 miles. While there's not really a trail down to it, the way is obvious. The Middle Boulder Trail can be seen far below, paralleling your route.

Middle Boulder Lake nearly equals East Boulder Lake in scenic spectacle, with a vast meadow on one side and a white headwall rising overhead. The trail bottoms out well away from the lake. Past a series of marshy meadows, it begins a killer ascent (900 feet in 1/2 mile, with no switchbacks and over bare rock), to the serpentine ridge overhead. A third of the way up, the trail passes a small bench upon which perch two exquisite, one acre ponds.

Middle Boulder Lake, like much of the East Boulder Trail, lies on private property.

The Middle Boulder Trail meets the Pacific Crest Trail amid an area of orange outcroppings, whitebark and foxtail pines. From the junction, it's 4 miles (right), to Mavis Lake. Happily, the PCT is designed to avoid steep grades and faint spots. You're still in the heart of cattle country, however, so bring sufficient water or carry purification.

The PCT continues through serpentine for another 3/4 mile, to the Telephone Lake turnoff. The latter petered out after 100 feet when I visited. I suspect that Telephone Lake is easily located by heading straight up the draw to the ridge top.

Beyond Telephone Lake, the PCT heads back onto granite. It's an impressive route, with crags rising overhead and a spectacular view of Mt. Shasta. The path alternates between woods and lush meadow, hitting the ridge top from time to time. It is highlighted by the vistas southward, first of Billy's Peak (above Bloody Run and Eagle Creeks), then of the Mt. Thompson/Caribou Peak cluster at the heart of the Trinity Alps. The view more than justifies the effort in getting there. Mavis Lake itself is not worth the long walk.

A mile past the Telephone Lake turnoff, the Bloody Run Trail appears on the left (south). If you're dying to check out the Eagle Creek Benches (and area of woods and meadows along Eagle Creek), this is the way to go. The Bloody Run Trail comes out at Doe Flat, between Stoddard and Doe Lakes (Chapter 7).

The Mavis Lake Trail comes in 4 miles from the Middle Boulder junction. West Boulder Lake, passed en route, has no trail access and can't be seen from the Pacific Crest Trail. The Mavis Lake Trail careens down a forested wall of white granite to the lake's densely wooded, brushy shore.

A side trail in the opposite direction from the Mavis Lake Trail ties into the Granite Creek Trail, Granite Lake (Chapter 7), and the North Fork of Coffee Creek (Chapter 2).

Mavis Lake didn't impress me much, being shallow, mucky and covering only 3 acres. Fox Creek Lake, 1/2 mile beyond Mavis Lake, is a little bigger and a couple hundred feet lower with a more meadowed shore. A rugged, faint way trail, supposedly, leads from Fox Creek Lake to Virginia Lake, a mile west, near the cirque headwall. Lovely Section Line Lake, high up in the granite crags between Mavis and Fox Creek Lakes, is reached from a tiny saddle on the PCT, 1/2 mile beyond the Mavis Lake junction.

I GET BUSTED

Despite being one of the lesser visited areas of the Trinity Alps, I encountered a surprising parade of passers-by on the Pacific Crest Trail, between Middle Boulder and Mavis Lake. Early in the day, I hiked for 2 miles with a fellow who started at the Mexican border, 1600 miles south.

He'd arranged for 27 food drops along the 2700 mile route — the next one at Ashland, Oregon. It's 10 miles off the PCT into Ashland, a town of 15,000 just over the state line. It struck me as a long way to go for some packets of dehydrated lasagna.

A few minutes later, I encountered another hiker who had started in Mexico. When I asked if he knew the guy I'd just spoken to, he frowned and grumbled something under his breath.

Soon after, a man in full Forest Service regalia— the Ranger in charge of the northern half of the Wilderness— came bounding up the path. We chatted for a few minutes, comparing notes on various trails.

That was when I got busted. When he asked if I had a Wilderness Permit, I tearfully confessed my guilt and pleaded for mercy. As punishment, he made me wait while he wrote one out.

Actually, he was quite nice. He explained that funding for trail maintenance relies on accurate visitor statistics. The free permits are required by law but he understood that when entering at a place like Callahan, they aren't always practical.

East Boulder Lake

East Boulder Lake Outlet

TANGLE BLUE LAKE

Destination: Tangle Blue Lake
Location: T39N-R7E-Sec. 20
USGS 7.5" Topo: Tangle Blue Lake, CA
Length: 3 miles
Water: Lots, but probably not good
Access: Fair dirt road
Season: June through October
Difficulty: Moderate to easy
Elevation: 4500 to 5700
Ownership: Shasta-Trinity NF
Phone: (916) 623-2121

Directions: *From I-5 at Yreka, follow Hwy 3 through Scott Valley. Past Callahan, turn right (staying on Hwy 3), towards Trinity Center and Weaverville. Take the first turnoff right, beyond Scott Mountain Summit, where the sign says "Tangle Blue Lake" and "39N20." From the turnoff, it's about 3 1/2 miles, past two major side roads, to the trailhead. Look for a bulletin board and a trail marker. The trail follows the gated road. Parking is ample.*

The miners and trappers who first explored most of Northern California, were by and large a pragmatic bunch, not given to poetic musing. Thus, place names in the region tend to be utilitarian and descriptive rather than fanciful. Hardly ever was a

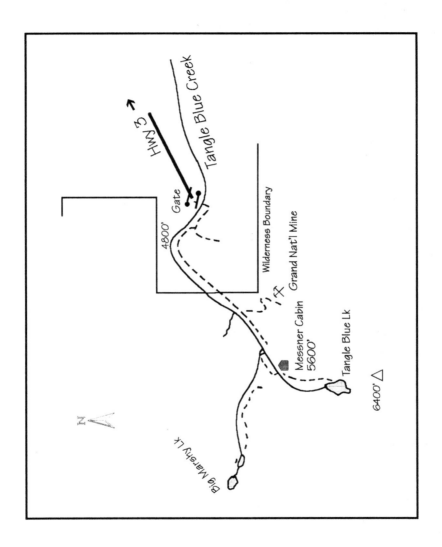

N

Hwy 3

Tangle Blue Creek

Gate
4800'

Wilderness Boundary

Grand Nat'l Mine

Messner Cabin
5600'

Tangle Blue Lk

6400' △

Big Marshy Lk

namer moved to poetry. And even then, the result tended to be a little hackneyed (Emerald Lake, Sapphire Lake).

Tangle Blue Lake alone, among the emerald and sapphire pools of the vast Klamath country, sports a moniker worthy of Whitman and Longfellow.

Given that it bears the region's prettiest name, the question remains: Do the trail and lake match it in beauty? The answer is a decided, "Sure, why not?" If nothing else, among the Trinity Alps' hundred or so glacial cirque lakes, Tangle Blue boasts possibly the shortest and easiest access.

Which brings up another question: Why couldn't I find the trailhead when I attempted to visit in 1988? On my latest visit, I encountered no difficulty whatsoever.

The Forest Service, it turns out, has installed several road signs since my earlier venture, partly in response to my negative feedback. The sign at the turnoff, the numbers marking the side roads, and the trailhead bulletin board, are all new.

In 1991, the Forest Service erected a fancy new sign at the turnoff from Hwy 3. In 1992, somebody ripped it down. A temporary sign, nailed to the denuded post, was similarly removed soon after.

Another 1988 problem was a plague of inaccurate maps. That, alas, remains the case. The only map correctly tracing both the access roads and the trail, strangely, is the Klamath National Forest map, where it overlaps Shasta-Trinity National Forest. If anything, it shows too much detail and is difficult to figure out.

For its first half, the path follows old mining roads. There is, in fact, no actual trail from the parking area, just a gate across the road. Walk past the gate, down to the creek and over the bridge. Beyond, the route climbs steeply uphill, then swings right and meets the creek again. Where a road takes off left, up the hill, about 1/2 mile up, continue straight, along the creek.

After a mile or so, beyond a second gate and the Wilderness Boundary sign, the scenery opens onto a large flat with some of the biggest incense cedars I've ever seen. Early miners, in their infinite originality, would have named this place Cedar Flat.

Uphill from the cedar (and Douglas-fir) flat, several wet, grassy meadows blanket the steep slope. A keen observer will spot patches of fly-eating darlingtonia plants scattered in the grass. These are rare "hanging bogs." Generally, bogs and swampy areas, where darlingtonia grow, occur in depressions or low lying sites. A hillside seep such as this usually does not provide enough water, consistently and over a wide area, to support a bog community.

While water abounds along the trail, I wouldn't drink it. Between hikers (the trail is quite popular), horses, habitation sites, old roads and (no doubt), grazing cattle, the risks are prohibitively high.

Despite the route's 1200 foot elevation rise, vegetation changes are minimal. At the trailhead, look for incense cedar, Douglas-fir, ponderosa pine, western white pine and white fir. Near the lake, the Douglas-fir and ponderosa pine fade out, while white pine and white fir become the dominant species. A few Shasta red firs sneak in as the lake is approached. By and large, however, the site isn't high enough to support a full compliment of upper elevation species.

In fact, it's hard to believe the trail rises 1200 feet. Much of it seems perfectly level and the upgrades aren't particularly steep or long.

Beyond the cedars, the trail bumps into the creek, continuing on the opposite bank. This crossing, to the creek's north side, is not reflected on the Trinity Alps or Shasta-Trinity map, even though the south bank is quite steep and probably never held a trail. The shallow creek is easily forded without getting wet.

Soon after the crossing, the path disappears in a maze of rock strewn gullies and side streams. The easiest way through is to follow the orange flagging (although the Forest Service hates flagging and removes it whenever they run into it). After crossing the main side creek, take a hard left back towards Tangle Blue Creek to rejoin the trail.

A couple miles from the trailhead, the route climbs to the edge of a large, grassy flat. It skirts it a ways, then drops back to the creek and crosses it a second time, at the ruins of Messner Cabin. From the cabin, it's a straight, fairly steep, 1/2 mile shot through the woods to the lake.

As you hike this last, south trending leg, the rocky spires capping the cirque headwall above the lake emerge in the distance. Then, while gray cliffs unfurl beneath the spires, sunlight dances through the trees, hinting at an impending large opening. Finally, the path breaks onto a large meadow, with the lake at the far end.

Tangle Blue holds its own in beauty among the Trinity Alps' many alpine glacial lakes. Being at a somewhat lower elevation than most, the glacier which formed it melted away earlier.

Thus, the 12 acre pool has progressed further in its evolution than higher lakes. The silting-in process is well along and the lake is shallow and choked with logs and branches fallen from the tree lined shore. Since the bottom is extremely mushy, I wouldn't try swimming.

Take particular note of the inlet, near the base of the head-wall. Like the Mississippi's mouth, a large silty delta is pushing into and gradually filling the lake. A lovely meadow decorates the formation.

The word Tangle, in the lake's name, correctly suggests abundant decaying vegetation in its waters. Since the water is therefore cloudy and algae laden, the Blue part of the name turns out to be merely wishful thinking. Maybe it was blue 100 years ago but it's greenish-brown now.

Don't worry, however. It's still well worth a visit— especially if you're a fisherman. Brook and rainbow trout by the dozens heralded our visit by leaping out of the busy, insect and frog laden water, in a choreographed salute. Several stayed for dinner.

Lance Podolsky at Tangle Blue Lake

BIG BEAR LAKE

Destination: Big Bear Lake, Little Bear Lake, Wee Bear Lake
Location: T39N-R7W-Sec. 34
USGS 7.5"topo: Tangle Blue Lake, CA
Length: 3 miles
Water: Lots
Access: Level gravel road
Season: May through November
Difficulty: Moderately difficult
Elevation: 3000 to 5800 feet
Use: Non-motorized only
Ownership: Shasta Trinity NF
Phone: (916) 623-2121

Directions: Take Highway 3 from Weaverville or south Yreka, to the the north end of Bear Creek Loop, north of Coffee Creek. The extremely roomy, well marked trailhead lies 2 miles up this wide, level, gravel road. It's 1 mile up from the loop's south end.

If I had to pick a single trail capturing the Trinity Alps's essence without involving a 10 mile hike, this would be it. The lake is the most beautiful of the Alps' outer lakes and the trailhead may be the most easily reached in the entire Wilderness.

My only problem with the Bear Lake Trail was that some things didn't quite "compute." Its length, for example, is listed variously as from 4 1/2 to 6 miles. I reached the lake in 1

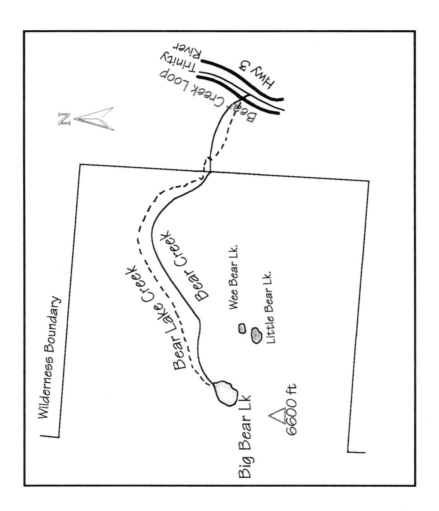

Wilderness Boundary

N

Big Bear Lk

Bear Lake Creek

Bear Creek

Wee Bear Lk.

Little Bear Lk.

6600 ft

Bear Creek Loop

Trinity River

Hwy 3

hour and 45 minutes, and estimated the distance at 3 1/2 miles. The Weaverville Ranger District recently re-measured the route at 3.09 miles.

With a 2800 foot elevation rise, a 3 mile trail should be horrendously steep. Although described as "arduous" in several references, I didn't find the going difficult at all.

Something is out of whack. Either the trail is longer than it seemed, steeper than it seemed, the listed elevations are wrong, or I passed through some mysterious time/space warp the day I visited.

Suffice to say, I found the excursion lovely throughout, highly varied and not unbearably strenuous. Granted, there are steep spots and the uphill trend rarely slacks off. But I disagree with the "arduous" designation and with allegations that the path is unbearably hot in summer due to its many exposed, brushy sections.

Hiking on an overcast October day, my perception may have been "clouded." Still, the path struck me as a nearly ideal balance between open and shaded areas.

Beginning in a dense, middle elevation forest above the canyon of Bear Creek, the trail hugs the stream for its entire length. Rising rather steeply at first, things level off near the bridge over Bear Creek. The crossing, an enchanted little deep woods spot, is not nearly as scenic as that to come. Beyond the bridge, the trail steepens, then levels off for a considerable distance.

For the first couple miles, the forest consists mostly of Douglas-fir and black oak. Scattered tanoak suggests a fair amount of rainfall. Diminutive but exquisitely flowered Pacific dogwoods add to the beauty, especially in spring. Occasional stands of knobcone pine indicate past fires or logging clearcuts, as do patches of manzanita brush.

This fairly level middle section reveals excellent views of the glistening white granite peaks on the south side of the creek. High up near their tops, a glacial cirque has been gouged into the rock, with an outlet crashing sharply into Bear Creek. This cirque houses Little and Wee Bear Lakes, which may be reached by hiking cross country to the southeast from the main lake.

Bear Creek canyon eventually narrow and curves south as white granite walls close in on either side. While the path steepens again here, the interplay of woods, open areas, side creeks and stone ramparts is appealing. Upper elevation mountain hemlock, white fir, Shasta red fir and western white pine populate the forested areas. Look for alder along the creek and ferns, willow, grass and coffeeberry lining the seeps and side creeks.

The last mile or so follows much closer to the creek. This section is steep, a little muddy and quite brushy, but the unfolding cirque ahead urges one on.

Immediately below the lake, the trail passes a couple of small, wooded glades with masses of azalea lining the path. Azaleas bloom in spring and occasionally in fall but not in summer.

Just beyond the azalea glades, the trail climbs up a rock face, passes more azaleas, and, at last, finds the lake. This last rock face is a gently rounded, glacially polished terrace. The creek fans out over it before forming a small waterfall.

All one can really say about the deep, 28 acre lake, is that it makes a fitting climax to a beautiful hike. White, billowing granite slopes circle 80% of the cirque, rising to a crown of jagged spires and minarets. Fishing is excellent and there's plenty of room to camp near the outlet.

***

To reach Little and Wee Bear Lakes, I'm told, contour around the slope on the south side of the Big Bear outlet until you enter the the mouth of the Little Bear cirque. Or follow the inlet creek uphill from Big Bear's southeast shore and climb to a small saddle at the ridge top. The 6 acre Little Bear Lake hides on the other side, one mile away and 400 feet higher than Big Bear. Tiny Wee Bear Lake occupies the same basin as Little Bear. This is not an easy trek.

STODDARD/DOE/GRANITE LAKES

Destination: Stoddard, McDonald, Doe, Granite Lakes; Stoddard
Meadows, Doe Flat, East Fork Coffee Creek
Location: T38N-R7W-Sec.18 (Stoddard)
T38N-R8W-Sec. 30 (East Coffee Ceek.)
USGS 7.5" Topo: Billys Peak, CA
Length: 2 miles (Stoddard Lake via Stoddard trailhead); 5 miles (Stoddard Lake via East Fork); 7 miles (Granite Lake via Stoddard); 9 miles (Granite Lake via East Fork.)
Water: Enough
Access: Long dirt road, bumpy near end
Season: June through October
Difficulty: Moderate to Difficult
Elevation: 3400 to 7200 feet
Use: Non-motorized only
Ownership: Shasta Trinity NF
Phone: (916) 623-2121

Directions: Take Highway 3 from Weaverville or Yreka. North of Coffee Creek, turn west onto Eagle Creek Loop (south end, the north end was closed as of 7/92). Proceed 1 mile to the signed turnoff on road 38N22. Follow it to the junction with 38N27 and continue on the latter to the trailhead (8 mi. from Highway 3). Or stay on Eagle Creek Loop 2 more miles to the junction with 38N27, at a Forest Service campground, and take it the entire route.

Park on the shoulder at the trailhead, which isn't large enough for the use it receives.

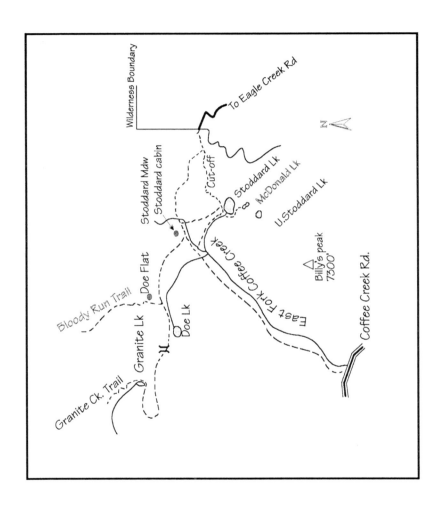

The East Fork Coffee Creek trailhead lies 7 1/2 miles up Coffee Creek Road and is very well marked, alongside the road, just over the East Fork bridge.

As one of several large, beautiful lakes adorning the periphery of the Trinity Alps Wilderness, Stoddard makes an ideal day-hike. An ambitious fishermen or sightseer could camp at Trinity Lake or Coffee Creek, fish the Trinity and visit Stoddard, Boulder, Tangle Blue, Big Bear and a bunch of other lakes in 3 or 4 days.

At 25 acres, just 5 lakes in the Wilderness exceed Stoddard's size. And the path to it is only 2 miles long. While the 8 mile dirt road from Highway 3 is dusty, and a little bumpy near the end, views of nearby Billy's Peak, along with the white uplifts around Big Bear Lake, across Eagle Creek, more than hold your interest.

Before starting out for Stoddard Lake, an apparently simple undertaking, readers should be aware of an array of options, muddled by some odd Forest Service signing.

The first decision is whether to hike from the Stoddard or the East Fork Coffee Creek trailhead. Since it's a 5 mile walk from the East Fork trailhead and only 2 from the Stoddard trailhead, and since the Stoddard begins 1600 feet higher than the East Fork, there should be no question. Still, the East Fork Trail is fairly popular and will be described shortly.

Presuming you opt for the Stoddard trailhead rather than the East Fork trailhead, the path's first 1/2 mile is choked with an astonishing variety of shrubs, including evergreen chinkapin, scrub tanoak and the rare Sadler oak. Look also for scrub liveoak, rhododendron, manzanita and other heath species in this steep, rocky region.

Much of the area lies within a serpentine rock formation, although the main summit of Billy's Peak, rising above the lake, is composed of greenstone; an ancient, metamorphosed lava. Serpentine adapted vegetation abounds along the trail.

After 3/4 mile, in a grassy flat, a side trail breaks away. The sign is down, so look for a small cedar with nails in it. The path to the left, which cuts a mile off the route to Stoddard Lake, is unmaintained and very steep.

If you continue straight ahead, rather than turning left, it'll take longer to reach the lake but the route is much gentler and prettier. It passes numerous darlingtonia bogs (an insect catching species related to the pitcher plant), plus close-up views of Big Bear Peak, across Eagle Creek, and far-off views of Mt. Shasta and Castle Crags.

Two miles from the trailhead, the longer route becomes the upper end of the East Fork Trail. It meets another turnoff to Stoddard Lake just past Stoddard Meadows, near the remains of Stoddard Cabin. At Stoddard Meadows, the sign in the direction leading back the way you came says, inexplicably, "Ripple Creek." Ripple Creek is nowhere near any of the trails, although the access road crosses it early on.

I'll describe the route from Stoddard Meadows to Stoddard Lake shortly, when I talk about the East Fork Trail. Meanwhile, we re-join the narrative back at the junction where the unmaintained cut-off trail veers off to the left.

From the cedar with nails in it, the cut-off trail winds steeply uphill. Along the way; between fallen logs and patches of Jeffrey pine, Western white pine, white fir and incense cedar; lurk numerous seeps, meadows and side creeks. I noted two bog areas, each with masses of darlingtonia rearing their cobra heads in quest of hapless insects.

According to the map, the route rises 1300 feet in the 1 3/4 miles between the trailhead and the crest above the lake. It then drops 500 feet in 1/4 mile. These numbers seemed greatly exaggerated when I visited. I'd estimate a rise of no more than 600 or 700 feet, with a drop of 200 feet.

With all that climbing, you'd expect to be rewarded by a great vista of the lake from the trail's summit. Alas, you're in for a disappointment. The trail tops out deep in the woods and neither the lake nor the tortured crags above it, comes into view until near the bottom.

Stoddard's vast azure shores are densely forested with lodgepole pine and the tree species noted above. The north bank, where the trail emerges, is steep and rocky while the opposite side is more level with colorful, open meadows. The best campsites are found along the wooded ledge near the outlet. At 85 feet, Stoddard ranks among the Wilderness Area's deeper lakes, home to a fair brook trout population.

Should Stoddard Lake prove boring (which I can't imagine), or if you manage to fish it clean, 4 acre McDonald Lake occupies the same basin, 1/4 mile south, with tiny Upper Stoddard Lake tucked in a rocky pocket overhead.

****

The East Fork Trail is a fairly popular alternative route to Stoddard Lake, not to mention Doe and Granite Lakes. Though steep, it follows an impressive rock gorge for 2 miles (occasionally along an old road bed), passes a couple mine sites, then hugs the creek for 2 more miles before veering right and heading uphill to the lake.

For reasons known only to the Forest Service, two parallel, 1 mile trails, 1/4 mile apart, connect the East Fork with Stoddard Lake. At the lake, they are signed, "Doe Lake" and "Stoddard Cabin." On the East Fork Trail, they are signed "Stoddard Lake, Road 38N27" and "Stoddard lake."

The sign at the first turnoff, reading "to Road 38N27," makes little sense. The only way to reach the road that way is via the supposedly closed cut-off trail. The shortest and easiest route from the East Fork to 38N27, would be straight ahead, following the "Ripple Creek" sign.

The second Stoddard Lake turnoff (from Stoddard Meadows), is the less steep of the two, gaining 300 feet in its mile, vs. 500 for its companion pathway.

****

The Doe/Granite Lake Trail leaves the East Fork Trail between the two Stoddard Lake turnoffs. It's 3 miles to Doe Lake and 5 to Granite Lake from the East Fork junction. This is not the same Granite Lake as that reached via Swift Creek (Chapter 15).

The Doe Lake Trail's first mile ascends a steep, forested hillside which burned in 1987. The route contains many level stretches and crosses a couple gushing creeks. But it includes some killer upgrades.

Eventually, the trail emerges at Doe Flat, with its expanse of grass and corn lily. A side trail labeled "Bloody Run Creek," connects to the Pacific Crest Trail after 3 miles, near East Boulder Lake (Chapter 4).

The easily followed path through Doe Flat contains a section where it crosses and recrosses a small creek several times. Watch out for mud and quicksand.

From Doe Flat, the trail enters a small cirque basin, with white rock outcroppings on either side. The next mile is rather frustrating as the route snakes through woods, up creeks and around alder thickets. You keep heading up steep rises, expecting to find Doe Lake at the top.

After it has penetrated as far as possible into this lakeless cirque, the trail exits the basin and enters another, hanging basin. From there, it's only one or two more false summits to the lake.

Though only 4 acres, Doe Lake richly deserves to be called a "Trinity Alps lake." A jagged, perpendicular granite headwall hugs two sides of the lake and snow lingers until mid-July. Mountain hemlock, Western white pine and Shasta red fir surround the lake.

The lake chart on the Forest Service Wilderness map lists the elevation of Doe lake as 7300 feet. On the map itself, however, it lies a couple squiggles below the 7200 feet contour, at about 7000 feet.

To reach Granite Lake, 2 miles away, continue along the trail as it climbs sharply out of the Doe Lake cirque. After leaving the basin, it scrambles down a rocky slope, then contours around a sparsely wooded hillside with views of Thompson Peak and the core of the Trinity Alps. Look for a charming, spring fed glade in this segment. In the final mile to the lake, the path surmounts yet another granite ridge, then descends rapidly to the lovely, 6 acre, pond lily clogged pool.

Granite Lake can also be reached via the Granite Creek Trail, which begins 5 miles up the North Fork of Coffee Creek (Chapter 2). It's 9 miles that way, the same as from the East Fork Trail.

BILLY'S PEAK TRAIL

Destination: Billy's Peak
Location: T37N-R8W-Sec. 1
USGS 7.5" Topo: Carrville, Billys Peak, and Tangle Blue Lake,CA
Length: 3 miles
Water: None
Access: Good gravel road
Season: June through October
Difficulty: Very difficult
Elevation: 4000 to 7274 feet
Ownership: Shasta-Trinity NF
Phone: (196) 623-2121

Directions: Take Highway 3 from Weaverville or Yreka to the Trinity
Lake area. The signed turnoff from Highway 3 is located west of the
highway, 1 1/2 miles north of Coffee Creek, 1/4 mile north of Trinity
Campground and 2 miles south of the south end of Eagle Creek Loop.
   It's 4 miles up a wide, somewhat steep, gravel road to the trailhead. Turn left at the first intersection and right at the next two. The
first intersection contains no trail sign, the second has a post where a
sign used to be and the third is prominently signed. About 50 cars
can fit at a logging landing 500 feet before the trailhead. The last 500
feet are extremely steep, with room for only one or two cars at the
trailhead itself. The trailhead is marked by a post but no bulletin board.

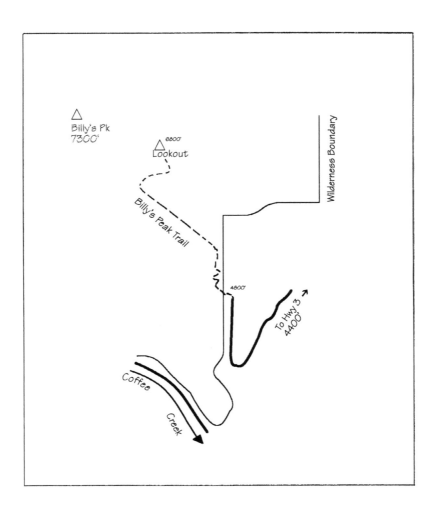

Billy's Pk
7300'

8800'
Lookout

Billy's Peak Trail

Wilderness Boundary

4800'

To Hwy 3
4400'

Coffee

Creek

This strenuous outing, rising 3300 feet in 3 miles, offers an easily accessible, early season entry into the heights of the outer Trinity Alps. Because the trail climbs the south face of an extremely steep, exposed slope, snow melts off quite early considering the 7274 foot elevation. Hiking on May 17th (of a drought year), I encountered only a couple rapidly dwindling snow patches near the summit. The north face was inundated with the stuff, however.

Should you venture forth before summer, bring a jacket no matter how warm the temperature and be wary of cold winds and rapid weather changes. Wear the jacket if it gets breezy, even if you end up drenched with sweat under it.

The view from Highway 3, near the north end of Eagle Creek Loop, reveals that there are actually two Billy's Peaks. The trail climbs the isolated, bell shaped outcropping on the left, where a fire lookout once stood. Billy's Peak proper is set back from and 1 1/2 miles north (right) of the lookout peak. Its imposing crags top out at 7400 feet.

To check snow conditions before starting out, the best south face view of the lookout peak occurs near the French Gulch intersection on Highway 3. The entire trail route and a large chunk of the actual trail can be seen from there. Proceed only if no snow— or nearly no snow— lingers on the south side.

From the trailhead, the Billy's Peak Trail shoots upward along an old skid road for 1/4 mile, then levels slightly as it begins a series of zig-zags up a wooded ridge. Despite past logging here, you'll find fat sugar and ponderosa pines keeping company with Douglas-fir, white fir and gnarled old incense cedars. In the frequent open areas, look for squawcarpet, manzanita, scrub tanoak, evergreen chinkapin and bittercherry. I noted tons of wildflowers, including paintbrush, iris, phlox, monkeyflower and a lone beargrass plant near the trailhead.

Views of the Trinity River, Highway 3, and the upper end of Trinity Lake gradually unfold to the southeast in this lower portion. This alternates with a southwesterly panorama of the outer Trinity Alps, visible across the steep canyon of Coffee Creek. The impressive row of peaks includes Red Rock Mountain and Ycatapom Peak in the Boulder Lake area. The cluster's highest summit, far to the south, is Gibson Peak at 8400 feet.

You'll know you're making progress when, after 1 1/2 miles, you cross for a final time to the Coffee Creek side of the ridge.

Shortly after, the steep-sided rock dome that is the trail's destination, pops into view, looking frustratingly far away. It disappears about 10 steps later.

The greenish tinge of the rock reveals that Billy's Peak is made of greenstone, a crumbly, ancient, metamorphosed lava. Greenstone is extremely common throughout Klamath Mountains geological province, to which the Trinity Alps belong. It is less common in the Trinity Alps than in other Klamath ranges.

For the next 1 1/4 miles, neither the trail's direction nor its moderately steep gradient varies more than a degree or two. The forest pretty much peters out as the path makes its way across brushfields broken by rock falls and outcroppings. It's a nearly vertical, 4000 foot drop into Coffee Creek from here.

About 2/3's of the way up this segment, the lookout summit reappears, this time as a row of cliffs atop a steep avalanche slope sweeping upward from the path. The slope, covered with rock, scree and low brush (mostly squawcarpet and manzanita), is dotted with widely scattered mountain hemlock and Shasta red fir. The trail can be seen gashing across the scree fields high overhead.

Your objective is the highest and largest of the cliffs. Just to its left, you'll note a small notch. The trail will climb a steep rockfall to the notch, then light out over the rock face to the left. If the narrow chute containing the rockfall appears clogged with snow, you could be in trouble.

Back at the base of the avalanche basin, abruptly and suddenly, the seemingly interminable straight-away above Coffee Creek ends with a sharp switchback and an imposing, if brief, glimpse of the main Billy's Peak summit, 1 1/2 miles north of the lookout summit.

The trail grows steeper and much rockier as it ventures across the avalanche slope. Another switchback soon leads to the base of the narrow chute with the rockfall inside. While the trail's builders attempted to construct a series of tight switchbacks up the loose rock, falling boulders have obliterated it in places (although the route is obvious). The path is choked with brush in other spots, and it may lie under snow in some others. The distance between switchbacks rarely exceeds 30 feet.

This section is difficult to represent on maps because maps show only the horizontal while the path rises 500 feet over a barely discernible horizontal span. The trail gradient here has been measured at 36%, placing it in the "killer" category. The gradient of the rocky slope which it climbs is closer to 100%.

This final, precarious stretch may be the second steepest pitch in this book (after the approach to Grizzly Lake– Chapter 1). It's safer than it looks, though, and fairly short. Lingering snow patches just below the summit offer the route's only water.

Amid grunting and straining, the path finally reaches the notch, which perfectly frames Mt. Shasta, far to the northeast. After swinging briefly left, the now faint trail climbs a narrow crack in the smooth rock face to the right. This may require the use of hands.

After 100 feet of rock climbing, the trail reappears on the left for the final short haul to the summit. You'll be glad you stuck it out. Past the lookout base, a wooden post and a survey cap mark the high point.

From this aerie, the ridge swoops down to a dramatic, knife edge saddle, then back up to the main crest of Billy's Peak. The entire Coffee Creek drainage is now visible. It culminates, on the western horizon, with the high peaks of the inner Trinity Alps– Caribou Peak and Mt. Thompson– peering over from behind Red Rock Mountain.

To the east, look for Mt. Shasta, plus Mt. Eddy and Castle Crags in the Trinity Divide range. The imposing view southward, of Trinity Lake and the outer Alps, has already been described.

Billy's Creek Trail. Note sign On Rock. 'This Way Please!'

Summit of Billy's Peak. Caribou Peak is just below the cross

Sugar Pine Lake

SUGAR PINE LAKE

Destination: Sugar Pine Lake, Battle Canyon
Location: T38N-R8W-Sec. 32
USGS 7.5" Topo: Ycatapom, CA
Length: 5 1/2 miles
Water: 2nd mile only
Access: Good gravel road
Season: June through October
Difficulty: Difficult
Elevation: 3200 to 6600 feet
Ownership: Shasta-Trinity NF
Phone: (916) 623-2121

Directions: Take Highway 3, from Weaverville or Scott Valley, to Coffee Creek. Follow Coffee Creek Road 6 1/2 miles to the well signed trailhead, a couple hundred feet down a side road. Coffee Creek Road is paved for the first 4 1/2 miles. The trailhead can accommodate a dozen cars.

The Sugar Pine Trail is memorable in that it gave my wife something new to worry about when I venture forth unaccompanied on weekend gallivants. More on that shortly. Its main selling point, like the paths up Granite and Billy's Peak, is it's test of physical stamina as it gains 3400 feet in 5 1/2 miles. The first 3 miles (rising 2800 feet), offer little besides anaerobic muscle burn, in the swelter of low elevation California heat.

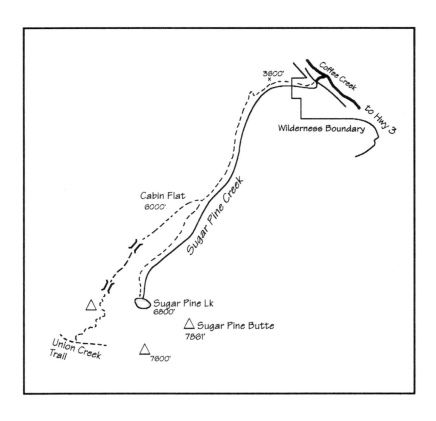

Coffee Creek

to Hwy 3

3800'
×

Wilderness Boundary

Cabin Flat
6000'

Sugar Pine Creek

Sugar Pine Lk
6800'

△ Sugar Pine Butte
7861'

△
7600'

Union Creek
Trail

The trail begins at Coffee Creek, at what was once an auto bridge leading to a network of logging roads. Once across the bridge, the path begins its relentless rise almost immediately. After following an old jeep road for 1/4 mile, it begins snaking its way through an endless woods.

According to the Forest Service map, the trail hugs Sugar Pine Creek its entire length. You only catch one or two glimpses of the creek, however. Most of the time, the path contours several hundred feet up, with the view blocked by dense forest.

Not that it's a bad forest. Some of the trees are huge and the species transition is fascinating. Look for low elevation species at first— madrone, black oak, tanoak, Douglas-fir, ponderosa pine, incense cedar, deerbrush ceanothus, manzanita, etc. Not to mention sugar pine.

After a couple miles, the middle elevation crowd takes over, including Douglas-fir, incense cedar, white fir, white pine, golden chinkapin, Sadler oak and snowbrush. Lodgepole and white pine adorn the high meadows while, approaching the lake, Shasta red fir and mountain hemlock dominate.

The first landmark is a switchback (the trail's only), 1 1/4 miles up. Soon after, several creeks scoot by in rapid succession. The second is biggest. While I drank from it and lived, it wasn't wise. This is a popular horse route and I noticed evidence of cattle in the high meadows. While I saw no cow spoor by the second creek, they had to have gotten to the meadow somehow. There's no drinkable water beyond the second mile after mid-July.

Shortly after the second creek, the trail passes an old fence. A quarter mile beyond that, a yellow tag nailed to a tree indicates that you're leaving the square-mile section of private property through which you've been walking.

Whoever put up the tag was slightly disoriented. It gives the location as the line between Sections 8 and 9, a point 2 miles southeast. You're actually on the line between Sections 31 and section 6.

Things really get messed up a mile later, beginning at another yellow tag. This one cites the location, probably correctly, as the line between Sections 7 and 12. This means the trail, as shown on the Forest Service map, is ever so slightly misdrawn. That's not the messed up part, though.

The map also shows nearly a mile between that section line and the junction with the Battle Canyon Trail at Cabin Flat.

From Cabin Flat, according to the map, it's 1 1/2 miles to the lake.

The Cabin Flat junction, however, miraculously appear 5 minutes beyond the yellow tree tag. "Wow," you think, "I've walked a mile in 5 minutes and I only have 1 1/2 to go." No such luck. The map is wrong. It's nearly 2 1/2 miles from the junction to the lake.

At Cabin Flat, the trail improves markedly. For one thing, it levels off. Except for a few stimulating upgrades, the going becomes pretty easy.

For another thing, the scenic quality takes a Baryshnikov leap. Cabin Flat is a lovely grass and corn lily meadow. The orange serpentine crags of the canyon wall tower overhead (the first time they've been visible), while the imposing spires of Sugar Pine Butte (7861 feet), can be seen in the distance, across the canyon.

The Battle Canyon trail out of Cabin Flat, is even steeper than the main trail. It rises 1000 feet in 1 mile to the ridge top, drops 600 feet to Battle Canyon, climbs 800 feet to a pass, then drops 1500 feet in 1 1/2 miles, to the junction with the Union Creek Trail, a mile from Union Lake (Chapter 10). It's 4 1/2 miles from Cabin Flat to Union Lake (5 1/2 if my assertion regarding map error is correct).

Several writers on the Trinity Alps list Sugar Pine Lake as a natural side trip from other destinations, via the Battle Canyon Trail. This makes no sense to me. It's 11 miles to the lake from the Union Creek trailhead and 12 from the Boulder Lakes trailhead (Chapter 13). Via Boulder Lake, you hit a 7300 foot crest at Foster Lake, then drop 1300 feet in 1 1/2 miles. Once at the bottom, you walk 20 foot across a grassy flat before climbing 1500 feet back up the Battle Canyon Trail.

On the Sugar Pine Trail, the lake lies only 5 1/2 miles away. Should you feel an urge to explore, hike to the ridge top between Battle Canyon and Union Creek. It offers a commanding view of Battle Canyon, the Union Creek basin, Red Rock Mountain, Parker Divide and the cirques of Union Lake and Bullards Basin, with Caribou Peak in the distance.

Granite bounders begin littering the Sugar Pine Trail well before Cabin Flat. Beyond, they increase markedly. The trail passes two more meadows, with lots of forest in between, before commencing its frustrating approach to Sugar Pine Lake.

This is one of those deals where you keep thinking the lake is just over the next rise but the path never seems to get there.

When a jagged, 1000 foot granite cliff appears in the distance, you figure the lake has to be nearby. The trail marches right up to the cliff base, then follows it for 1/2 mile.

Eventually, the lake appears, covering 9 acres at the base of a vertical headwall. A rockfall decorates the far shore, with a terraced rock face beside it, on the flank of Sugar Pine Butte. For the most part, the shore is steep, brushy and very bouldery. The area around the trail, in the woods, boasts some lovely campsites above the outlet creek.

The trail more than vindicates itself on the return trip. Often, on steep trails, the hike down is as slow the way up, especially if the tread is rocky and uneven. This is an ideal downhill trail—steep but not to the point of treacherousness and with a wide, soft tread. After a 4 hour hike to the lake, I was back at my car in 2 1/2 hours.

A STRIKING STORY

During my visit, I stood in an open and bouldery area, at the foot of the cliff, about 1/4 mile from the lake, when a lightning storm suddenly hit. One thunder clap nearly knocked me over. It felt like my eardrums had imploded into my medulla oblongata while the accompanying lightning appeared to hit the ridge top, directly overhead.

My fingers crackled afterwards, and air was filled with electricity.

Charged with adrenalin and electricity, with thunder and lightning crashing all around, I ran the last 1/4 mile to the lake, stayed 8 seconds (long enough to get a picture), and got the heck out of there.

It began hailing just as I hit the highest of the three meadows. Soon after, it turned to rain, which continued all the way back to the trailhead. I'd started out in bright sunshine, with a predicted high of 105 and not a cloud in sight. But then, the peaks of the Trinity Alps have given birth to many a summer thunderstorm.

At the Coffee Creek store, the sun shone and nobody believed my explanation of how my clothes and hair got drenched. They figured I'd fallen into a creek somewhere and was ashamed to admit it.

Landers Lake

UNION/LANDERS/FOSTER LAKES

Destinations: Bullards Basin, Dorleska Mine, Union Lake, Landers Lake, Parker Divide, Foster Lake, Lion Lake.
Location: T38N-R9W-Sec. 34
USGS 7.5" Topo: Caribou Lake and Ycatapom, CA
Length: 6 miles (Union Lake), 8 1/2 miles (Landers Lake), 8 miles (Lion Lake).
Water: I'd love some (lot's, actually, plus lots of cows)
Access: Good gravel road.
Season: June through October
Difficulty: To the Union Lake — easy to moderate, every place else more difficult
Elevation: 4400 to 7300 feet
Ownership: Shasta-Trinity NF
Phone: (916) 623-2121

Directions: From Weaverville or Yreka, take Highway 3 to the community of Coffee Creek. Follow Coffee Creek Road 10 1/2 miles to the well marked trailhead, alongside the road. There's room for a dozen cars and plenty of turnaround space. The trail leads up a gated logging road.

This was my very last hike in researching this book. I concluded my Trinity Alps summer on the highest of possible highs–atop a windswept, granite crest between two of the most splendid, little known lakes the Trinity Alps has to offer. The entire Trinity

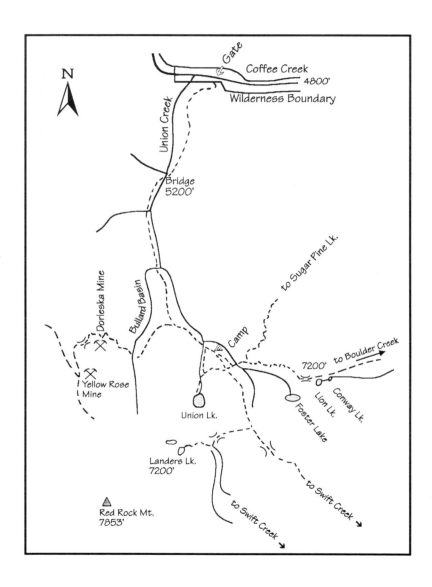

N

Gate

Coffee Creek
4800'

Wilderness Boundary

Union Creek

Bridge
5200'

to Sugar Pine Lk.

Dorleska Mine

Bullard Basin

Camp

to Boulder Creek

7200'

Yellow Rose
Mine

Lion Lk.

Conway Lk.

Foster Lake

Union Lk.

Landers Lk.
7200'

to Swift Creek

Red Rock Mt.
7853'

to Swift Creek

to Swift Creek

Alps range stood for a final bow to the west of my perch while Mt. Shasta bade a farewell salute on the east— even as the first storm of winter gathered on the horizon.

This "peak" experience was slow in coming, however. The first 2 lakes on the 4 lake, 22 mile hike didn't particularly impress me. Also, I nearly went home, skipping Foster and Lion Lakes, after seeing a bear 1/4 mile from where I'd set up camp. (More on my ursine encounter shortly.)

For its initial 4 miles, the Union Creek Trail ranks as the Champs Elysees of Trinity Alps pathways. Following an abandoned roadbed, a half dozen horses could march side by side up its gentle grades. Fairly heavily traveled by hikers and riders, it rises only 1700 feet in 5 miles. This is not to imply that the path doesn't have an occasional rough spot or steep pitch.

The most notable feature of the first 2 miles are an old pumpchance (pond), by an azalea lined creek; a stagnant, 1 acre lake; and a grove of fat sugar pines with the most intensely red bark I've ever seen. The section rises moderately for 1 1/2 miles, then drops gradually for 1/2 mile, to a wooded creek crossing with a lovely campsite.

The mile 2 crossing offers the first opportunity to examine Union Creek. The steel and concrete bridge spanning the creek was built before they closed the road —no horse could carry those I- beams— even though it was constructed (in 1967) for foot traffic.

The creek is strewn with boulders and lined with massive slides and earth failures. This is partly because it's a steep, unstable area and partly the result of mining in Bullards Basin. The notorious 1964 flood, which forever altered many streams in the region, also played a role.

For miles 3 and 4, the trail wanders boredly alongside the creek, through park-like woods of Douglas-fir, white fir, ponderosa pine and sugar pine, with occasional grassy openings. Towards the end of mile 4, observant hikers are treated to a brief but tantalizing peek up the skirt of Bullards Basin, a lakeless cirque one basin over from Union Lake.

The road ends at the brushy, rocky crossing of Bullards Creek (mile 3 1/2), then picks up again for 1/2 mile before ending for good at another creek crossing. The trail into Bullards Basin peels off at mile 4 1/2, after the basin's barren, serpentine headwalls have faded into the distance. The side trip is described later in the chapter.

Back on the Union Creek Trail, the first of two Union Lake turnoffs show up 1/2 mile past the Dorleska Mine junction. It's a mile through woods and boggy darlingtonia meadows to the 3 acre, 6050 foot elevation lake. The path rises only a couple hundred feet.

Union Lake reminded me of a girl I used to know– extremely shallow. Not to mention brushy, stagnant and full of muck and dead trees. A crumbling cirque of jagged serpentine, tumbling from Red Rock Mountain, surrounds the pond. A huge, beautiful campsite sits on a shaded hillock beside the lake, with plenty of pasture nearby.

The 1 mile Union Lake Trail splits halfway down, with the second tine of the "Y" rejoining the Union Creek Trail 1/2 mile past the first turnoff. In between the two Union Lake turnoffs, the main trail divides at an unmarked fork. Rock ducks suggest the right hand prong as the correct route. That direction leads to a four-way intersection, with signs pointing to the second Union Lake Trail, the path you just came up (from Coffee Creek Road), and trails to Foster Lake and Parker Divide. Take the Parker Divide Trail for Landers Lake.

Bearing right at the unmarked intersection follows a path alongside Union Creek. It rejoins the main trail at another un-marked junction, where the Foster Lake Trail crosses the creek.

I camped at a fine campsite at the first unmarked junction, 5 1/2 miles from the trailhead. A campsite at the second un-marked junction has been fouled by cattle.

The four-corners intersection sits in a grassy field dotted with Jeffrey pines. The main valley swings from east to south here. To the north, across Union Creek, rises the serpentine ridge behind Sugar Pine Lake (Chapter 9). Immediately east, a mas-sive slope of polished granite soars 1500 feet above the valley. A narrow cleft in the granite formation leads to a rock bench 1000 feet overhead. Foster Lake sits in judgment on the bench, 1 1/2 miles away.

***

It is 1 1/2 miles from the four-corners junction (7 from the trailhead), up the Parker Divide Trail to the Landers Lake turn-off. En route, the 6100 foot high valley widens considerably, culminating in a semi-circle of barren, yellow crests. The tree population (white pine, Shasta red fir, mountain hemlock, foxtail pine and whitebark pine), dwindles to practically nil, except in shaded pockets.

At the Landers Lake turnoff, the Landers Lake Trail climbs due west while Parker Divide, straight ahead to the southeast, crosses a 6800 foot ridge about a mile away. Beyond Parker Divide, the trail hooks into Parker Creek, the Poison Canyon Trail (Chapter 14) and the Swift Creek Trail (Chapter 15).

I noted some of the biggest foxtail pines I've ever seen where the Landers Lake Trail takes off uphill. A treeline species, foxtail pines are considered big if they top 10 feet. These reached 60 to 70 feet.

The 3/4 mile climbout from Union Creek offers a middling workout, although it goes by pretty quickly. If you expect Landers Lake to greet you at the summit, you're sadly mistaken. That lies another 3/4 miles off.

The summit does treat visitors to a vista of Red Rock Mountain, Swift Creek and, far to the left, massive Gibson Peak. Several hundred feet down, a brilliant grassy meadow– but no lake– perches atop a raised flat. The trail leads to the meadow's lower end, where Landers Creek falls into the Swift Creek Valley. A side trail at this charming, verdant spot follows Landers Creek down the mountainside.

The Landers Lake Trail skirts the meadow and climbs a red rock outcropping to another lakeless flat. Then it climbs more rocks to a third and fourth meadow. Just when you're about to scream in disgust, Landers Lake appears on the left, against a craggy extension of Red Rock Mountain. A side trail right leads to a pond at the base of the mountain's main summit.

As with Union Lake, I found Landers Lake a little disappointing– and a little odd. The 6 acre pool sits in an eroded, treeless basin, at the foot of an extremely jagged outcropping. It is surrounded by– and full of– ugly black boulders with little shoreline vegetation. With no outlet, the shallow lake tends to be quite stagnant. Since it shrinks markedly over the summer, when I visited in September, after a series of droughty years, it had dwindled to only 3 acres.

"THE BERNSTEIN BEAR"

After my exhausting Landers Lake safari, I hiked back down the Union Creek Trail, looking forward to dinner and a well deserved night's sleep in my tent. Until that moment– in 22 years of hiking in southern Oregon and northern California– I'd never seen a bear on the trail, only from the car a couple times.

When I first spotted the giant, absolutely monstrous black creature, it puttered idly around a dry field, 200 feet away, as

I emerged from a clump of trees at the crest of a little rise. I stopped when I saw it, while I attempted to decide whether to back up, wait, hide, proceed or panic. I ended up hollering, to warn the bear of my presence.

When the animal failed to respond, I yelled again, still with no response. My third, much louder holler, provoked a startled double-take. The bear looked at me, then lumbered off in the opposite direction.

Early that evening, a herd of cows wandered through my camp while I rested in my tent. Power mad from my meeting with the bear, I yelled at them and they ran off, just as the bear had done.

That night, I dreamed I heard something outside my tent. Not knowing if it was a bear of a cow, I hollered once again. Except being a dream, I only dreamed I hollered. On realizing that, I hollered again, this time for real, only to discover that it too was only a dream holler....

****

From the Bullard's Basin/Dorleska Mine turnoff, 4 1/2 miles from the Union Creek trailhead, it's 2 miles to Dorleska Mine, 3 miles over the ridge top to Yellow Rose Mine and 5 to Big Flat.

Rusted machinery, decaying buildings, huge rock piles and the remains of stamping mills litter the turn of the century gold mines. In hard rock gold mining, ore containing gold bearing quartz (hopefully), was pulverized in a stamping mill. They ran the resulting grit through a mercury bath which picked up only the gold. Then they simply boiled away the mercury.

The treeless, 7200 foot summit between Bullards Basin and Big Flat offers an excellent panorama of the Salmon River's upper South Fork. The entire Josephine Creek cirque can be seen from the spot, including Josephine Lake (Chapter 12).

***

If Landers and Union Lakes proved disappointing (although hardly unmitigated disasters), Foster and Lion Lakes more than compensated. Soon after boulder hopping across the narrow Union Creek, I encountered a cluster of cottonwood trees, unusual at this elevation (6100 feet), in the middle of a meadow. A sign informed me that the Sugar Pine Lake Trail (Chapter 9), branched to the left while my objective, Foster Lake, lay to the right.

From the reality of the junction, I could not understand why that route to Sugar Pine Lake is frequently recommended as a side trip from Foster Lake. Not only are the two 7 miles apart, it's necessary to descend 1200 feet in a mile from Foster Lake, walk 500 feet cross the flat, then climb 1500 feet in 1 1/2 miles.

My advice: If you visit Sugar Pine lake, use the Sugar Pine Lake trailhead. It's quite steep but reaches the lake in 5 1/2 miles instead of 12 from the Boulder Lake trailhead (Chapter 13), or 11 from the Union Creek trailhead.

I have no problems with the Boulder Lake trailhead as an alternative route to Foster Lake. It's 7 miles from the Boulder Lake trailhead to Foster Lake, including a 2 mile stretch which ascends 1900 feet. Via Union Creek, it's 7 1/2 miles, with the steepest pitch rising 1000 feet in 1 mile.

The Foster Lake Trail from Union Creek negotiates a seemingly vertical slope marked by granite outcroppings hundreds of feet high, with wooded pockets and manzanita slopes. The route zig-zags alongside a large gully, capped by a white rock terrace.

Near the beginning of the climb, the path crosses the only pure water since the trailhead, coursing down a lively side creek. While I couldn't imagine cattle venturing up the steep slope, I purified the water anyhow when I filled my canteen.

High overhead, the beautiful white shelf— looking like a dam made of igloo bricks— beckons hikers onward and upward. A spectacular waterfall spills over its edge until mid-summer, when the lake outflow dwindles to an ooze down the blocky rock face.

Eventually the brush fields, boulder fields, forest patches and sheer rock faces, the trail mounts, then crosses the bench. Unlike at Landers Lake, this is no false summit. As soon as you reach it, you're at the lake.

The trail, however, never actually gets to the lake. From the bench, it immediately starts up the rocks, marked by rock ducks, to the crest between Foster and Lion Lakes. Watch for a side path leading to the lake's sheltered outlet.

The secluded flat between the outlet and the bench's rim, contains Foster Lake's best campsite— one of the loveliest ever. In fact, Foster Lake ranks near the scenic top among Trinity Alps lakes. The pear shaped, 6 acre pool sits in a deep cirque, with angular granite blocks rising straight up out of the water.

Were one to paint a mental picture of the most perfect cirque lake imaginable, it would look pretty much like Foster Lake. Either that or Lion Lake.

It's about 1/4 mile, and a 200 foot rise, from Foster Lake to the ridge crest overhead. The round, 3 acre Lion Lake sits in an east facing basin immediately below. Its outlet creek flows through a narrow, vertical slit into diminutive, lily pad choked Conway Lake.

From the ridge top, with its rounded boulders and windswept foxtail pines, Lion Lake perfectly frames Mt. Shasta, on the eastern horizon. The view in the other direction is even better. Beyond Foster Lake, you look down on the Union Creek Valley and across to the Union Lake, Bullards Basin and Landers Lake cirques. In their midst rises Red Rock Mountain, while Caribou Peak's white mass towers in the distance. Beside Caribou Peak, Sawtooth Mountain cuts the heavens on the far side of the Stuart Fork Valley.

It was a fitting ending to a memorable summer.

Lion Lake, with Mt. Shasta in the background.

CARIBOU LAKES TRAIL

Destinations: Snowslide Lake, Little Caribou Lake, Middle Caribou Lake, Lower Caribou Lake, Caribou Lake, Sawtooth Ridge
Location: T37N-R9W-Sec.18
USGS 7.5" Topo: Caribou Lake,CA
Length: 10 miles
Water: Surprisingly little
Access: Good gravel roads
Season: June through October
Difficulty: Moderate
Elevation: 5000 to 7400 feet
Use: Non-motorized only
Ownership: Klamath NF
Phone: (916) 468-5351

Directions: Take Highway 3 from I-5 south of Yreka, via Scott Valley, or from Weaverville. Turn west on Coffee Creek Road and follow it 19 miles to Big Flat Campground. Coffee Creek Road is wide, level and gravel surfaced. The campground/trailhead is roomy and well developed. Obtain a free Wilderness Permit at the Coffee Creek Ranger Station.

The magnificent Caribou Lakes Trail, penetrating to the very core of the Trinity Alps amid deeply cut glacial valleys and white granite upthrusts, practically defines the word "spectacular." World

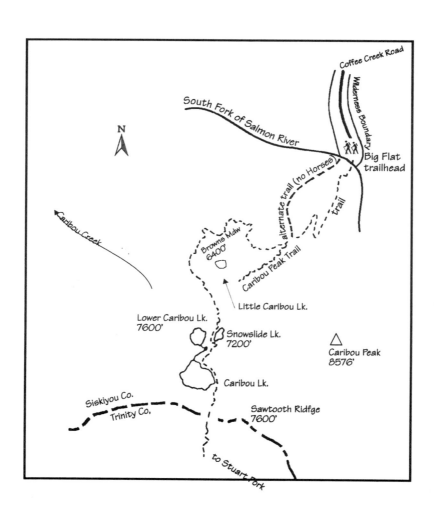

class views abound of Thompson Peak, highest in the Alps' jumbled maze of sawtoothed ridges.

Although Thompson Peak thomps out at only 9002 feet, it contains the only active glaciers west of the Sierra/Cascade chain and south of the Washington Olympics. Sizewise, Caribou Lake, at 72 acres, clobbers its nearest Trinity Alps competitor by 29 acres.

The Caribou Lakes Trail begins at the Big Flat trailhead, campground and parking area near the end of Coffee Creek Road. A sign directs hikers left, down an old road across a grassy ravine. The trail crosses a wide creek (the South Fork of the Salmon River), then starts uphill, switching steeply back and forth for the next 3 miles.

The path along the river to the right, at the crossing, also leads to Caribou Lakes, rejoining the main trail after 3 miles. This "no-horse" alternative is a little shorter, much rockier and quite a bit steeper.

The main item of scenic interest on the first 3 miles, is the panorama of the Salmon River's upper South Fork valley. As can be seen from the trail, the river has its source in the Trinity Alps' largest (but not deepest), glacial cirque, surrounded by the glacially sculptured peaks and ridges of Sawtooth Ridge (Chapter 12). A sharp eye will pick out Big Flat, the trailhead area and the continuation of Coffee Creek Road beyond the closed gate.

How, you might ask, did Coffee Creek Road get from following Coffee Creek, which flows into the Trinity, to the Salmon River, which flows in the opposite direction into the Klamath? If you pay careful attention as you drive the road, you'll note that it crosses a barely perceptible divide on Big Flat proper, a mile before the Big Flat trailhead. At some point, I've been told, the Salmon River eroded its way headward onto Big Flat and actually stole the upper South Fork valley from Coffee Creek, redefining the Siskiyou-Trinity County line in the process.

Back on the Caribou Lakes Trail, its designers must have felt it would be overwhelming to hikers to blast them with the region's full beauty all at once. So it's doled out a little at a time, building to a crescendo.

First, there's the view of the aforementioned upper South Fork valley. Then you approach, but never quite reach, a beautiful granite rock face. After 3 miles, past a grassy flat (Caribou Meadows) containing the junction with the Caribou Peak Trail and the upper end of the "no-horse" trail from Big Flat, the path picks its way over a huge outcropping of glacially polished granite. At mile 5, it crosses Brown's Meadow, a sea of corn lilies and alder brush splayed up a hillside.

The steep Caribou Peak Trail leads from Caribou Meadows to the summit, and most of the way to 3 acre Little Caribou Lake, situated outside the Caribou Basin, 1000 feet above the trail junction. There is no path directly to the lake so it's necessary to contour around when the Caribou Peak Trail draws level with the cirque opening.

Back on the Caribou Lakes Trail, its only drinkable water (don't quote me), trickles out a pipe a few hundred yards past Brown's Meadow. A mile beyond, Thompson Peak finally comes into view. 1 1/2 miles later, the lakes appear, inside a cirque across a tremendous glacial valley.

The write-home vistas begin where the trail comes around a bend and Thompson Peak emerges in full splendor. The afternoon sun glistens blindingly off its glaciers and polished white rock. Sparkling, jagged dikes, radiating from the summit, look like a giant, diamond tiara. Immense ravines assault the mountain's northern flank. Caribou Creek, 2000 feet beneath your feet, rushes through a "U" shaped chasm with hanging side valleys. By the time melt water from the Thompson Peak glacier arrives at Cecilville, 20 miles distant, it has dropped 7000 feet.

For the next couple miles, the route continues climbing, at one point inching around a huge white cliff resembling a wall of icicles. You don't know until you get there, how the trail plans to cross the expanse.

Occasional patches of western white pine, lodgepole pine, mountain hemlock and Shasta red fir line the trail. I also noted a single Brewer spruce, 1/2 mile above Snowslide Lake.

Soon, Caribou Lake emerges in the distance, inside a giant, steep walled cirque left of Thompson Peak. Then Lower Caribou Lake appears, in a granite bowl, under a waterfall gushing from the main lake.

Granite carved by glacial ice has a softly rounded, pillowy look. Thus, Lower Caribou Lake, 1/2 the main lake and nearby Snowslide Lake, all appear set into a giant, rather rumpled, down comforter of white satin.

At one point on the trail, both the main (upper) and the lower lake can be seen, beneath an immense granite slope rising up to a razor ridge on the left. It's impossible to imagine where

Snowslide Lake, immediately left of Lower Caribou Lake, might fit in. But a third cirque magically emerges from the granite wall. Between miles 7 1/2 and 9, the trail drops 500 feet, to a narrow, pillow ridge between Snowslide and Lower Caribou Lakes.

My wife nominates Snowslide as the prettiest of the Caribou Basin lakes (Middle Caribou Lake is a 1/2 acre pond next to Lower Caribou Lake). The main lake's beauty is slightly diminished because its cirque cuts a band of boring, crumbly schist on one side.

At 10 acres, Snowslide Lake is the smallest of the trio. It's surface, 6700 feet above sea level, lies 200 feet above the 22 acre lower lake and 150 feet below Caribou Lake. White slopes shoot up 1000 feet from Snowslide's eastern shore, culminating in a row of stone spires that resemble a giant marimba.

Expect a continuous stream of hikers and horses on this extremely popular route. The campground at Snowslide Lake, on a rocky hump separating Snowslide from Lower Caribou Lake, tends to be busy and crowded. The upper lake also attracts many campers but offers more room to spread out.

The trail up from Snowslide to the much larger Caribou lake, winds through a maze of marshmallow granite to Caribou's eastern shore. Again, sawtoothed ridges careen down to a series of gentle meadows and glacially rounded granite outcroppings. Brook and rainbow trout fishing excels in all lakes.

For a glimpse of the two most beautiful lakes you're ever likely to experience, continue up the trail an 11th mile, to the pass 700 feet above Caribou Lake. It's steep, of course, but not very long. Views of the Caribou Basin and Thompson Peak should keep your mind off the panting and perspiration.

From atop the narrow, high ridge, the trail plunges into the valley of the Stuart Fork (Chapter 18). The astonishingly deep, "U" shaped glacial valley is framed by the sheer, 3000 foot wall of Sawtooth Ridge on one side and 8800 foot Sawtooth Mountain on the other, with the flat green expanse of Morris Meadows in between. It brought to mind the final scene from "The Sound of Music."

On the map, it appears 3/4 of a mile from the ridge to the Stuart Fork Trail. In that span, however, the trail drops 2500 feet. I contented myself with merely peering down. Which was fine since it was possibly the most beautiful scene I've ever witnessed.

The Stuart Fork Trail culminates at the deep cirque shared by Emerald and Sapphire Lakes. For a peek at them, scramble west along the ridge for 1/4 mile. You can't help feeling like a piece of dental floss as you climb between and around the ridge's protruding sawtooth spires. It soon pays off, though. The most exquisite lakes on Earth quickly appear, 3000 feet straight down the south face of Thompson Peak. Sapphire lake, higher of the pair, covers 43 acres and reaches a depth of over 200 feet.

Sawtooth Ridge!

WARD LAKE/SAWTOOTH RIDGE

Destinations: Kidd Creek Divide, Ward Lake, Horseshoe Lake, South Fork Salmon River, Sawtooth Ridge, Salmon Lake, Tri-Forest Peak, Josephine Lake
Location: T37N-R9W-Sec. 18
USGS 7.5" Topo: Caribou Lake and Siligo Peak,CA
Length: 6 miles (to Ward Lake and Sawtooth Ridge)
Water: Very little (treat first!)
Access: Excellent gravel road
Season: June through October
Difficulty: Difficult
Elevation: 5000 to 7600 feet
Ownership: Klamath NF
Phone: (916) 467-5757

Directions: Take Highway 3 from Yreka or Weaverville to the town of Coffee Creek. Follow Coffee Creek Road 19 miles to the gate, 1/4 mile past Big Flat Campground. There's room for 6 or 8 cars along the shoulder near the gate; or park at the campground, which accommodates at least 50 cars. The trail follows the road.

One fact of life for outdoors writers is that they lose credibility if they describe too many places as, "the most beautiful I've ever been." In the Trinity Alps, unfortunately, Grizzly Lake, Caribou Lake, Sapphire Lake, Canyon Creek, Deer Creek Pass and Papoose Lake line up in a virtual dead heat for that singular honor.

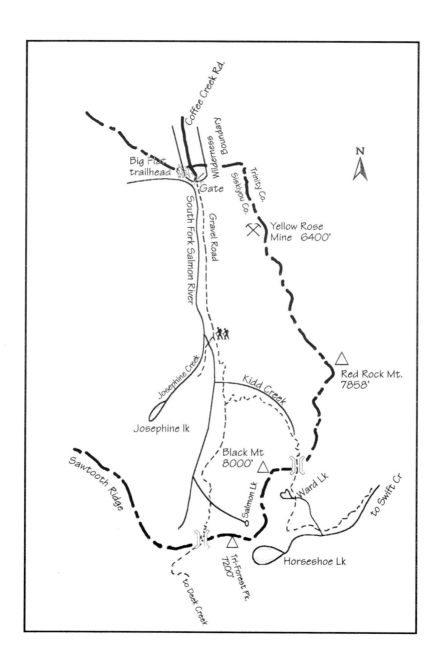

When I climbed the Kidd Creek divide and Sawtooth Ridge and tried to formulate suitable words to express its overwhelming beauty, the dreaded phrase, "it's the most beautiful place I've ever been," kept weaseling into my thoughts. While I eventually came up with a more apt description, the incident underscores the many wonders in store for those taking time to explore the Trinity Alps' lesser trails.

If you must know, the most beautiful place I've really ever been was Dead Horse Point, at Utah's Canyonlands National Park.

Aside from being— perhaps— one of the most beautiful places I've ever been, my excursion to Kidd Creek and Sawtooth Ridge stands out for two reasons. First, I hiked 19 miles in a one day, non-camping trip, making it by far this book's lengthiest day-hike. Second, between the Kidd Creek divide and Sawtooth Ridge, I climbed 4800 feet, beating out Grizzly Lake and Granite Peak by a fair margin, as the book's climbingest chapter.

More precisely, I climbed 2600 feet, descended 500 feet, re-climbed 500 feet, descended 2200 feet, climbed 1700 feet and descended 2100 feet.

The trail (several trails, actually), begins at the locked gate across Coffee Creek Road, 1/4 mile past Big Flat Campground. The popular Caribou Lakes Trail (Chapter 11), takes off from Big Flat. Just before Big Flat, Coffee Creek Road leaves Coffee Creek and begins following the South Fork of the Salmon River.

No trailhead markings adorn the gate, just a sign warning that only patrons of Josephine Creek Lodge may drive past that point. It's a lovely, easy, 2 mile stroll along the slightly uptrending road to the actual marked trailhead. The road winds through a beautiful forest of Douglas-fir and white fir, opening every once in a while to wide, green meadows.

The highly fishable river, for the most part, runs well away from the road and is not visible. The same cannot be said of the white granite, 8500 foot flank of Caribou Peak, towering overhead. As you walk, a huge cleft in Caribou Peak gradually comes into view. You soon find yourself peering straight up the Josephine Creek cirque, with its perfectly formed headwall.

Eventually, a sign alongside the road announces, "Kidd Creek, Ward Lake, Swift Creek." Nearby, a trail trails off into the woods on the left.

If you stay on the road, it's 1/2 mile to Josephine Creek Lodge— reservations only. Renting a cabin at this lovely retreat will save you 4 miles of hiking (2 miles each way). Patrons are also permitted to undertake the short, difficult climb to Josephine Lake, inside the Josephine Creek basin. At 17 acres, the privately owned lake is a miniature version of Sapphire Lake.

Although the road sign fails to mention it, the Kidd Creek trailhead is also the Sawtooth Ridge trailhead. The Sawtooth Ridge turnoff lies a mile up the path. The reasonably level first mile snakes through woods and across several dry (usually), cobbly creek beds. Eventually, it inscribes a short series of steep switchbacks and passes a house, a road and Kidd Creek before hitting the junction.

The Kidd/Sawtooth junction lies 3 miles from the gate and 400 feet above it, at 5400 feet. From there, it's 3 miles to Sawtooth Ridge, 3 to the Kidd Creek divide and 3 1/2 to Ward Lake (the sign claims 4).

The sign pointing towards Sawtooth Ridge also says "Tri-Forest Peak." The latter rises just east of the Sawtooth Ridge Trail crest. As the name suggests, the 7600 foot summit lies in Klamath, Shasta and Trinity National Forests. It was named, I presume, before they combined Shasta and Trinity National Forests.

The junction sign also claims it's 4 1/2 miles back to Big Flat. Actually, it's between 3 and 3 1/2 miles to the Big Flat Campground. Either the signmaker had a bad case of Forest Service math or the sign refers to Big Flat itself, not the Campground.

From the junction, the Kidd Creek Trail's initial mile winds steeply though the woods in interminable switchbacks. Eventually, it crosses a point of rock and approaches the deep gorge of Kidd Creek. According to the Wilderness map, the path fords the creek here. In the real world, it never crosses Kidd Creek, following the south bank clear to the summit.

As the trail climbs above the rock point, a huge cliff comes into view, with scree fields and avalanche slopes at its base. The path gradually makes its way around this impressive structure. Soon after, topping a small rise, the giant, virtually treeless Kidd Creek basin unfolds.

The orange serpentine summit of Red Rock Mountain (7853 feet), borders the basin on the left while Black Mountain's black schist outcropping (8098 feet), forms its right hand flank. All this color contrasts markedly to the prevailing white granite visible on the other side of the South Fork valley.

It's nearly a mile across the basin's rolling meadows, and a 600 foot climb, to the crest of the encircling cliffs. Most of the rise occurs in the last 1/4 mile. The climbout ascends a series of ledges, then charges straight up a rock fall. The final pitch jumps onto the nose of a rocky side ridge, zig-zagging back and forth several more times.

What a view from the top! I hiked along the rim a couple hundred feet, to some small outcroppings. It made a perfect aerie in which to rest, eat lunch and take pictures.

The most obvious landmark from my vista point was Ward Lake, a horseshoe shaped, 5 1/2 acre pool tucked in the woods at the base of Tri-Forest Peak and Black Mountain. It's 1/2 mile, and a 500 foot drop, to the lake. Six-acre Horseshoe Lake occupies the pocket just south of Ward Lake. According to the Forest Service, expect yellowjackets at Horseshoe Lake and bears at Ward Lake.

The most popular route to Ward Lake follows the 9 mile Swift Creek Trail, from the same trailhead as the Granite Lake Trail (Chapter 15).

Beyond Tri-Forest Peak, the Deer Creek valley can be seen. Look for Siligo Peak, Gibson Peak's sprawling granite upwelling and, in between, Deer Creek Pass (Chapter 17). At your feet, the Swift Creek valley drops swiftly past Thumb Rock and Ycatapom Peak (Chapter 14). Trinity Lake is not visible but Mt. Lassen is, on the southeastern horizon.

***

The Sawtooth Ridge/Tri-Forest Peak Trail begins back at the junction, 3 miles from the gate and a mile from the trailhead. Unlike the Kidd Creek Trail, it rises only slightly its first 1 1/2 miles, contouring through an old growth forest of white fir, Shasta red fir and white pine, well above the valley floor. There are many campsites in this area. There are also several roads and old trails scattered around.

A series of downhill pitches signal that the full basin, in all its grandeur, is about to unfold for the first time, at a large meadow. Sawtooth Ridge's white spires comprise the basin's right hand wall while a jumble of rock types— mostly schist and greenstone— make up the left side. Your objective is a small, wooded notch at about 11 o'clock. Reaching it requires ascending 1200 feet in the last mile, to the 7100 foot crest.

Halfway across the meadow, the path veers left and takes off up a grassy slope, then a gully, then another grassy slope, then a wooded slope. It then drops briefly but steeply down to a creek– the route's only water in late August. For the terminally energetic, it's a mile– and a 1500 foot rise– up this creek to 1 1/2 acre Salmon Lake (which can also be reached from the top of Tri-Forest Peak). There is no trail.

Beyond the creek crossing, the path wends its precarious way up a series of outcroppings, coming out on a bench marked by glacial striations and an incredible view. The tiger fang serrations of Sawtooth Ridge, blending into Caribou Peak's rounded, milky flanks, from here, look remarkably like the cliffs and domes surrounding the Yosemite Valley. Both the South Fork and Yosemite Valleys are flat bottomed basins which once housed massive glaciers, although the South Fork valley lacks Yosemite's encircling waterfalls.

As you peer down from this awe inspiring perch, see if you can find the spot where the valley transitions from Coffee Creek, which flows east into the Trinity River, to the South Fork of the Salmon, flowing west into the Klamath.

Also, look for the mouth of the Kidd Creek basin, somewhere on the right. The South Fork valley is bordered on both sides by hanging valleys, sliced off by the advancing glacier. The Kidd Creek basin's mouth is such a hanging valley, which explains why the initial approach is so steep compared to that of the South Fork valley.

If reaching this spot got your blood pumping, things are about to get much more strenuous. The path climbs another side ridge or two, then zooms up a last, nearly vertical pitch in a dozen switchbacks which jump from gray outcropping to wooded terrace to gray outcropping.

At the summit, you're greeted by a fine view of the Deer Creek drainage. The trail becomes the Willow Creek Trail, which connects with the Deer Creek Trail after 2 miles.

Between the saddle and the beginning of Sawtooth Ridge, on the right (west), the ridge line is level, grassy and dotted with trees. It's an easy, 1/2 mile stroll along the rim to the rocks, and a short climb from there to the Deer Creek/Stuart Fork divide. The divide offers a view of Morris Meadows, Thompson Peak and Emerald Lake, from 3000 feet up.

Following the ridge line left, instead of right, from the saddle, will take you on a steep, brushy, 1/2 mile climb to the top of Tri-Forest Peak. Give it a shot if being in three national forests at once is your idea of a good time.

BOULDER LAKES

Destination: Boulder Lake, Little Boulder Lake, Tapie Lake, Found Lake, Lost Lake.
Location: T37N-R8W-Sec.16
USGS 7.5" Topo: Ycatapom,CA
Length: 1 1/2 miles
Water: No water
Access: Long dirt road
Season: June through October
Difficulty: Easy even though uphill
Elevation: 5350 to 6100 feet
Use: Non-motorized only
Ownership: Shasta Trinity NF
Phone: (916) 623-2121

Directions: Take Highway 3, from Weaverville or Yreka, to a well marked turnoff west, just south of Coffee Creek. It's 11 miles to the very roomy trailhead. The last 3/4 mile of the dirt access road is a little rough and narrow.

This is an ideal trail for those wishing to experience the Trinity Alps' high lakes with a minimum of hiking. Both Boulder and Little Boulder Lakes compare favorably to many in the Wilderness (although, admittedly, little compares favorably to such treasures as Sapphire, Grizzly or Papoose Lakes– all at the end of long, difficult trails).

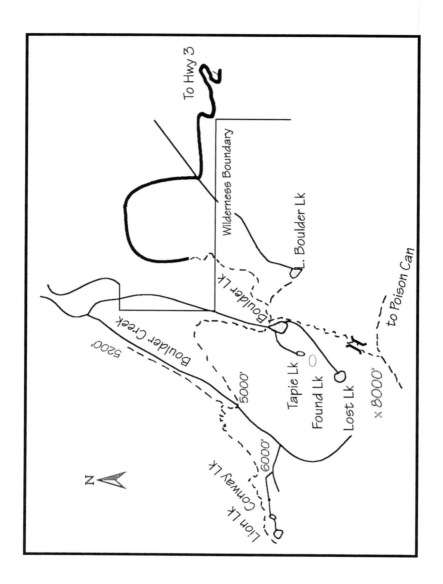

To Hwy 3

Wilderness Boundary

L. Boulder Lk

Boulder Lk

to Poison Can

Boulder Creek

5200'

5000'

x 8000'

Tapie Lk

Found Lk

Lost Lk

6000'

Conway Lk

Lion Lk

N

Of the many logging roads nibbling at the Trinity Alps from Highway 3, the well graded dirt road to the Boulder Lakes trailhead may be the most scenic. It winds steeply upward for 11 slow miles, crossing creeks and logging operations while peering out across the Trinity River and neighboring Billy's Peak.

Approaching the trailhead, several near peaks are revealed, in a maze of granite outcroppings. The craggy ridge cut by the Boulder Lake cirque is seen from the road as blending from white granite on one end, to red serpentine on the other.

While logging operations may slow your drive slightly, bear in mind that they paid for the road. A decade ago, visiting Boulder Lake required a steep, 7 mile hike from Coffee Creek. The stacks of slash and hardwood logs are called YUM piles. The initials stand for "yarded unmerchantable material." Dragging such debris to the landing reduces the fire and insect danger and prepares a bed for planted seedlings.

The last 3/4 mile to the trailhead, though driveable, is steep, narrow and rough. The trailhead area, by contrast, brings to mind a supermarket parking lot.

Although the trail climbs steadily to a ridge top, the distance is short and the grade gentle and well shaded. The woods are composed of western white and lodgepole pine, plus Shasta and white fir. Sadler oak dominates the understory.

I noted a single mountain hemlock, 1/4 mile above Little Boulder Lake. Common in the Siskiyous and Marbles, the species begins to fade out south of the Russian Mountains. It occurs sporatically in the Trinity Alps, abounding around Callahan Summit but nearly absent in many areas to the south.

After 3/4 mile, the path crosses a gentle crest and begins to circle into the Boulder Lake cirque. This down side is a little steeper and shorter than the up side. It's also far more scenic, revealing a series of granite domes at the cirque's head (Tapie Peak and Cub Mountain are most prominent). A steeply terraced canyon cuts between the domes.

The shore of the 8 acre main lake is densely wooded while pond lilies decorate much of the lake. With its exquisite, tightly composed domes, terraces, trees, azaleas, pond lilies and water; the scene brings to mind a Japanese water color.

The trail comes out near the lake's outlet, on a beautiful wooded flat. From there, it's a tortuous 4 miles to Conway, Lion and Foster Lakes. Although I chose to describe those lakes in Chapter 10, Boulder Lake is just as good a route, being a mile shorter than Chapter 10's Union Creek Trail. From either direction, it's a steep uphill trek to the 7300 foot crest above Foster Lake.

A side trail around Boulder Lake's east shore leads to the higher terraces of the Boulder Lake cirque, and to the Poison Canyon Trail (Chapter 14). To tap into Tapie Lake or find Found Lake, contour west, beginning just below the north side of the ridge between Boulder Lake and Poison Canyon, through a small glade and out around the barren slopes of Tapie Peak. It's 1/2 mile to 2 1/2 acre, granite lined Found Lake (and to Lost Lake, its companion pool at the base of the headwall in the same basin).

Tapie Lake, 1 1/2 acres, is visible a few hundred feet downhill from Found Lake, and 1/4 mile away, at the bottom a gully, on another granite ledge.

On the way back to your car, a 1/2 mile side trail breaks off at the ridge top between Boulder Lake and the trailhead, to Little Boulder Lake. It's a steep drop into the tiny bowl, over open, rocky outcroppings.

The 4 acre pond at the bottom is a hidden gem, with a wooded, rocky shore choked with azaleas. A polished, snow white granite slope, several hundred feet high, rises out of the water on one side. Like it's big sister, Little Boulder's shallow water supports a community of pond lilies. Both lakes offer outstanding fishing and picnicking.

Lilly Pad Lake

Destination: Poison Canyon, Lily Pad Lake, Shimmy Lake
Location: T37N-R8W-Sec.26
USGS 7.5" Topo: Ycatapom,CA
Length: 3 1/2 miles
Water: Plentiful
Access: Wide gravel road
Season: June through October
Difficulty: Moderate
Elevation: 4200 to 6300 feet
Ownership: Shasta-Trinity NF
Phone: (916) 623-2121

Directions: Follow Highway 3 from Yreka or Weaverville to Trinity Center. There, take the clearly marked Swift Creek/Lake Eleanor/Poison Canyon turnoff and proceed 8 miles to the Poison Canyon trailhead (called the "N. Fork Swift Creek" trailhead on Forest Service maps). Plenty of parking and turnaround room is available along the wide road near the trailhead.

My main reason for including this trail is the fact that I'm intrigued with the word "Ycatapom," the name of the lovely, 7596 foot granite dome which dominates much of the Poison Canyon Trail. While it's clearly of Indian origin (supposedly meaning "leaning mountain"), it evokes (in my bizarre mind, at least), images

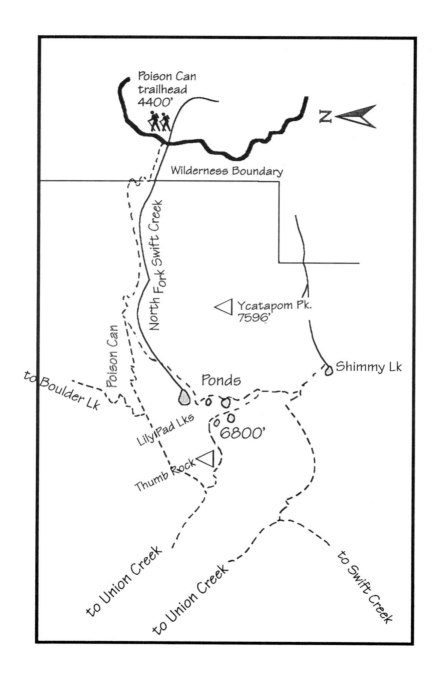

Poison Can
trailhead
4400'

N

Wilderness Boundary

North Fork Swift Creek

Poison Can

Ycatapom Pk.
7596'

Shimmy Lk

to Boulder Lk

Ponds

Lily Pad Lks

6800'

Thumb Rock

to Union Creek

to Union Creek

to Swift Creek

of someone frightened by a feline cheerleader ("Eek, a cat with pom-poms!").

Never mind.

The steep but short (3 1/2 miles) trail takes in some surprisingly worthwhile scenery. Unfortunately, the aptly named lake isn't good for much besides looking. Swimming and fishing are out due to the masses of pond lilies (Not that there aren't plenty of catchable trout in this teeming pool, it's just hard to find the water).

Were I to recommend a short hike to a charming lake full of lily pads, it would more likely be Boulder Lake (Chapter 13), which holds a slight edge in prettiness and whose trail is easier and shorter.

The lake chart on the Forest Service wilderness map, strangely, lists the distance to Lily Pad Lake as 8 miles, while the trailhead sign claims 3 miles. From the map and hiking time, I believe it's slightly more than 3 miles but certainly no more than 4.

Why, you might ask, does this book include a trail which I can offer no compelling reason to take? The answer is that I try to write from the perspective that most readers will not hike most of the trails. Thus, some chapters are simply meant to be read and enjoyed, not necessarily hiked, with me doing the walking and the reader doing the imagining.

This is a chapter where you can just sit back and relax by the fireplace on a housebound winter's evening, and let your mind wander to exotic places you'd like to visit but probably never will. To experience the beauty of Lily Pad Lake and Ycatapom Peak, in all their remoteness and serenity, you need only close your eyes.

The trail begins in an old clearcut high above the North Fork of Swift Creek. While the entire path follows this creek, the first 2 miles contour hundreds of feet up the hillside, well removed from the canyon floor.

The clearcut appears to have been planted with ponderosa pine 10 or 15 years ago. Despite the exposed south slope conditions, I'd have planted Douglas-fir (with shade cards), since pines are only a minor component at this elevation. While the pines' growth is only so-so, native conifers (Douglas-fir, white fir and incense cedar), are coming up nicely. Meanwhile, certain brush species; Sadler oak, evergreen chinkapin, thimbleberry, dogwood, deerbrush and snowbrush; are positively thriving in the harvest area.

Deerbrush ceanothus is notable because for eleven months out of the year, it is one of the most nondescript brush species in the West. For one month each spring, however, it suddenly becomes "California lilac" and people drive for miles to witness its pink, white and purple floral display. The flowers will suds up in water and can be used as an aromatic soap.

When I taught woody plant identification at our local community college, one of my students had a terrible time remembering the name "ceanothus." He kept calling it "ceanora," which I decided I liked better. Aside from deerbrush, snowbrush is also a "ceanora," as are squawcarpet and whitethorn.

From the clearcut to the junction with the Thumb Rock Trail, 2 1/2 miles from the trailhead, the woods thin out only rarely and contain some huge trees, including one of the fattest, gnarliest cedars I've ever seen. You know you're in a climax forest when the understory consists mainly of vanillaleaf and snowberry.

Soon after the clearcut, the trail makes a series of 6 switchbacks, ending at the unmarked Wilderness Boundary. The path's first mile is quite steep. The second mile, happily, levels considerably.

About 1 1/2 miles up, a small clearing appears, with an excellent first glimpse of the granite cliffs of Ycatapom Peak, your constant companion for the rest of the journey. After that, it's back into the woods, and a crushing end to any hope that the trail will remain level. From the clearing to the junction, the route is even steeper than the first mile. It does, however, pass several side creeks and springs.

Look for delphinium, monkshood, cinquefoil, willow, mountain alder and bittercherry at the creek crossings.

A half-mile beyond the clearing, the deep valley of the North Fork of Swift Creek suddenly ends at a box canyon. A wall of white granite poses a formidable barrier at its head, which explains all the climbing the path has been doing. Above, the creek waters course through the much smaller, narrower and rockier gorge of Poison Canyon. The trail offers only fleeting, tree screened glimpses of this drama, however.

After following Poison Canyon for 1/2 mile, the trail works its way to the west side of Ycatapom Peak as it crosses several large meadows. At the far end of the meadows, it arrives at the junction with the Thumb Rock Trail. A right turn here takes you near the top of Thumb Rock, and to Boulder Lake, Parker

Divide, Union Lake (Chapter 10), and just about anywhere else in the Wilderness. So, theoretically, would a left turn.

It's an easy mile, leftward, from the junction to Lily Pad Lake, through meadows and across boulder fields, with ever improving views of Ycatapom Peak. When the North Fork of Swift Creek is finally crossed– the puniest of trickles during my August visit– it means the lake lies just ahead.

The lake, as noted, is choked with pond lilies. The surrounding basin, on the other hand, can only be described as exquisite. The lush and lovely scene looks like something the artist Monet might have dreamed up.

Open, grassy meadows, encircling the 2 acre pond, are dotted with judiciously placed tree clumps (Shasta red fir, lodgepole pine, Western white pine and mountain hemlock). Graceful, terraced walls of white rock rise up on three sides of the airy basin, culminating in 7735 foot Thumb Rock, to the southwest.

A campsite adorns the lake's south end, in a clump of trees, at the edge of the grass, at the foot of a smoothed rock slope with water fanning out over it. South of the lake, around the west side of this rock, grass and granite slope gently upward to a cluster of ponds ponds set in a lush high meadow.

The trail completely petered out at the campsite when I visited, and I had a difficult time following it from there. The route is fairly evident, however. Eventually, it picks up again and climbs past the ponds and out of the basin.

From the rocky summit, 500 feet above the ponds, it's 1/2 mile and a 300 foot drop to the Deer Flat Trail. A Right turn at Deer Flat takes you to Swift Creek via Parker Creek. If you hang a left, you'll arrive at 1 1/2 acre, stagnant, bug infested Shimmy Lake in 1/2 mile (and another 300 foot drop).

Paul Bernstein at Granite Lake.

GRANITE LAKE

Destination: Granite Lake, Swift Creek, Mumford Meadow, Bear Basin, Sunrise Creek, Twin Lakes, Seven-Up Peak, Parker Creek, Ward Lake.
Location: T36N-R8W-Sec.21
USGS 7.5" Topo: Covington Mill and Ycatapom, CA
Length: 5 miles to Granite Lake, 8 miles to Bear Basin, 10 miles to Ward Lake
Water: Plenty
Access: Good gravel road
Season: June through October
Difficulty: Moderate
Elevation: 4000 to 6000 feet
Use: Non-motorized only
Ownership: Shasta Trinity NF
Phone: (916) 623-2121

Directions: Take Highway 3 from Weaverville or south Yreka to the Swift Creek turnoff at Trinity Center. Follow the good quality gravel road 6 miles to the roomy trailhead. The trail begins at the lower parking lot beyond the horse trailer area.

Granite, that gleaming white, smoothly rounded rock from the earth's core, abounds in the Trinity Alps and contributes greatly to the region's beauty. Thus, the word "granite" turns up frequently in local place names.

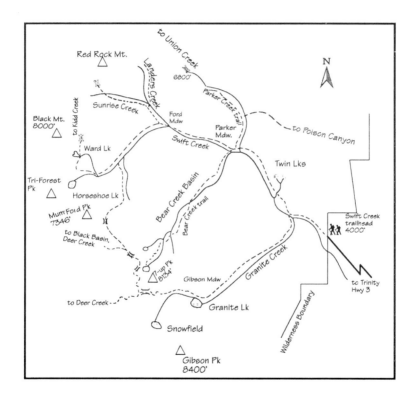

Red Rock Mt.

to Union Creek

6800'

Landers Creek

Parker Creek trail

Sunrise Creek

to Kidd Creek

Black Mt.
8000'

Ford
Mdw

Parker
Mdw.

Swift Creek

to Poison Canyon

N

Ward Lk

Twin Lks

Tri-Forest
Pk

Bear Creek Basin

Horseshoe Lk

Bear Creek trail

Mumford Pk
7346'

Swift Creek
trailhead
4000'

to Black Basin,
Deer Creek

Granite Creek

7-up Pk
8134'

Gibson Mdw

to Trinity
Hwy 3

to Deer Creek

Granite Lk

Wilderness Boundary

Snowfield

Gibson Pk
8400'

While Granite Lake may not boast the most original name, it ranks among the wilderness area's prettiest bodies of water. The trail offers much variety and many points of interest. It is the shortest and best destination reached off the Swift Creek Trail, the most extensive and popular trail network and drainage system in the eastern Trinity Alps.

From the trailhead, the path to Granite Lake scoots sharply down to beautiful Swift Creek, which it follows for 3/4 of a mile. The wide, rushing, boulder strewn stream lives up to its name and I was sorry to have to turn away from it.

Swift Creek flows through a serpentine area of white and Jeffrey pine. Side creeks along the trail are home to azalea fringed bogs where fly eating darlingtonia's rear their cobra-like heads. At one point, the creek cuts an immense, steep sided gorge. From the trail along the top, one hears crashing water and can almost make out a huge waterfall.

The Granite Lake Trail leaves Swift Creek over an elaborate metal bridge. Once across, the path makes a right turn up Granite Creek.

The next 2 miles are a little frustrating as the trail punches rather steeply through a dense Shasta fir forest. Glances ahead for evidence of the Granite Lake cirque or Gibson Peak seem continually frustrated. The only highlights here are a sizeable waterfall on the main creek and a couple maidenhair fern grottoes.

Eventually, the scene opens out to a series of lovely, if narrow, meadow areas alternating with small forest clumps. To the right rises a naked, grassy ridge culminating in cinnamon colored, weathered serpentine.

The ridge must be quite unstable since it has littered the canyon with boulders the size of elephants. Hundreds of smashed trees lie jackstrawed on the ground nearby, as though the mountain was playing a game of nine-pins with the forest.

Long, level terraces in this section alternate with steep rock faces. The beautiful creek, fringed with alder, willow, grass and wildflowers, cascades through the open country in a progression of low falls. At last, the sawtoothed spires above Granite Lake emerge in the distance.

A mile from the lake, the trail inscribes a series of switchbacks up a narrow spot in the canyon. At the top, the lush, pond dotted expanse of Gibson Meadow unfolds. It's a little less than a mile across the meadow and up a couple more terraces to the lake cirque.

Granite Lake rests in a sprawling basin ringed in granite minarets. Gibson Peak's white frosting dominates the scene. At 8400 feet, Gibson peak ranks among the highest in the Trinity Alps. It may also be the Wilderness Area's most massive mountain structure, in terms of volume. As viewed, for example, from the Kidd Creek divide (Chapter 12), it clearly occupies more room than any other peak in the region.

The 18 acre lake at its northeast base, though beautiful, is a little disappointing. The side of the lake away from the cliff is choked with virtually impenetrable alder brush. Only one small spot on the shore is easily reached and that has a very steep bank. Campsites are well away from the water.

If you can get through the brush to the good fishing spots, you will be amply rewarded. Not by me, though.

From the lake, the trail can be seen climbing 1600 feet in 1 1/2 miles to an inviting pass leading to the Deer Creek Trail, just below Deer Lake (Chapter 17). The pass climbs a corridor resembling a stairwell, with granite on one side and serpentine on the other. It descends, on the other side, via a similar stairwell groove.

***

As noted, the Swift Creek Trail ranks among the most popular in the Wilderness. Numerous side paths, leading to any number of fascinating places, branch off from the main trail in the 7 miles between the trailhead and Mumford Meadow. The path gains only 1500 feet in those 7 miles, as it marches through forests of giant Douglas-fir and white fir. Here is a very sketchy summary of the Swift Creek Trail's many options:

A mile past the Granite Lake turnoff, the trail crosses the outlet from Twin Lakes, a pair of lily pad ponds hiding 1/2 mile up the hill in a sea of darlingtonia bogs and serpentine. There is no path and the way is steep and brushy.

A four-way junction, connecting to Parker Divide and Bear Basin, comes front-and-center 4 miles from the trailhead, just past an impressive gorge at the mouth of Parker Creek. The Parker Creek Trail leads over Parker Divide to Union Creek and Landers Lake. You can also reach Landers Lake by continuing up Swift Creek other 2 miles and following the steep, low quality Landers Creek Trail past Sunrise Creek.

Personally, were I dying to stick a toe in Landers Lake, I'd use the route described in Chapter 10. The Sunrise Creek Trail, branching off the Landers Creek Trail, comes out at Yellow Rose Mine above Big Flat.

Past the of crowded campsites at Foster Cabin and Mumford Meadow, the Swift Creek Trail climbs past red serpentine out-croppings, floral meadows and darlingtonia bogs to Horseshoe and Ward Lakes (Chapter 12). Yet another side trail, 2/3's of the way from Mumford Meadow to Horseshoe Lake, branches south, ascends a very steep ridge, then drops into the Black Basin mining area and, ultimately, the Deer Creek Trail.

The other main side route off Swift Creek offers a challenging and highly scenic loop from Gibson Lake, if you have a couple days. The Bear Basin Trail leaves the Swift Creek Trail at Parker Creek, just below Parker Meadow. It climbs steeply for a couple miles, through a narrow, wooded canyon, then emerges at a series of large meadows bordered by serpentine cliffs.

At the head of the basin, the path ascends the orange flank of Seven-Up Peak (8134 feet), loops through a tiny but deep, lakeless cirque housing a permanent snowfield, and comes out on the ridge above Deer Creek. A fork just past the cirque allows you to either drop into Deer Creek via Black Basin, or circle up and around Seven-Up Peak, connecting to the pass above Granite Lake after a mile.

Granite Peak Summit.

GRANITE PEAK TRAIL

Destination: Granite Peak
Location: T35N-R9W-Sec. 14
USGS 7.5" Topo: Covington Mill,CA
Length: 4 1/2 mi
Water: Sparse
Access: Good dirt road
Difficulty: Very difficult
Elevation: 4100 to 8091
Season: June through October
Use: Non-motorized only
Ownership: Shasta-Trinity NF

Directions: Take Highway 3 from Yreka or Weaverville, to the Trinity Lake area. Between Stoney Creek and the Estrellita Marina, look for the turnoff to the Granite Peak Trail. Follow the dirt road 3 miles to a huge parking area on an old logging landing. On the Forest Service map of the Trinity Alps Wilderness, this trailhead is mislabeled Stonewall Pass. Do not accidentally take the real Stonewall Pass road, 3 miles south.

The Granite Peak Trail is impossible to describe without feeling tongue-tied. As a reporter, however, it's my duty to try. If the news that the mountain is "real pretty– with a terrific view," somehow falls flat, blame it on the inadequacy of our language.

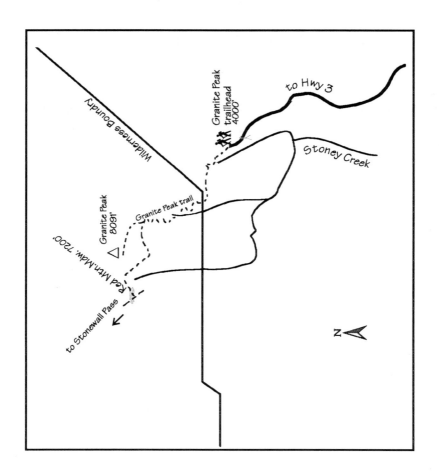

I could evade the issue by bowling readers over with statistics. To seekers of physical challenge, this path, soaring 4000 feet in 4 miles, ranks as a genuine killer. It left me achy and limping for three days (although admittedly, I'd done little hiking that particular summer).

Granite Peak, at 8091 feet, is by no means the Trinity Alps' highest. That honor goes to 9002 foot Thompson Peak. The trail, however, is the loftiest in this book since the region's most prominent peaks generally require off-trail scrambling to surmount.

The Granite Peak Trail also holds the record for most switchbacks. On the map, it resembles a seismograph read-out after an earthquake. I lost count after 50 of them.

Virtually the entire trail route is visible to northbound motorists on Highway 3, coming up from Weaverville. Granite Peak, charging directly out of Trinity Lake, is the summit on the right, made of granite. To its left rises the cinnamon hump of Red Mountain, with Stonewall Pass in between.

The trail's first mile inauspiciously follows an old road up a series of foothills. A middle elevation forest of Douglas-fir, incense cedar, sugar pine and black oak shades the area. One by one, these species fade away as the elevation relentlessly soars.

After a mile, the route mutates into actual trail. For the next 1 1/2 miles, it works its way around to the peak's south face, up a slope pocked with giant boulders and airy stands of pine and cedar. Trinity Lake soon comes into view far below and remains visible to the summit.

At 2 1/2 miles, the path hits an immense avalanche gully, with a picturesque stream running down the middle. Far above, the emerald meadows and blocky granite facets of the summit beckon like the Gardens of Babylon. (It's not really the summit but it's comforting to pretend).

The trail spends 1/2 mile zig-zagging up this fascinating, brush choked, nearly vertical ravine; bouncing off the Shasta fir/white pine forests on either side. The ravine contains every high elevation brush species imaginable —squawcarpet, bitter-cherry, manzanita, oceanspray, snowbrush, evergreen chinkapin, azalea, etc. Masses of wildflowers, changing colors from season to season as different species pass in and out of bloom, choke the thinner-soiled sites.

Beyond the ravine, 3 1/2 miles from the trailhead, the path reaches a false summit. This enchanted spot, with its precarious rock formations and open meadows, offers the first glimpse of the true summit's jagged skyline, 1500 feet overhead. Of interest here is a huge, classical "balancing Rock," right out of a Road Runner cartoon.

Continuing relentlessly upward from the false summit, this time out in the open, the path criss-crosses a nearly perpendicular white granite slope, decorated with wildflowers (Indian paintbrush, pennyroyal), brush (pinemat, heather), and an occasional stunted Shasta red fir.

Finally, rounding a ridge top, a view of the inner Alps unfolds that will melt even the most cynical observer to maple syrup. Immediately north and west, the bleak, orange expanse of Red Mountain is revealed. The green splotch of Red Mountain Meadow, below Stonewall Pass' rocky lip, stands out like an oasis on the barren serpentine upwelling.

(When I finally visited Red Mountain Meadow, a couple years later, I was disappointed. Siligo and Van Matre Meadows, on the other side of Stonewall Pass, are much lusher and prettier. See Chapter 17)

North of Red Mountain, high above the Stuart Fork valley, the brooding inner Alps– notably Thompson Peak and Sawtooth Mountain– can be seen. Although only a little higher than the outer Alps, their glistening slopes and radiating mazes of jagged spires– liked a huge, jeweled crown– place them among the most majestic peaks anywhere.

It's 3/4 of a mile from the false summit to the junction with the trail to Stonewall Pass, Stoney Ridge and Deer Creek. The Granite Peak summit lies another panting 1/4 mile to the right.

After reaching the lookout base on the summit ridge's southern end, scan the horizon for Shasta and Lassen, the Sacramento Valley, the Sierra Nevada, Weaverville and Granite Peak's kissin' cousin immediately north, Gibson Peak.

Closer at hand, a couple of stunted foxtail pines nestle among the crest's spires and crags; along with oceanspray, fireweed and tasteful clusters of mountain hemlock and Shasta red fir. Foxtail pine is native mainly to subalpine areas of the southern Sierra. After a 600 mile gap in its range, it turns up again in scattered sites in the Trinity Alps and Marble Mountains.

Hikers often spend the night atop Granite Peak before venturing home or on into the Alps. I'm told that on exceptionally clear nights, moving headlights along I-5 in the Sacramento

Valley can be seen far in the distance. All in all, it's not a bad payoff.

Monument Peak.

DEER LAKE/STONEWALL PASS

Destination: Deer Lake, Summit Lake, Luella Lake, Diamond Lake, Deer Creek Pass, Siligo Meadows, Little Stonewall Pass, Echo Lake, Van Matre Meadows, Stonewall Pass, Red Mtn. Meadows, Anna Lake, Long Canyon, Bee Tree Gap, Bowerman Meadows.
Location: T35N-R5W-Sec.15
USGS 7.5 Topo: Siligo Peak and Covington Mill, CA
Length: 19 miles (Stonewall Pass trailhead to Stuart Fork junction via Summit Lake. 18 miles via Deer Lake)
Water: Plenty, all over
Access: Long gravel road
Season: July through October
Difficulty: Difficult
Elevation: 4400 to 7600 feet
Ownership: Shasta-Trinity NF
Phone: (916) 623-2121

Directions: Take Highway 3 from Weaverville or Scott Valley to the Stonewall Pass trailhead turnoff. Follow the signs up the occasionally bumpy gravel road, 6 miles to the roomy parking area at a logging landing. The trail's other end lies 8 miles up the Stuart Fork Trail (Chapter 18). The latter is reached off Highway 3, 3 miles up Trinity Alps Road. A third entry, via Long Canyon Trail, is also accessed from a signed turnoff on Highway 3. All 3 turnoffs lie just north of the Stuart Fork Bridge, near the south end of Trinity Lake.

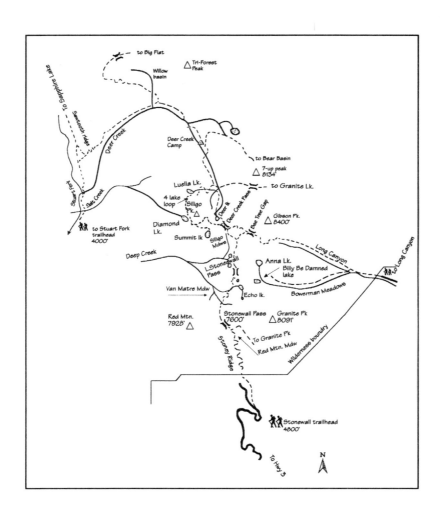

to Big Flat

Tri-Forest
Peak

Willow
basin

To Sapphire Lake

Sawtooth Ridge

Deer Creek

Deer Creek
Camp

to Bear Basin

7-up peak
8134'

Stuart Fork

Salt Creek

Luella Lk.

4 lake
loop

to Granite Lk.

Silligo
Pk.

Deer lk.

Deer Creek Pass

Bee Tree Gap

Gibson Pk.
8400'

to Stuart Fork
trailhead
4000'

Diamond
Lk.

Summit lk

Silligo
Mdw

Long Canyon

Deep Creek

L. Stonewall
Pass

Anna Lk.

Billy Be Damned
lake

To Long Canyon

Van Matre Mdw

Echo lk.

Bowerman Meadows

Red Mtn.
7928'

Stonewall Pass
7600'

Granite Pk
8091'

Wilderness boundry

To Granite Pk
Red Mtn. Mdw

Stoney Ridge

Stonewall trailhead
4800'

To Hwy 3

N

Were it up to me, the Deer Creek/Stonewall Pass Trail would be called the Serpentine Trail. It not only makes its way through the Trinity Alps' most extensive serpentine rock formations, it may be the twistiest, most serpent-like path in the entire wilderness, both horizontally and vertically.

When I followed this gorgeous, underrated route, so completely different from the rest of the Trinity Alps, I began at the far end, where the path meets the Stuart Fork Trail at Morris Meadows. We left cars both at the Stuart Fork trailhead and the Stonewall Pass trailhead.

While I advocate no particular route, I feel the Stonewall Pass trailhead makes a better terminus than entry. As an entry it takes 6 boring miles of uphill switchbacks to get anywhere. The elevation gains 2700 feet between the trailhead and Stonewall Pass, although dozens of switchbacks ease the grade considerably. Those beginning at the Stonewall Pass end hit the trail's two steepest pitches in the down direction but miss some of its most dramatic surprises.

Many folks enter the Deer Creek area via Long Canyon. Here are some mileage comparisons between Long Canyon, Stonewall Pass and the Stuart Fork trailhead: Deer Creek Pass via Long Canyon - 7 miles; Deer Creek Pass via Stonewall– 11 miles; Deer Creek Pass via Stuart Fork– 14 miles; Echo Lake via Long Canyon– 8 miles; Echo Lake via Stonewall – 8 miles; Echo Lake via Stuart fork – 16 miles.

***

While the Long Canyon trailhead lies 900 feet below the Stonewall Pass trailhead, the Long Canyon trail reaches quality scenery much more quickly.

The Bowerman Meadows Trail branches off two miles up the Long Canyon Trail. The meadows begin a mile from the junction, 2 rugged miles below Anna and Billy Be Damned Lakes. Long Canyon proper, with its marshy, rock enclosed meadows, starts shortly past the Bowerman junction and culminates in a floral meadow near Bee Tree Gap, 5 1/2 miles from the trailhead.

The Bowerman Trail to lovely lake Anna, with it's serpentine bowl and views of Bowerman Canyon, is extremely rugged. Many visitors prefer to reach Lake Anna either by contouring along the ridge from Bee Tree Gap (south, 1 mile), or by climb-

133

ing the gully on the south side of Long Canyon, a mile below Bee Tree Gap.

***

I shall describe the Deer Creek/Stonewall Pass Trail as I hiked it, beginning at Morris Meadows on the Stuart Fork Trail. From there, it's only 1/2 mile to the first of many hellacious uphill climbs, this one rising 700 feet in 1/2 mile.

The next four miles aren't nearly as bad, gaining 1000 feet to reach the 6000 foot mark. This section contours high above the precipitous canyon of Deer Creek, with its slide scarred walls. It alternates between forest and meadow, with many side creeks and abundant wildflowers (corn lily, delphinium, etc.).

After 3 miles, the Deer Creek Trail meets the Willow Creek Trail. The latter leads over Sawtooth Ridge to the South Fork of the Salmon River (Chapter 12).

You know you've made progress when the Deer Creek Trail crosses Deer Creek, then crosses it again 1/4 mile later. From there, it's less than a mile to the junction with the Black Basin Trail, Deer Creek Camp and one of the most exquisite high mountain scene I've ever witnessed.

The view sneaks up on you. You come around a bend, tired and impatient, and there it is —two craggy peaks of gray granite (Gibson on the left at 8400 feet, and Siligo on the right at 8162 feet). They frame an unnamed, 8000 foot summit of orange serpentine. At your feet spreads a vast meadow dotted with clumps of Western white pine. Deer Creek, now a rushing alpine brook, courses through the middle.

Deer Creek Pass lies only 2 miles from where you're standing. The trail rises 100 feet in the first of those miles, then soars a horrendous 1600 feet in the second. The gap just left of the orange summit is Deer Creek Pass while the trail from Summit Lake enters via the notch to the right of the same peak.

From Deer Creek Camp, a tiny flat by the creek with a sparse clump of stunted pines, one can stare at this divine panorama from their campfire as the sun sets.

The trail fords Deer Creek a third time a few hundred feet beyond Deer Creek Camp. It then makes its way up through the meadow to a major junction with the Summit Lake Trail on the right (west), the Granite Lake Trail on the left (east), and the Deer Creek Trail straight ahead.

The Granite Lake Trail climbs a deep trough formed at the seam between the granite of Gibson Peak and the serpentine of Seven-Up Peak. It looks just as impressive on the other side, where it comes down at Granite Lake (Chapter 15).

I missed the turnoff to the Summit Lake Loop, just before the Granite Lake turnoff. The loop climbs a brushy gully, gaining 1000 feet in 3/4 mile, to Luella Lake. It then contours around the backside of Siligo Mountain, past Diamond Lake, to 13 acre Summit Lake, the area's largest. Set in a deep basin, the rock lined pool lacks a creek outlet. While a steep spur leads to the shore, most visitors are contented with the view from above.

Beyond Summit Lake, the loop enters the magnificent Deer Lake cirque, holding a contour far up the barren, orange, scree draped headwall. It rejoins the Deer Creek Trail just before Deer Creek Pass.

Since the headwall retains snow until very late in the season and the path is gouged into a steep, north facing slope, passage can be treacherous before July. Most hikers– a remarkably determined lot – manage to get through.

Back at the lower junction, where the Summit Lake Loop leaves the Deer Creek Trail, the Deer Creek Trail gains 1200 feet in 3/4 mile as it climbs a series of gray rock ledges alongside the crashing waters of the Deer Lake outlet.

The 4 1/2 acre lake perches at 7200 feet, in a nearly treeless basin. A small meadow near the inlet and some willow brush near the outlet comprise virtually the only vegetation.

It is 1/4 mile and 400 feet up the red rock crags from the lake to Deer Creek Pass, the trail's high point. On our June 21st visit, we found the last few hundred yards under snow and ended up climbing over boulders, off the trail, to avoid the steep snow banks. We did the same at Little Stonewall Pass and Stonewall Pass.

Not a speck of snow decorated the south face of Deer Creek Pass –or any of the others. South of the pass, the red serpentine takes over completely, except for the steep backside of Gibson Peak.

Serpentine is actually a waxy greenish black. Because it contains a high amount of iron (not to mention nickel and chrome), it weathers to the more familiar orange hue.

Once over Deer Creek Pass, hang a right for Siligo Meadows and Little Stonewall Pass. The latter rises far in the distance, to the southeast. The trail left, to Long Canyon, crosses Bee Tree Gap after 1/2 mile.

Lovely Siligo Meadows, with its deep yellow-greens, contrasts strikingly with the brilliant red-orange of the rock. The path across the meadows, and elsewhere in the area, peters out in spots. Look for rock ducks, and for blazes on the few trees (mostly Western white pine, plus a few lodgepoles near Deer Creek Pass). With such a paucity of trees, you can usually spot the trail heading out the other side of the valley.

Little Stonewall Pass lies at the far end of Siligo Meadows. While extremely steep, the approach isn't nearly as treacherous as it looks from Deer Creek Pass.

Just beyond Little Stonewall Pass, a sign points to Echo Lake. An exquisite lake appears soon after. A jumble of red rock surrounds the pool, and a boulder peninsula juts into it. At the far end rises an almost vertical headwall, with a large snowbank dropping to the water's edge.

Only after eating lunch did we discover that this was not Echo Lake. The real lake lies 1/8 mile away, just over the low rock ridge forming our lake's southeast shore. At 2 1/2 acres, Echo Lake boasts much lingering snow and an extremely steep headwall.

Echo Lake cannot be seen from the trail. Nor can yet another small pond buried high in the Echo Lake headwall. For the truly foolhardy, a climb up Echo Lake's 900 foot headwall takes you to Billy-Be-Damned Lake, above Bowerman Canyon, after 1/2 mile.

Past Echo Lake, the trail drops to Van Matre Meadow, bottoming at 6700 feet before rising one final time to 7400 foot Stonewall Pass, 1/2 mile away. The path disappears several times and contains long sections of flowing water. It badly needed water-barring and maintenance.

The sign at Stonewall Pass announces the "Salmon-Trinity Primitive Area," which hasn't existed since the creation of the Trinity Alps Wilderness in 1992.

Atop the pass, our third of the day, the gray fortress of 8091 foot Granite Peak (Chapter 16), comes into view, along with Red Mountain Meadows and, far below, Trinity Lake. I preferred Siligo Meadows to Red Mountain Meadows.

An extremely steep 3/4 mile later, we passed a sign lying on the ground beside a rock duck. It said "Deer Lake –5 miles, Highway 3– 6 miles." Since it's 6 miles from Highway 3 just to the trailhead, we knew the sign had to be be wrong. On the map, it appears to be 2 1/2 miles from Red Mountain Meadows to the Stonewall Pass trailhead. It turned out to be, yes, 6 miles. Even at a brisk downhill pace, it took nearly 3 hours.

The sign and rock duck, we surmised, marked the junction with the Granite Peak Trail. We saw no trail taking off from there, however. The Granite Peak Trail's other end, near the top of Granite Peak, is well signed and maintained.

The final descent to the Stonewall Pass trailhead worms its way down Stoney Ridge above Stoney Creek. The first three miles lie pretty much in the open, amid serpentine and brush-fields. Eventually the path enters the woods and cools off a little. The only point of interest is a huge waterfall, far in the distance about halfway down.

The only water between Stonewall Pass and the trailhead occurs 2 miles from the trailhead, at a large side creek which probably runs all summer. We were extremely glad to see it.

DEER 'CREAK' PAST

Deer Creek is well named. A half dozen of the beasts circled constantly as we ate dinner at Deer Creek Camp, and prowled our camp all night long. They seem to crave salt like some people crave opium. Nothing we did caused them to back off more than a few feet. Then they'd resume their relentless circling, edging ever closer until we ran them off again.

My companion, Brian Boothby, had washed his shirt in the creek and hung it up to dry. We laughed, at first, when one of the deer began chewing on it. After a few minutes, however, we decided it wasn't a good idea to let him make a meal of it. That was when Brian yelled and tossed a stick at the animal.

His efforts scared it off, all right, except it took the shirt with it.

Emerald lake.

The outlet of Emerald Lake.

EMERALD/SAPPHIRE/ALPINE LAKES

Destination: Alpine Lake, Morris Meadows, Emerald Lake, Sapphire
Lake, Mirror Lake, Smith Lake, Deer Creek Tr.
Location: T35N-R9W-Sec.20
USGS 7.5" Topo: Siligo Peak, Caribou Lake, Thompson Peak,
Mount Hilton, CA
Length: 14 miles (Sapphire Lake), 4 mile side trail (Alpine Lake)
Water: Plentiful
Access: Excellent paved and gravel road
Season: June through November
Difficulty: Moderate to Sapphire; difficult to Alpine Lakes
Elevation: 2900 to 6100 ft.
Ownership: Shasta-Trinity NF
Phone: (916) 623-2121

*Directions: Take Highway 3 from Weaverville or Yreka to Trinity Alps
Road, near the Stuart Fork Bridge on Trinity Lake. Follow the road 3
miles, through the resort, to the trailhead parking area just past
Bridge Campground. You'll find a horse corral and parking for about
20 cars.*

I've dreamed about hiking to Emerald and Sapphire Lake for
20 years, since first moving to California. From photos, they
looked like the two most beautiful alpine lakes on Earth. The map
placed them at the very core of the Trinity Alps Wilderness, in a

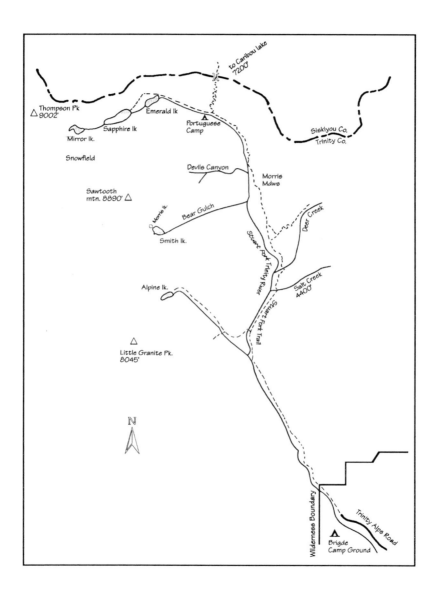

to Caribou lake
7200'

Thompson Pk
9002'

Emerald lk

Sapphire lk

Portuguese
Camp

Mirror lk.

Siskiyou Co.
Trinity Co.

Snowfield

Devils Canyon

Morris
Mdws

Sawtooth
mtn. 8890'

Morris lk.

Bear Gulch

Deer Creek

Smith lk.

Stuart Fork Trinity River

Alpine lk.

Salt Creek
4400'

Stuart Fork Trail

Little Granite Pk.
8045'

N

Wilderness Boundary

Trinity Alps Road

Brigde
Camp Ground

deep glacial cirque between the region's two highest and most splendid peaks, Thompson Peak and Sawtooth Mtn.

In 1988, I came tantalizingly close to Emerald/Sapphire when, on a trip to Caribou Lake, I took the short side trip to the crest of Sawtooth Ridge and looked down on my dream lakes from 7400 feet. The photos hadn't lied.

On June 20, 1992, at 9:45 AM, my 20 year quest came to an end. The journey, which I'd put off for so long, went remarkably smoothly and the 14 miles from the trailhead to Sapphire Lake zoomed by with surprising speed.

In the 8 miles between the trailhead and Morris Meadows, the path remains largely in the woods. It contours high above the Stuart Fork for the first two miles, then drops to the bank every once in a while. This section alternates between long, level stretches and gentle to moderate upgrades. The 1400 foot rise in 8 miles amounts to only 350 feet per mile. You'll find plenty of campsites and many side creeks.

This initial section generally lacks panoramic views. Landmarks include the side trail to Alpine Lake and the crossing of Deer Creek. Deer Creek's narrow rock gorge, spanned by a wooden foot bridge, is so impenetrable that the Deer Creek Trail (Chapter 17) doesn't begin until a mile past the creek mouth.

The significance of Deer Creek is that it marks the beginning of "The Wall," a nearly vertical, 3000 foot high formation that wraps around the east and north face of the Stuart Fork valley from Deer Creek to Thompson Peak. The Wall is shown on the map as Sawtooth Ridge.

Morris Meadows begin at the second of two Deer Creek Trail turnoffs. At Morris Meadows, a vast emerald expanse of grass and corn lily unfolds. The Wall, in all its granite massiveness, comes into view for the first time here, with 8889 foot Sawtooth Mountain looming to the west.

Sawtooth Ridge and Sawtooth Mountain, I should point out, are completely unrelated. In both cases, the description is appropriate, if not very original.

Morris Meadows lie opposite the gaping maw of Bear Gulch, cut into the Sawtooth Mountain's gray flanks. Smith Lake, a gorgeous, 24 acre pool at the head of Bear Gulch, can be reached by the foolhardy by fording the Stuart Fork and following the gulch uphill for 3 miles, to a cirque basin at 7000 feet. There is no trail and the route is marshy, full of sheer rock faces, and dangerous.

Most Smith Lake visitors scramble over from Alpine Lake, discussed later in the chapter.

The Stuart Fork Trail through Morris Meadows braids a bit, with many false paths. There are many side creeks and muddy patches. A huge campsite lines the edge of the trees to the west.

At 4400 feet, the meadows aren't particularly high. While most of the oaks, common near the trailhead, have faded away; ponderosa pine, dogwood and maple continue in abundance. Such middle elevation trees as white fir and Western white pine are beginning to take over.

My biggest botanical surprise was the presence of quaking aspen, beginning at Morris Meadows and continuing for the next 3 miles. While mundane in the Cascades and Sierra, it's only the third place I've seen them in the Klamath Mountains region. The others were at Trail Gulch Lake (Chapter 2), and in Oregon, near the summit of Mt. Ashland.

I'd been warned of rattlesnakes in Morris Meadows. Sure enough, we spotted one curled up in the grass under a tree. It was just as anxious to avoid us as we were to steer clear of it.

We were also treated to a rare close-up look at a cougar, sauntering along the trail 50 yards ahead of us in the woods just past the meadows. While the species was unmistakable, the color seemed a trifle off— dark brown instead of buff tan. It moved away as we approached, giving us something to ponder when we made camp soon after.

From Morris Meadows, it's 3 miles to Portuguese Camp. The trail climbs only 500 feet in this section so level stretches remain plentiful. The forest gradually melts away, replaced by brush (chokecherry and snowbrush), and rock outcroppings. Portuguese Camp appears just before the side trail to Caribou Lakes, 1 1/2 miles from Emerald Lake.

The Caribou Lakes Trail, between the Stuart Fork and the pass atop Sawtooth Ridge, spans only about 3/4 mile horizontal distance, during which it rises 2500 feet. With switchbacks, it's actually 2.2 exposed, south facing miles to the pass, which is still plenty steep. Also called the Suicide Pass Trail, I'm told it's in quite poor condition. Nevertheless, many people use it.

A half-mile beyond the Caribou Lake turnoff, the Stuart Fork Trail begins climbing boulders and rock faces, dotted with Brewer spruce and Western white pine, alongside a series of cascades spilling from the mouth of Emerald Lake. Fortunately, the 600 foot rise is concentrated into a very small area. Since there are almost no campsites at either lake (well...a couple if you stretch a point), carrying up a full pack would be pointless.

Emerald Lake's 21 acres are flanked on two sides by sheer granite cliffs. Its basin is a little wider than Sapphire Lake's but the lake is smaller. Gold miners at the turn of the century built a rock dam at the creek mouth but it's since collapsed.

Rusted machinery strews the site. Climb out on the white rock ledge to view the waterfall just below the outlet.

After contouring around Emerald Lake's north side, the trail shoots up another 600 feet, over more white boulders and rock faces. Like its companion, the Sapphire Lake outlet contains an impressive, stairstep waterfall. Except it's much more difficult to obtain a good close-up view.

If you liked Emerald Lake, you'll adore Sapphire Lake. The cliffs on either side are higher, steeper and closer in. I counted (in late June), six waterfalls tumbling down the sheer south wall into the lake. As with Emerald Lake, the outlet was once dammed.

Some Sapphire Lake statistics: At 43 acres, it ranks second in the Trinity Alps to Caribou Lake (Grizzly Lake runs a close third). Sapphire's 200 foot depth makes it by far the deepest in the wilderness.

My friend Glenn McNeil, who is much more audially oriented than I (I'm nearly all visual in my aesthetic preferences), tells of a March snowshoe trip to Sapphire Lake. He says one of the great experiences in his life was walking out on the frozen water on a crisp, sunny morning, and listening to the noise of the creaking ice reverberate off the canyon walls.

Two small glaciers lurk in the imposing, banded headwall at the Emerald/Sapphire basin's upper end. To sneak a peek at the larger one, take the cross country trek to Mirror Lake. The lake is perched on a ledge at the base of the vertical spires and glaciers ringing the cirque, 1/2 mile beyond and 500 feet above Sapphire Lake. Although the hike around Sapphire Lake can be a challenge, Mirror Lake shines as one of the loveliest 14 acre water bodies imaginable.

To reach Mirror Lake, follow a way trail as far as you can around Sapphire Lake's north shore. It looks impossible but isn't (although a boat would make life much easier). You'll end up scrambling through brush and over rocks, 100 feet above the lake. On reaching the level basin floor at the head of Sap-

phire Lake, follow rock ducks and way trails up the talus slope —
or follow the Sapphire Lake inlet creek– to Mirror Lake.

As much as I enjoyed my visit, Emerald and Sapphire Lakes
can only be fully appreciated from the top of Sawtooth Ridge,
on the Caribou Lakes Trail. From there, both Thompson Peak
and Sawtooth Mountain can be seen, with their glaciers and
radiating ridges, rising directly out of the basin. Neither peak
is visible from the lakes.

The ridge top view reveals the Emerald/Sapphire cirque as
the deepest and most perfectly formed in the Trinity Alps, ap-
pearing to have been excavated from the massive upheavals
by a giant ice cream scoop. It is possible to trace the extent
of the glacier responsible. It probably ended about a mile south
of Morris Meadows, 7 miles from the headwall, where the flat
bottomed valley gives way to a "V" bottom profile.

***

The Alpine Lake Trail branches from the Stuart Fork Trail
at mile 5. Unlike Smith Lake, no good views of the gulch housing the lake may be had from the Stuart Fork Trail. An excellent
campsite marks the trail junction, however.

Although the Alpine Lake Trail rises an exhausting 2600 feet
in 4 miles, the biggest impediment lies in crossing the Stuart
Fork, near the junction. A concrete, low water bridge washed
away years ago.

On my June 19th visit, I found the water waist deep and
the current barely manageable. While I could have made it
across and wouldn't have drowned if I fell, I didn't want to risk
ruining or losing my camera. The Forest Service rule of thumb
on this crossing is July 1.

Once across the Stuart Fork, the trail climbs the steep opposite bank and loops into the canyon of Alpine Creek, rising
800 feet in its first mile. At the end of that mile, it meets the
Boulder Creek Trail to Canyon Creek.

Beyond the Boulder Creek junction (stay right), the route ascends at a stiff but fairly even pace, eventually leaving the
woods and heading out onto the white rock above Alpine Creek.

A half-mile from the lake, the path negotiates a last, steep
pitch alongside a waterfall. It then levels off at a lovely meadow,
in the deep lake basin's lower end. The narrow, 14 acre lake
lies just beyond the meadow, at 6100 feet, 2000 feet below
the summit of Little Granite Peak.

The best (but far from good), route to beautiful Smith Lake follows a side creek uphill to the right, just below Alpine Lake. It's only about a mile, and a 1000 foot rise, to a saddle between Alpine Creek and Bear Gulch. From the saddle, contour left around the mountainside until Smith Lake (and tiny Morris Lake, in the same basin), comes into view. Smith Lake is 800 feet higher than Alpine Lake. Several way trails marked with rock ducks make things at least a little easier.

Granite Peak, from Rush Creek Trail.

Rush Creek Trail ridge - towards Monument Peak.

RUSH CREEK LAKES

Destinations: Rush Creek Lakes, East Weaver Lake, East Fork Lake
Location: T34N-R9W-Sec.4
USGS 7.5" Topo: Rush Creek Lake, CA
Length: 7 miles
Water: At lakes
Access: Easy
Season: June through October
Difficulty: Difficult
Elevation: 4000 to 6600 feet
Ownership: Shasta-Trinity NF
Phone: (916) 623-2121

Directions: Take Highway 3 from Weaverville or Scott Valley to the Trinity Lake area. The well signed turnoff is located near the south end of Trinity Lake, three miles south of the Stuart Fork Bridge. It's 2 1/2 miles up the good quality dirt access road (muddy in spots in wet weather), to the trailhead, which can accommodate 4 or 5 cars on the shoulder. Kinney Spring Camp, 1 1/2 miles from Highway 3, has a single picnic table and no toilets or water.

According to a chart on the Forest Service map of the Trinity Alps Wilderness Area, the Rush Creek Lakes Trail meets its namesake lakes after 5 miles. If this is correct, I must have hiked it on a heavy gravity day. In fact, the trail length is 7 miles. Nor is this the only inaccurate distance listed on their chart, which

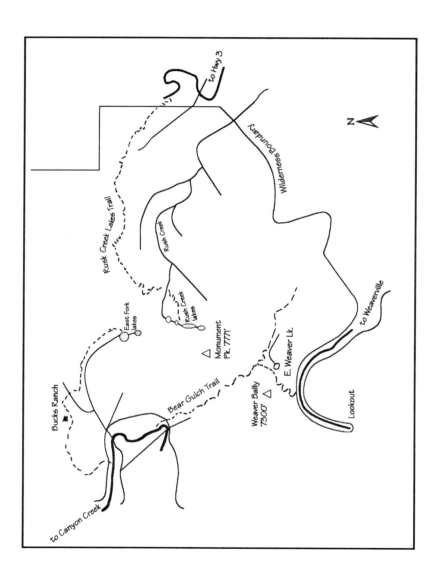

N

to Hwy 3

Wilderness Boundary

Rusk Creek Lakes Trail

Rush Creek

Rush Creek lakes

East Fork lakes

Monument Pk. 7771'

to Weaverville

Bucks Ranch

Bear Gulch Trail

E. Weaver Lk.

Weaver Bally 7300'

Lookout

to Canyon Creek

shows the Big Bear Lake Trail at 6 miles, rather than the correct 3. If they're going to mess up, they should at least overestimate, not underestimate. The error makes the route sound like a simple day-hike. While it can certainly be done in a day, I recommend spending the night.

Given the sustained upgrades in the trail's first 6 miles, I'm amazed that it only gains 2600 feet– a moderate 400 feet per mile. With all the climbing I seemed to be doing, the path should have ended up on the moon. The fact that this was my first outing of the year, after a sedentary winter with lots of good food and drink, might have factored into the situation.

While I hiked the trail on May 3rd of a freakishly dry year and ran into tons of snow the last mile, the lakes normally become accessible in late May or early June. The surrounding basin and peaks, however, often are not snow-free until late July or early August. The access road officially opens May 1 due to the trailhead's low elevation.

The walk begins with a series of quick switchbacks that take you to the top of the ridge which will be your home for the next few miles. Usually, the path runs just below the crest, grazing it every once in a while.

Despite the trail's lofty perch, there are no vistas to speak of the first 2 1/2 miles; only woods of Douglas-fir, white fir, sugar pine, ponderosa pine, California black oak and bigleaf maple. The only thing worth mentioning in this segment is a hard left turn made in the middle of a small patch overgrown with deerbrush. It could possibly be missed.

Things get interesting at 2 1/2 miles, when the path rounds a bend and the needle spires of 7771 foot Monument Peak, and its associated summits, pop into view for the first time, peering from behind a wooded ridge. The white granite Monument Peak group is the Trinity Alps' southernmost cluster of high peaks. The Weaverville basin can be viewed immediately south.

Where Monument Peak first appears, the trail shoots briefly uphill in an almost perpendicular pitch, eventually leveling off as it sidehills across a steep brushfield with a tantalizing view of Monument Peak's row of high, craggy outcroppings.

Look for a rock duck marker at the far end of the brushfield where the trail– at about mile 3– hits the ridge top. The path looks like it's about to follow the ridge around to the left. Instead, it doubles back to the right and downhill.

The next mile is by far the easiest. Mostly in the woods, it alternates between commanding panoramas of the Stuart Fork Valley and ever improving views of Monument Peak, with its blocky, flatiron rock formations. On the Stuart Fork side, look for Granite Peak and Red Mountain above the mouth of the valley, with Tri-Forest Peak, Sawtooth Mountain and Thompson Peak at the head. Mt. Shasta turns up once or twice, far in the distance, to the right of Granite Peak.

At mile 4, the trail emerges from the woods at the base of a large, manzanita covered knob. A 1000 foot cliff, truncating one side of the knob, plummets into the Stuart Fork (there's a great view of this spot from the Stonewall Pass Road. See Chapter 17). From the knob, a knife edged, east-west rim connects to another, higher knob. The looming gray wall of Monument Peak lies just to the right of this higher, emerald green button.

Look for a grove of Brewer spruce, just over the rim on the Stuart Fork side, where the path emerges from the woods and knob and cliff come into view.

This is the most grueling spot on the trail's "in" direction. Not bothering with switchbacks, the path shoots upward at a nearly 100% grade, for about 1/8 mile, to the knob's summit. It then lights out across the exposed, manzanita covered knife-rim, leveling off only a little.

I found the knife-rim interesting as well as beautiful. During my May visit, its south face contained no snow whatsoever, while the north side was stuffed clear to the top, like a nose in flu season. The path disappeared into north side snow a couple times, but the route was easily followed off the trail.

The journey attains its high point at the knife-rim's far end. From there, the path contours around to the south side of the higher knob. At mile 6, it re-enters the woods and rushes downward 600 feet in 1/2 mile, to Rush Creek. This, needless to say, is the return trip's most strenuous pitch.

Beyond the creek, the trail takes off for its final 1/2 mile, across vast boulders and billows of white granite, gaining back 400 of the 600 feet it just lost. Eventually, the tiny, meadowed basin containing the two lower ponds, each about an acre, magically pops into view. Here the trail ends.

The 4 acre main lake occupies a bench 1/4 mile up the basin, at an elevation 300 feet higher than the lower lakes. The expanse of white rock, soaring up to the angular spires atop Monument Peak, rises directly out of the waterfall fed upper lake. If Boulder Lake (Chapter 13) reminded me of a Japanese water color and Lily Pad Lake (Chapter 14) recalled the works of Monet, the Rush Creek cirque, with its headwall jumble of tilted cubes, could have been painted by Picasso or Kandinsky.

**

According to Glenn McNeil, only a sissy would use the Rush Creek Lakes Trail. He suggests two alternate routes.

The first begins just before the Weaver Bally lookout, at the end of road 33N38, which takes of north from Highway 299, immediately west of Weaverville. Just before the road hits the ridge, 1 1/2 miles from the lookout, an extremely steep trail takes off, dropping down to 1 acre East Weaver Lake. From the lake, another trail climbs to another ridge, then drops into Bear Gulch and Canyon Creek (Chapter 20).

At the crest of the Bear Gulch Trail, 2 miles from the trail-head, a faint, occasionally non-existent way trail takes off to the north, through brushfields, giant Shasta red fir forests and out onto the rocks. It is 1 1/2 miles to a gap just before the main rise of Monument Peak. From there, work your way down-hill and west, into the lake basin.

An easier (?) route uses the trails past Buck's Ranch and East Fork Lake, off Canyon Creek Road. Three miles before the Canyon Creek trailhead, turn up Big East Fork Road. Follow it to trailheads at Maple Mine or Dedrick, both of which lead to Buck's Ranch. Glenn discovered the route while living and mining at Buck's Ranch.

From the ranch, it's 2 miles to the 2 acre, rarely visited East Fork Lake, with its bouldery shores and rock islands. From there, it's 1/4 mile and a few hundred feet, up the eastern hill-side to the ridge top. Once atop the open ridge, follow it to the right, until the Rush Creek basin and the trail from Highway 3 appears. Scramble down to the trail, mark the spot where you came out, and turn right.

Glenn, by the way, made both these treks in mid-winter, on snowshoes, with a full pack.

Wedding Cake, Boulder Creek Lake.

Canyon Creek near Upper Canyon Creek Falls

CANYON CREEK/BOULDER CREEK LAKES

Destinations: The Sinks; Lower, Middle and Upper Canyon Creek Falls; Lower and Upper Canyon Creek Lake; "L" Lake; Boulder Creek Lake; Forbidden Lake; Kalmia Lake.
Location: T35N-R10W-Sec.17
USGS 7.5" Topo: Mount Hilton, CA
Length: 8 miles to Lower Canyon Creek Lake; 2 mile side trail to Boulder Creek Lake.
Water: All over the place.
Access: Mostly paved road
Season: May through October
Difficulty: Moderate to Canyon Creek; difficult to Boulder Creek.
Elevation: 3100 to 5750
Ownership: Shasta-Trinity NF
Phone: (916) 623-2121

Directions: Take Highway 299 from Redding or Eureka to Junction City, 8 miles west of Weaverville. At Junction City, turn onto Canyon Creek Road (marked by a green city street sign). Follow the road 13 miles to the Canyon Creek trailhead. The first 12 miles are paved, the last is gravel. The trailhead area accommodates at least 100 cars.

The Canyon Creek Trail, so I'd been told, is the most popular– and allegedly the most scenic– in the entire trail riddled Trinity Alps Wilderness. The huge trailhead parking lot bore out the

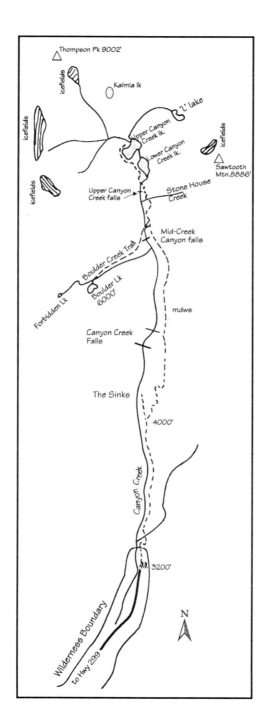

Thompson Pk 9002'

icefields

icefields

Kalmia lk

'L' lake

Upper Canyon Creek lk.

icefields

Lower Canyon Creek lk.

Sawtooth Mtn. 8886'

icefields

Upper Canyon Creek falls

Stone House Creek

Mid-Creek Canyon falls

Boulder Creek Trail

Forbidden Lk

Boulder Lk 6000'

mdws

Canyon Creek Falls

The Sinks

4000'

Canyon Creek

3200'

Wilderness Boundary

to Hwy 299

N

first assertion when I pulled in on a Memorial Day weekend. I was lucky to find a parking place.

As to whether Canyon Creek is also the Trinity Alps' most scenic pathway, my answer is an unqualified "probably." While the far ends of the trails to Caribou, Grizzly and Emerald/Sapphire Lakes may be a tad more spectacular, Canyon Creek boasts more areas of gentler, artistic beauty. Both the gentle/artistic and the truly spectacular are spread throughout the trail's length.

But why nit-pick? The fact is that Canyon Creek makes even Yosemite look like a back alley. Furthermore, because the Canyon Creek Lakes occupy one of the region's few south facing glacial basins, and they lie at rather low elevations (about 5600 feet), access opens up several weeks earlier than most other lakes.

From the trailhead, the path ascends steeply for a few hundred yards, then levels off high above a wooded canyon, amid a jungle of canyon liveoak, black oak, madrone, Douglas-fir, sugar pine, ponderosa pine, incense cedar and other low to middle elevation species.

As a one-time Forester, I found myself drooling over the giant, perfectly formed Douglas-firs lining the trail's lower reaches. "Number one peelers," the mills would call them.

After 1/4 mile, the trail crosses a large stream, then doubles back on the opposite side. It's been following Bear Creek, not Canyon Creek, it turns out. During my late May visit, all creeks fairly surged with moisture and I soon reconciled myself to constantly wet shoes.

A row of high rocks across Bear Creek looked just a little too far apart to walk comfortably in my precarious backpack. Instead, I opted for another row of stones a few feet upstream, closer together but slightly submerged. The six major creek fordings, at up to knee depth, required for this journey, were mitigated by the fact that all offered firm footing without a trace of slime.

Beyond the Bear Creek crossing, the trail heads steeply uphill, then curves around a wooded ridge top to meet Canyon Creek for the first time. The next 1 1/2 miles follow a nearly straight, level pitch a couple hundred feet up from Canyon Creek.

Two and 1/2 miles from the trailhead, you'll hit a couple of steep switchbacks heralding the side trail to "The Sinks." When I visited, the first drinkable water since Bear Creek gurgled across the path just before the turnoff. Rest assured that dozens of potable streams await.

At The Sinks, Canyon Creek disappears underground (during low water), into a maze of giant boulders. A couple good campsites may be found at the end of the steep, 1/4 mile side path.

The mile following The Sinks turnoff is the trail's most difficult as it breaks out onto the white boulder and rock slopes. In a series of switchbacks, it gains several hundred feet in elevation. According to the Wilderness map, the path rises 1200 feet in 3/4 mile here, then drops 800 feet. That seemed way out of kilter with reality and the Forest Services later verified that the map may be in error. I estimate the rise at 500 feet, with intermingled level stretches, followed by a 100 foot drop.

The purpose of this sudden rise is revealed when the roar of Lower Canyon Creek Falls appears in the distance. The falls' height looked to be about 200 feet.

The surrounding mountains become increasingly impressive from here on, as summit after rocky summit is revealed, rising thousands of feet overhead. Frequent crashing streams can be followed from high snowfields, down entire mountain flanks, often through deep gorges and over waterfalls, to Canyon Creek.

After a mile of climbing, the grade levels off and re-enters the woods at a rock point near the top of the falls. Look for an occasional Brewer spruce for the next few miles. Look also for white fir. Wherever there is Brewer spruce, you will always find white fir. The oaks and madrones of the lower elevations are now long vanished.

The next mile (the 5th from the trailhead), hugs the shaded banks of the now passive Canyon Creek. This easy stretch is rife with campsites, culminating in Upper Canyon Creek Meadows. There are no campsites in the meadows themselves, a swampy field overgrown with corn lily. The most remarkable campsite hides inside a huge boulder. A chunk missing from boulder's bottom side is large enough to accommodate a dozen people. A similar boulder/shelter occurs at Stonehouse, a couple miles up the trail.

Past the meadows, the trail alternates between level woods and steeper excursions onto the granite at the base of the mountain slope. At mile 6 1/2, amid a beautiful Douglas-fir forest and a quiet side stream, you'll come to Middle Canyon Creek Falls.

A short side trail to the 100 foot high mini-Niagara was unmarked when I visited. Look for it immediately past the side creek near the falls. The side path climbs for 200 yards, then emerges onto a smooth rock face halfway up the falls.

I chose this exquisite spot, 1/8 mile from the Boulder Creek Lakes junction, to camp for the night. I figured to visit Canyon Creek Lakes and Boulder Creek Lakes in the morning without pack, then return, gather my gear and head home. Several good campsites lie between the Middle Falls and the junction.

According to a sign at the parking area, it's 8 miles to Lower Canyon Creek Lake and 9 miles to Boulder Creek Lake. The Boulder Creek Trail seemed shorter, not longer, than the final leg of the Canyon Creek Trail.

Continuing along Canyon Creek, the path winds through the woods for another 1/2 mile (past a slightly tricky spot where it makes a right angle turn while a false trail continues straight), then cuts uphill beside Stonehouse Creek.

Here, the track leaves the woods and makes its way around the base of– then to the top of– a granite ledge. Stunning vistas of Sawtooth Mountain, third loftiest in the Trinity Alps at 8884 feet, now appear to the northeast. "Sawtooth," unfortunately, doesn't quite describe the row of giant, pointed, cream-colored spires aligned along the ridge top, 3000 feet overhead. "Tigertooth" fits a little better.

Soon after, the trail passes one of the loveliest of the trip's more "artistic" locations. At the base of 50 foot Upper Canyon Creek Falls, the water fans out over a gently sloping, glacially smoothed rock face. At the bottom, it collects into a shallow, sandy pool. On the pool's banks, a cluster of high elevation trees (Western white pine, mountain hemlock and Shasta red fir), shelter some of the route's most coveted campsites.

Nearby rises a second ledge, much higher than the first, over which the Upper Falls tumble. As the trail makes its way to the top, it appears as though the Lower Lake is about to emerge. Rounding the smooth granite crest, however, only trees can be seen, with yet another ledge beyond. The lake, rest assured, does lie atop this third ledge.

Between the rim of the ledge above the Upper Falls and the point where the trail takes off up steeply uphill to the right (up the middle of a small side creek), a new, alternate path has been constructed to the Lower Lake. Marked only by a small sign pointing left that says "trail," it is easily missed.

The old trail ends on the south side of the Lower Lake outlet. To reach the Upper Lake from there, one must ford the sometimes torrential outlet, which drops immediately into a series of treacherous cascades.

The new trail, past Stonehouse, fords Canyon Creek at a much more amenable spot. It ends up atop the smooth, barren ledge on which the lake is set.

As gorgeous at the 14 acre Lower Lake may be, with its picturesque conifer clumps, blue water and white boulder shore, the upper lake is prettier– not to mention larger (25 acres). To reach it, follow a way trail less than 1/4 mile around the Lower Lake's north shore, to the top of yet another low ledge.

At the upper lake, the vista to the west opens out dramatically. Three small glaciers feed the lake from near the top of Thompson Peak, highest in the Trinity Alps at 9002 feet and Mt. Hilton, the second highest peak at 8964 feet. Run-off from the glaciers tumble down a tremendous glacial valley, culminating at Upper Canyon Creek Lake. An intermediate ridge blocks the view from the Lower Lake.

The more eastern, steeper inlet to Upper Canyon Creek Lake flows down Sawtooth Mountain through "L" Lake, a 2 acre, kidney (or "L") shaped pool inside a narrow, steep walled cirque. To reach "L" Lake, follow a brushy way trail, or the inlet creek, upstream for 1/2 mile and a 600 foot elevation rise.

**

According to the Fish and Game Angler's Guide, to reach 1 acre Kalmia Lake, a mile from "L" Lake and 900 feet higher, "Hike towards 'L' Lake, then through the timber to the gap between Canyon Creek and Stuart Fork. Work around in a (north) westerly direction on the Canyon Creek side to the lake."

Right. It sounds easy enough, until you actually get there and crane your neck up at those forbidding granite barriers. Still, there is a rather inviting gap in the ridge, as you look back from "L" Lake. Just maybe...

**

Whatever you do, don't miss the 2 mile side trip to Boulder Creek Lakes, which branches off 6 1/2 miles from the Canyon Creek Trailhead. It's only 2 hours out of your life.

After 1/8 mile, the Boulder Creek Trail fords Canyon Creek. I found the fast moving water about knee deep and didn't bother with the log crossing, 1000 feet upstream. I'm told hikers have been killed trying to wade this creek in high water, however. The 4500 foot elevation here makes the spot accessible as early as March or April.

On the far bank, follow the left trail (the path right leads to the log crossing). After winding over some rocks into the Boulder Creek valley, the path levels off for a considerable distance, making its way through a series of grassy meadows.

Where the trail begins its steep climb at the end of the meadows, about 3/4 mile up, one of the Trinity Alps' most incredible panoramas appears. At the valley's far end, a perpendicular cliff, 500 feet high, runs from one wall to the other. A waterfall rivaling Yosemite's Bridal Veil plummets over the edge. Turn around here if you like but do get a look at the falls.

I'm sorry to report that you must ascend the highest cliff to reach the lake. And no, the waterfall is not the lake outlet. The outlet flows through the narrow canyon dividing the cliff in half, just to the north (right) of the waterfall.

The next 1/2 mile zig-zags wildly up a loose, brushy slope. Finally, after crossing a small creek, the path apparently ends at the polished rock face of the cliff rim. After scrambling up the rock face, the trail reappears amid a surreal landscape of vistas and giant boulders.

I pondered hard about ways to describe the cream colored peaks, almost completely covered with white snow, which towered overhead. Not nearly as jagged as Sawtooth Mountain, I finally decided it reminded me of a huge slice of frosted birthday cake. On checking the map, however, I discovered my idea was not original. The peak is called The Wedding Cake.

From the nearly treeless shelf atop the cliff, Boulder Creek Lake can be seen in the distance, 1/8 mile away. It looks to be a 5 minute walk. Before heading there, take a few minutes to explore the cliff edge. You should be able to work around to a perch almost directly above the high waterfall seen from the valley.

As close as the lake looks, a steep sided, 100 foot deep chasm of loose rock blocks the route. The pathway across is marked by rock ducks (cairns). If you lose the exact path, I'm told its best to stay to the right of the waterfall. The crossing is much easier without a backpack.

The 5 acre, sinuous shored lake, set amid rounded, glacially polished granite, differs little from other area lakes. Which is to say, it's absolutely lovely.

As at Upper Canyon Creek Lake, another, smaller pool lurks in the crannies of the cirque headwall above Boulder Creek Lake. It's called Forbidden Lake and it's even harder to reach than "L" Lake. For me, the name said it all. I found it difficult to find, full of mosquitoes and nearly dried out.

NORTH FORK TRINITY/PAPOOSE LAKE

Destinations: North Fork Trinity R., Bear Valley Meadows, Papoose Lake.
Location: T35N-R11W-Sec. 6
USGS 7.5" Topo: Mount Hilton, Thurston Peaks, CA
Length: 14 miles
Water: Lots
Access: Long, fair gravel and dirt road
Season: May through October
Difficulty: Easy to moderate
Elevation: 3500 to 6600
Ownership: Shasta-Trinity NF
Phone: (916) 623-6106

Directions: Take Highway 299, between Eureka and Redding, to Helena, 15 miles west of Weaverville. Immediately west of the North Fork bridge, turn up East Fork Road and proceed 17 miles, following signs to Hobo Gulch Campground and the North Fork trailhead (shown on the Wilderness map as the Hobo Gulch trailhead). There's parking for 15 cars at the trailhead, many more near the horse packer area and the campground.

While I believe every trail in this book to be a scenic block-buster —otherwise it wouldn't be included— the Trinity Alps boasts 5 areas in particular which rank as world-class, Maslovian "peak" experiences. All lie in a tight cluster around the core of the range,

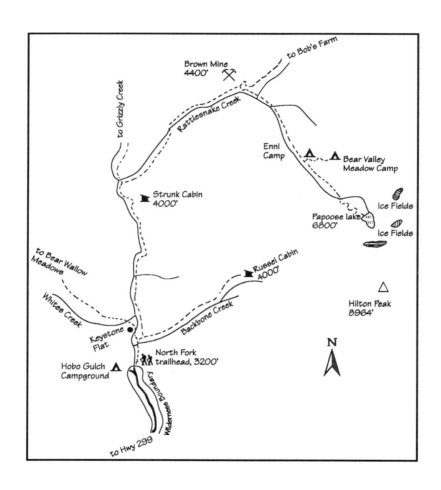

near Thompson Peak and Sawtooth Mountain. They are, however, forever separated by these impossibly rugged and imposing peaks and each must be approached from a different direction.

Of the 5 areas (Grizzly Lake, Caribou Lakes, Canyon Creek Lakes, Emerald/Sapphire Lakes and Papoose Lake), Papoose is the most westerly, most isolated and lies at the end of the longest trail. It offers by far the best fishing en route, in the Trinity River's North Fork.

The single, spectacular destination of the Papoose Lake Trail climaxes a leisurely journey which rises only 2100 feet in the first 13 miles. Like Grizzly Lake, the final mile, from Bear Valley Meadows to the Lake, soars 1000 feet up a glacial headwall to a hanging basin surrounded by glacierettes and topped by Mt. Hilton, the Trinity Alps' second loftiest summit at 8964 feet. The Canyon Creek Lakes lie just over the summit.

Just before the turnoff from Highway 299 to the trailhead access road, at Helena, you drive over a bridge labeled "North Fork Trinity River." The road up the North Fork is called East Fork Road, however. After 4 miles, the pavement ends and the route climbs 7 or 8 miles to a ridge top. It then crosses the ridge and follows the canyon on the other side to the North Fork trailhead.

How can the North Fork be on both sides of the ridge at the same time? A mile from 299, the North Fork veers west and crosses under the road, which continues straight ahead along what is now the East Fork.

At the road summit, you're greeted by an impressive vista of the south end of Limestone Ridge, rising across the North Fork canyon. The ridge can be reached via the New River Divide and White's Creek Lake Trails, described in this chapter. Or it can be visited from the Green Mountain trailhead (Chapter 22).

Despite its reputation for low use and isolation, the North Fork/Hobo Gulch trailhead area was a madhouse when I visited, the first weekend of hunting season. An eighth mile before the trailhead, where the road to Hobo Gulch Campground branches left, a commercial horse packer has set up operations. It's 1/4 mile from there to the campground, down a narrow road which drops to the canyon floor.

I found the Hobo Gulch Campground unappealing, despite the riverside location and old growth forest. It is seemingly unmaintained and the dustiest place I've ever been. Since I arrived late in the day (after a 5 hour drive from home), I hiked upriver a mile before turning in for the night.

From the trailhead, the path wanders high up the canyon, through a forest of giant Douglas-fir, with an understory of vine maple and dogwood. White oak in the rare open areas attests to the fact that above the cooling overstory, the canyon bakes like a Dutch oven in summer.

A path up from the campground joins the main trail after 1/4 mile. After 3/4 mile, the gently rising route crests out and begins dropping, crossing Backbone Creek at mile 1, near a large campsite decorated with an old car axle.

Just past the cobbly Backbone Creek crossing, a sign directs hikers either uphill right or downhill left, both to Papoose Lake. Uphill right climbs steeply up the nose of a ridge for 1/4 mile, then bears left and contours high up the canyon. The Backbone Creek Trail, taking off near the junction, follows the side creek 3 miles to the remains of Russell Cabin.

The left hand trail at the Backbone Creek junction, signed "Papoose Lake—Low Water Route," quickly drops down to and crosses the North Fork. This is not a good route to Papoose Lake no matter what the water level. Use it only if heading for Bear Valley Meadows, White's Creek or the New River Divide.

They must mean "Very Low Water Route." I visited in late September, well into an extended drought, at a time when the water couldn't possibly get any lower. While I managed to boulder hop across, it took some precariously long steps to accomplish this with dry shoes. Any other time of year would require taking your shoes off and fording. Prior to mid-July, it's probably wise to avoid this route.

The high trail drops back down to the water after a mile. From there, it's 3 miles to Rattlesnake Camp and the next major junction. And a fine 3 miles it is, with very little rise and frequent encounters with the North Fork—a productive trout and steelhead stream. This section boasts many large flats and campsites, beneath a canopy of old growth Douglas-fir, sugar pine, oak and madrone.

Past the remains of Strunk Cabin, you arrive at Rattlesnake camp. Turn right, up Rattlesnake Creek, for Papoose Lake, 9 miles distant. To continue up the North Fork, boulder hop or wade across Rattlesnake Creek. This will lead you directly into Chapter 1 and, ultimately, Grizzly Lake, 14 miles upstream.

Things change drastically on Rattlesnake Creek, and not just because you're now heading east instead of north. For one thing, the gradient begins to picks up, although it's still far from steep. While the trail's first 5 miles rise only 400 feet, the first 4 miles of Rattlesnake Creek gain 600 feet, to 4200 feet (still 2400 feet below the lake elevation).

Rattlesnake Creek's most notable feature is the intense gold mining activity. The area is riddled with tailings, pits and rock piles, dating from the last century and continuing to the present. Mining was the one activity exempted in the 1967 Wilderness Act and there are still a few permits to drive motorized vehicles and equipment into the area.

While the trail follows an old road bed through parts of the Rattlesnake Creek Canyon, miners drove straight up the middle of the North Fork to reach it. Most mines are now inactive and overgrown with alder brush and the area is healing.

The Rattlesnake Creek Canyon has a few narrow spots as it makes its way past Martin's Gulch to where it crosses to the north bank. You'll likely get your feet wet before emerging on the road to Brown's Mine on the other side.

At Brown's mine, look for a profusion of rusting junk and the turnoff to the Bob's Farm Trail, discussed in Chapter 1. While this route appears to offer a shortcut to Grizzly Lake, it's horribly steep, brushy, exposed and not recommended.

Shortly beyond Brown's Mine, the trail crosses Mill Creek and bends to the southeast. From here on, it's a straight shot to Papoose Lake. The path breaks into the open and steepens considerably as views of Hilton Peak, the 8964 foot summit dominating the region, gradually take center stage. In the 4 miles from Brown's Mine to Bear Valley Meadows, the trail rises 1400 feet, to 5600 feet.

At Enni Camp, a trail takes off left, leading to Bear Valley Meadows Camp, 1200 feet up the mountainside and nowhere near Bear Valley Meadows. This is not the way to Papoose Lake. The Bear Valley Meadows Camp Trail has been officially deactivated, especially since much of the route burned in one of the many forest fires which swept Northern California in 1987.

The true trail, and the actual Bear Valley Meadows, lies at the head of Rattlesnake Creek Canyon, in a wide basin surrounded by greenstone cliffs and ledges, with a boulder strewn floor.

Unlike Grizzly Meadows, Bear Valley Meadows are vast and beautiful—except I couldn't help wondering why they're called Bear Valley Meadows, not Rattlesnake Creek Meadows.

If the region's pioneers had their way, they'd have named every creek, mountain, meadow and lake after the area's most famous carnivore.

Twelve miles from Hobo Gulch, the trail finally gets serious. Just beyond Enni Camp and the meadows, it begins a strenuous switchback ascent up gullies, through brush fields, over boulders and around rock ledges while rising 1000 feet in 1 1/2 miles. Though well used and marked with occasional rock ducks, it's mostly a scramble trail and not nearly as obvious as the route from Grizzly Meadows to Grizzly Lake.

This is one of those places where the trail climbs a series of benches and you keep thinking the lake is at the top—only to discover another, and yet another bench still to be climbed.

When you finally arrive at the 28 acre lake, entering the basin at a ridge 100 feet above its narrow, "V" outlet, you find yourself inside what may be the most enclosed glacial cirque in the entire wilderness. Soaring cliffs wrap around 3/4's of the basin, with white granite on one side and greenstone on the other. Permanent snowfields and glacierettes decorate the high ledges just below the summit of Mt. Hilton, 2300 feet straight up the rock walls.

(Actually, Mt. Hilton is set back a little. The highest point on the cirque rim is only 8911 feet).

You'll find some great campsites, mostly to the right of the lake. The lake itself boasts a rocky shore lined with grass and, in season, a profusion of wildflowers (paintbrush, monkeyflower, etc.). A granite ledge jutting into the water offers a great spot to launch your quest for the elusive brook trout.

***

If you plan to visit White's Creek, Bear Wallow Meadows or the New River Divide, cross the North Fork via the low water trail at Backbone Creek, 1 mile from the North Fork trailhead. Presuming you make it across, you'll find yourself in the dense, cathedral forest of Keystone Flat. A half-mile later, the White's Creek Trail to Bear Wallow Meadows takes off left and makes its way up White's Creek.

Two miles after that, beyond a series of pools and benches, the path leaves the alder lined canyon and heads up a rocky, serpentine slope. The forest continues to be dominated by low elevation species—Douglas-fir, black oak and canyon liveoak.

After much zigging, a little zagging, and a several hundred foot rise, the trail arrives at a little gully choked with willow and alder, just beyond a small side creek, 3 1/2 miles from Keystone Flat. This is Bear Wallow "Meadows." While I observed neither meadows nor wallowing bears, I wouldn't bet on the continuing absence of our ursine friends.

Beyond Bear Wallow Whatchamacallit, the path contours far above White's Creek for a mile. It then climbs steeply for 1/2 mile, with excellent views of the North Fork and the high peaks to the east. At mile 6 from Keystone Flat, Hunter's Camp appears, in a wooded glade beside a small spring.

Shortly past Hunters Camp, the path finally reaches its objective—the New River Divide, at a 5600 foot saddle on Limestone Ridge, amid a majestic white fir forest. A left turn here will land you at White's Creek Lake (Chapter 22) after 2 miles. A right turn leads onto the New River Divide Trail, which follows the ridge top for 10 miles, past Cabin Peak and Rattlesnake Lake (puddle), to the main crest of the Salmon Range, just east of Mary Blaine Mountain (Chapter 23). From there, it's 5 more miles to Cecil Lake and the long, dirt road down to Cecilville, on the South Fork of the Salmon.

We're talking wilderness here. And I don't mean the weekend carnival wilderness found at places like Canyon Creek. I mean real wilderness, where you're far more likely to encounter a bigfoot than another human.

GREEN MOUNTAIN/LIMESTONE RIDGE

Destinations: Brushy Mtn., Ladder Camp, Limestone Ridge, White's Creek Lake, Devil's Canyon, Big French Creek.
Location: T35N-R8W-Sec.19
USGS 7.5" Topo: Thurston Peaks, Jim Jam Ridge, Del Loma, CA
Length: 1 1/2 to 14 miles
Water: A little
Access: Very remote dirt and gravel roads
Season: May through November
Difficulty: Difficult
Elevation: 5200 to 7000 ft. (1700 ft. at Devil's Canyon trailhead)
Ownership: Shasta-Trinity NF
Phone: 1-916-623-6106

Directions: Turn off Highway 299, between Weaverville and Eureka, at French Bar, 5 miles west of Big Bar and 30 miles west of Weaverville. Follow the signs along roads 5N13 and 5N04, 13 miles to the Green Mtn. trailhead. The gravel and dirt roads are well maintained but winding, steep and long. The last mile is quite narrow but easily driveable. The trailhead area accommodates about three cars. Turnaround room is barely adequate for a small vehicle. Trailers should continue straight, to where the road loops back on itself a mile further down.

Were Limestone Ridge located in New Jersey, it would probably be a National Park and people would travel thousands of

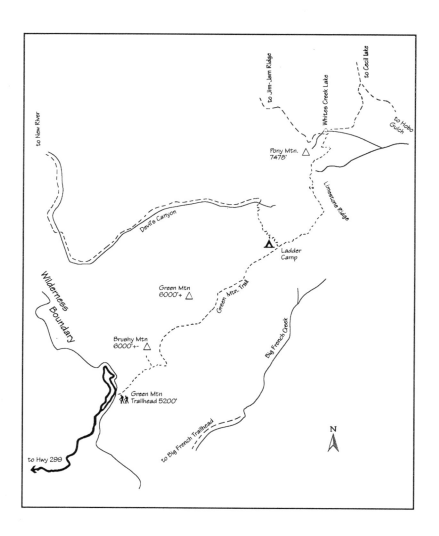

to New River

to Jim-Jam Ridge

to Cecil lake

Whites Creek Lake

to Hobo Gulch

Pony Mtn.
7478'

Limestone Ridge

Devil's Canyon

Ladder Camp

Wilderness Boundary

Green Mtn
6000'+

Green Mtn. Trail

Brushy Mtn
6000'+-

Big French Creek

Green Mtn
Trailhead 5200'

to Big French Trailhead

N

to Hwy 299

miles for the opportunity to bask in its splendor and magnificence. In the Trinity Alps, however, it's just a minor, out-of-the-way outcropping whose main appeal lies in its location away from high use areas.

The western 2/3's of the vast Trinity Alps Wilderness offers a world far different from the spectacular peaks and glacial cirques of its eastern portion. It is characterized by long trails, miles of rugged emptiness and only a few prominent summits. Within this seldom visited region, the Green Mtn. Trail stands out like an exploding skyrocket.

Views of Limestone Ridge pop up several times along the interminable, winding drive from Highway 299 to the trailhead. Ten miles from the turnoff, the entire range comes into view, above the canyon of Big French Creek. It's hard to believe that the jagged peaks, topping out at 7400 feet, are completely isolated from the more famous ranges to the east.

A lovely, easy trail up Big French Creek, takes off 3 miles up road 5N13, near the first major switchback. From the 1800 foot elevation trailhead, the year round route winds for 7 miles (gaining only 600 feet), through old growth forest and grassy flats.

Limestone Ridge is part of a geological formation within the Klamath Mountains system, called the "Western Paleozoic and Triassic Plate." While extremely complex, it hasn't been studied nearly as extensively as other Klamath ranges such as the eastern Trinity Alps, the Marbles, or even the North Yolla Bollys.

Like the marble in the Marble Mountains, limestone, a fossil bearing marine sediment subject to cave erosion, occurs in the Trinity Alps only as isolated lenses. I don't know if there are caves in Limestone Ridge but it wouldn't surprise me. The Forest Service is reluctant to reveal such information and may not even know. The American Speleological Society keeps much better records on such things. It also wouldn't surprise me if many caves in the vicinity were as yet undiscovered.

From the trailhead, it's 1 1/2 miles to the 6100 foot summit of Brushy Mountain, during which the path rises 900 feet through a forest almost entirely of white fir and Shasta red fir. Just before the trail begins to drop back down, a side path takes off to the left. Although unmaintained and overgrown in spots (with snowbrush and chokecherry), it's worth 10 minutes of your life.

The side trail leads to the flat, grassy summit of Brushy Mountain, with a commanding view of the round topped, 6400 foot Green Mountain and the jagged Limestone Ridge beyond. The New River canyon dominates the western expanse, although most of the peaks in that direction are low and uninteresting.

Back on the main trail, in the 1/2 mile beyond Brushy Mountain, the path plummets to 5200 feet, the trailhead elevation. It bottoms out at Panther Camp, then contours around to a saddle between Brushy and Green Mtn., through alternating forest and brush. Past the saddle, the route begins a gentle climb, missing the summit of Green Mtn. by a goodly distance.

Beyond Green Mtn., the trail follows a mostly wooded, up and down ridge to Ladder Camp, 6 miles from the trailhead. There's little to be seen at Ladder Camp and the springs which once welcomed pioneer travelers has long since dried up.

The path finally begins its ascent of Limestone Ridge beyond Ladder Camp, contouring gradually out onto its exposed flanks over the next 1 1/2 miles, to Hanger's Roost (6400 feet), a wooded campsite along a creek.

From there, the climb grows considerably more serious, attaining the trail's 7000 foot crest, at a narrow saddle between two outcroppings, a mile later. At the crest, spectacular views of high peaks abound in every direction, with the inner Trinity Alps unfolding to the east. Pony Mountain, the 7478 foot climax of Limestone Ridge, rises a mile to the northwest.

Follow the path another 1 1/2 miles to Whites Creek Lake, a charming but miniscule puddle in a small, treeless glacier cirque on the east flank of Pony Mountain, 10 miles from the trailhead. This extremely rocky pitch drops 1200 feet from the crest.

***

When I conceived this chapter, I envisioned Ladder Camp as the major junction on a 14 mile loop from Brushy Mtn., through the intriguingly named Devil's Canyon. From Ladder Camp, the intersecting Devil's Canyon Trail drops 1600 feet in 1 1/2 miles, then follows the canyon bottom for 7 miles to a trailhead on the New River.

The canyon's name, I concluded, has to do with the quality of the trail therein, not the scenery. The path was described to me as faint and unmaintained and the canyon brushy and uninteresting. Worse, the Devil's Canyon trailhead is either nonexistent or extremely well hidden. In fairness, the map does not show it as a developed trailhead.

It's nearly a 50 mile drive from the Green Mtn. trailhead to the Devil's Canyon trailhead. The route passes one of the most spectacular stretches of Highway 299, high above the Trinity River. Between Burnt Ranch and Hawkins Bar, look for an overlook with a spectacular view of the crashing New River gorge, where it joins the Trinity.

At Hawkins Bar, you'll find a turnoff marked "Denny." Follow it over the bridge to Highway 402. It's 19 tortuous miles to Denny Campground, Ranger Station and village (no store), with its open meadow and cluster of houses. The one lane road is blacktopped to a bridge spanning the New River, 3 miles past Denny.

On the map, the trailhead lies just before a bridge, where Devil's Canyon Creek spills into the New River on the opposite bank. Between the creek mouth and the bridge stands a 50 foot high, perpendicular rock face.

I found the trailhead at the map location to be unusable because (1) it is a posted mining claim and (2) the trail fords the New River, waist deep when I visited on June 15th.

An employee at the Big Bar Ranger Station later instructed me that to reach the Devil's Canyon Trail, park on the far side of the bridge, bushwhack over the top of the perpendicular rock face, then climb down to and across the creek.

Instead, I scratched Devil's Canyon off my list. I don't regret the drive, however. A couple other trails near Denny bear mentioning. The Jim Jam Ridge Trail starts at 3800 feet and meets Whites Creek Lake and Limestone Ridge after 7 miles. The East Fork Trail explores that branch of the New River while the New River Trail picks up the river 3 1/2 miles north of Devil's Canyon.

Salmon Mountain Summit, Trinity Alps.

Salmon Mountain trail, Trinity Alps.

SALMON Mt./DEVIL'S BACKBONE/MARY

Destinations: Salmon Mountain; Indian Rocks; Red Cap, Knownoth-
ing, Rock, Water Dog Lakes; Devil's Backbone, Red Cap
Prairie, South Trinity Mountain, Mary Blaine Meadow.
Location: T38N-R7W-Sec. 16
USGS 7.5" Topo: Salmon Mountain, Youngs Peak, Dees Peak,Trinity
Mountain, CA
Length: 2 1/2 to 14 miles
Water: OK
Access: Long, good gravel road
Season: June through October
Difficulty: Moderate
Elevation: 5600 to 6957
Use: Non-motorized only
Ownership: Klamath, Shasta Trinity, Six Rivers NF
Phone: (916) 468-5351

*Directions: Take Highway 96, the Klamath River Road, from I-5 or
Highway 299, to the town of Somesbar. From there, follow the
Salmon River Road to the town of Forks of Salmon (17 miles). There,
turn up the South Fork Road towards Cecilville. Just past Forks of
Salmon, immediately over the bridge, road 10N04 takes off right (before the bridge and left, if coming from Cecilville). 14 miles up, where
10N07 runs into 10N04 a second time, turn right, onto 10N07 and fol-*

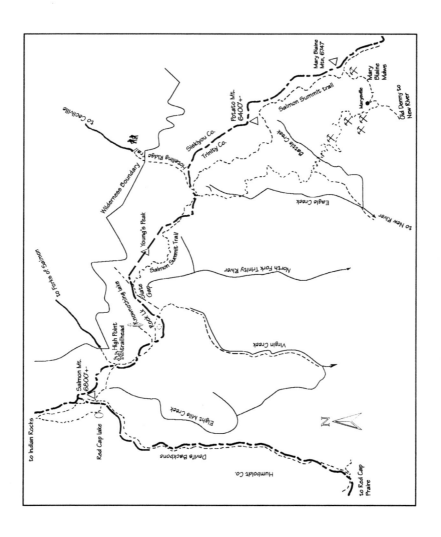

low it as far as you dare. It's about 1/3 mile from his last junction to the unmarked trailhead.

To understand the significance of Salmon Mountain, the Trinity Alps' westernmost peak, one must first understand why some consider the main rise of the Trinity Alps as two ranges, even though it's a single chain. This can best be seen from the Caribou Lakes Trail, 30 miles away on range's eastern end. From there, the system keeping such magnificent watch over California's vast Salmon River country is revealed in its entirety.

As seen from the Caribou Lakes Trail, the range's eastern end is higher and composed largely of white granite. West of the Thompson Peak area, the granite fades out. The range's remainder, along the same ridge, is composed mostly of greenstone and schist. These ancient, crumbly, gray/green or tan, metamorphosed rocks underlie much of the nearby Siskiyou and Marble Mountains as well as the western Trinity Alps.

Many maps call only the range's eastern, granite based portion the Trinity Alps. It's western half is usually labeled the Salmon Mountains. The Salmon Mountains' highest summit is...Salmon Mountain.

This western region is seldom visited and certainly can't compete with the splendor of Grizzly Lake or Canyon Creek. Still, it's a fascinating area characterized by long trails, astonishing pockets of scenery and infinite solitude.

One such "scenic pocket" is Salmon Mountain, whose 7000 foot crest drains into the Salmon, Trinity and Klamath Rivers and straddles 3 National Forests; the Klamath, Shasta - Trinity and Six Rivers. It offers vistas in all directions of some the most "back" back country the Golden State offers.

The drive to the Salmon Mountain trailhead peers down on the Salmon River, Nordheimer and Knownothing Creeks. In 1970, it was a steep, 10 mile hike to Knownothing Lake. Today, it's a 2 mile stroll from the trailhead at the end of road 10N07 (if you visit, go to nearby Rock Lake, instead. The trail is much easier to follow, the shore isn't nearly as brushy and the fishing is better).

Road 10N04 winds steeply for a couple miles as it ascends High Point Ridge from Forks of Salmon (a picturesque village which should not be missed by those who enjoy exploring California's backroads). The road levels off on the ridge top. For the next 8 miles, the wide, gravel route is fairly level, passing through vast burned (in 1987, naturally) and clearcut areas.

Road 10N04 meets road 10N07 after 14 miles. The latter is a poor quality firebreak along the ridge top. Turn right at this junction, then left, for the trailhead. It lies 1/3 of a mile from 10N04, up a very steep, sandy road. Park where you feel comfortable. Salmon Mountain rises blatantly to the right, a sharply contrasting bit of scenery amid the logging and forest fire desolation.

The trailhead is unmarked. Where the road ends, look for a Wilderness Area sign on the left. The trail takes off from there, trending upward through the woods, 1/2 mile, to a small, grassy opening. The grassy opening is a crucial spot, marked only by a signless post. Avoid, for now, the more obvious trail uphill and straight ahead, which leads to Rock and Knownothing Lakes.

Instead, take a hard right and head downhill 50 feet or so, until you come to an old road. Follow it a mile into Shasta Trinity National Forest, through wet alpine meadows of corn lily, yarrow, monkshood and arnica. Not to mention grass, willow and the sickeningly sweet smelling snowbrush.

I was struck by the distinct lack of tree diversity along the trail, noting only Shasta red and grand fir, plus a few incense cedars.

The path drops into the muddy meadows, then climbs out on the other side. Shortly after re-entering the woods, you'll come to two trail junctions, the first for Devil's Backbone (south), the second for Red Cap Lake. Stay right at both for Salmon Mountain, Indian Rocks and points north.

Beyond the Red Cap Lake turnoff, the route grows quite steep for a mile, remaining mostly in the woods. You'll soon see Red Cap Lake far below, a tiny lily pond in a miniature glacial cirque.

The path breaks into the open just below the Salmon Mountain summit. A glance to the rear reveals the gray domes of Devils Backbone, forested on the east and barren on the west. Ahead lies the narrow ridge between the Salmon and Klamath Rivers. Neither river is visible.

At the trail's high point, scramble uphill right to climb the peak, up a barren slope of scree and manzanita brush. It's only a couple hundred feet to the rim of a small, lakeless glacial cirque where a vertical rock face plunges several hundred feet to a lovely meadow.

The final summit lies a few hundred yards south, at a large rock cairn. Reaching it involves making your way up a series of steep, staircase outcroppings. It's not difficult.

The view from this centrally located aerie exceeds all expectations. Most impressive is the glaciated horn of Thompson Peak, highest point in the Trinity Alps, to the east. And no, you can't see the ocean.

It's 2 miles from Salmon Mountain to Indian Rocks, an outcropping similar to Salmon Mountain, which rises above the the cirque of Nordheimer Lake.

Salmon Mountain and Indian Rocks can also be reached (in about 3 miles), from the Salmon Summit trailhead in Six Rivers National Forest. Take the Klamath River Road to the town of Orleans, between Somesbar and Hoopa. Turn onto road 80100 at Orleans, then hang a left onto the long, winding road 10N01.

***

A couple other trails in the vicinity of Salmon Mountain bear mentioning. First is the Devil's Backbone trail, which runs for 7 miles along a ridge, through woods and across exposed rock, between the junction near Red Cap Lake and the far end of the Red Cap Prairie Trail.

Second is the Red Cap Prairie Trail, reached either from Devil's Backbone or road 10N02. The latter begins on road 80100 out of Orleans. From the 10N02 trailhead, the trail's first 3 miles climb steeply to Horse Trail Ridge. The path then passes through a maze of rocky summits, past Red Cap Prairie, Water Dog Lakes (water dogs are salamanders), and North Trinity Mountain (6362 feet). It's 7 miles from the trailhead to North Trinity Mountain

Finally, for the truly adventurous, the Mary Blaine Trail (my designation. Actually, it's part of the Salmon Summit Trail), can be followed from the same trailhead as Salmon Mountain, out of Forks of Salmon. Head towards Rock Lake instead of Salmon Mountain. It's 1/1/2 miles to the lake and 14 to Mary Blaine Meadow.

This remarkable path follows the crest of the Salmon Mountains past Young's Peak, Potato Mountain and Mary Blaine Mountain. All are in the 6700 foot range. Most of the time, the trail contours somewhat below the crest, to the south, but it does hit it every now and then.

Hardly anybody uses this pathway, except for bears. Expect it to be rough, extremely brushy, unmaintained and nonexistent in spots, with barely enough markings to get you through. It peters out completely at Slate Gap, 1 1/2 miles past Rock Lake, but you should pick it up at the gap's east end.

At Slate Gap, the trail passes the upper end of the 15 mile Virgin Creek Trail, which comes out at the New River trailhead, above Denny, described in Chapter 22.

Just past Mary Blaine Mountain, a side trail drops into beautiful Mary Blaine Meadow, in an area of limestone and red serpentine. Nearby can be found several gold mines, dating from the turn of the century. There are also some cinnabar mines, left over from a W.W. II attempt to develop a domestic source of nickel and chrome, potentially recoverable from serpentine soils. As I write, the U.S. imports 100% of its nickel and chrome.

Not far from the meadow lies two town sites, Old Denny and Marysville (the latter named, I presume, for Mary Blaine). All traces of both have been removed by the Forest Service, in line with the 1967 Wilderness Act. Personally, I see no sense in dismantling legitimate historical sites.

In the vicinity of Marysville, several trails lead to the North Fork of the New River, emerging at a trailhead above Denny. One can also loop back to the Salmon Summit Trail from Marysville, or continue east to Cecil Lake (Chapter 21), Grizzly Lake (Chapter 1), etc.

Six miles can be lopped of the Mary Blaine route (and 2 added), by using a trailhead off Hotelling Ridge. From the South Fork Salmon Road, turn south, up Methodist Creek, two miles west of the Hotelling Campground. About 1 1/2 miles up, the road makes a sharp switchback right, uphill to Hotelling Ridge. The unmarked trailhead lies 12 miles up, near the road end. You'll find the 2 mile connecting path to the Mary Blaine Trail steep and very faint in spots, but negotiable.

BRIGADOON CREEK TRAIL (Fiction)

Destination: Bogus Lake, Brigadoon Cave
Location: T34N-R11W-Sec.23
USGS 7.5" Topo: Helena, CA (Fiction)
Length: 3 miles
Water: Just enough
Access: Wide gravel road
Season: Any
Difficulty: Easy to very difficult
Elevation: Indeterminate

Directions: Take Highway 299 from Redding or Eureka to a turnoff 10 miles west of Weaverville. Look for a purple and green highway sign. The trailhead lies 1 mile up a gravel road. There's parking for exactly one car at the trailhead.

I'd often heard tales, usually late at night in the bars and poker rooms of Yreka and Weaverville, of the elusive Brigadoon Creek Trail. But I never actually located it on the map, saw it written up or met anyone who'd taken it. I even looked for it a couple of times, only to conclude that such efforts were a waste of time.

The problem, so the men at the bar informed me, was that like its mythical namesake, the Brigadoon Creek Trail appears only sporatically. Once a single car travels up the access road and parks at the trailhead, the window closes. After that, trail and access road disappear for anywhere from a few months to several years.

Needless to say, I was extremely surprised to stumble across it that morning of July 14, 1992. I'd driven past the turnoff at least 100 times, over the years, without noticing it. The trail, of course, was waiting specifically for me and would have been invisible to anyone else. Many readers of my books are convinced that more than a few of the paths I write about fall into the same category. I categorically deny it, however.

Suffice to say, though it's not for everybody, I highly recommend the Brigadoon Creek Trail. It took only a few hours and contained what may be the most spectacular scenery I've ever witnessed. It hardly mattered that when I returned to my car, a week of Earth time had elapsed.

Until a few months prior to my jaunt up Brigadoon Creek, my lifelong obsession with wilderness trails was one of the main things motivating me in our otherwise dreary world. But when faced with having to hike 15 such trails in a few weeks, just to satisfy some publisher in Los Angeles, my enthusiasm wore thin.

I found myself wondering exactly what all my hikes were accomplishing. Thus, while en route to my umpteenth trailhead of the summer, when a green and purple sign saying "Brigadoon Creek Trail– 1 Mile" suddenly appeared by the highway, I greeted it with less than unbridled excitement. It was just one more bit of drudgery in my overloaded itinerary.

From the very first step, however, the trail easily topped any I'd ever been on. Alternating between woods and meadow, it followed a sparkling stream lined with tules and cattails. The teeming fish life consisted of Sierra golden trout, sockeye salmon and goldfish. And I never saw so many butterflies in one place. Or songbirds. The green valley surrounding Brigadoon Creek reminded me of the woods where the Seven Dwarfs lived.

After an hour or so, the forest faded into the background as the trail wound its sinuous way around a series of cliffs, boulders and rock outcroppings. I ended up atop a rock ledge, at the edge of a spectacular floral meadow.

Up to then, the trail had been perfectly level, without a single rise or dip. When I looked back from the ledge, however, the forested expanse of the valley through which I'd just traveled, spread out far below. Stray clouds and mist tendrils clung to its floor, slowly dissolving in the afternoon sun. From the look of it, I'd gained at least 5000 feet elevation.

Either that, or the mountain had descended to meet me.

Not far from my vantage point, a huge waterfall crashed over the ledge. The meandering creek above housed just as many golden trout as it had down below.

Wildflowers filled the high meadow, like lollipops in a candy store. Species of gentian and lady slipper made up the bulk of the display. The sparse tree population consisted of a few windswept bristlecone pines and a lone cypress. Although I restrained myself, the perfumed air unleashed an urge to sing, dance and do handstands.

It was only 1/4 mile, following the stream, to Bogus Lake, which appeared shimmering at the foot of a cliff.

Pointed rock spires, like a wall of inverted icicles, soared 1000 feet straight up from the lake's far end.

Despite the exquisite scenery, the wildlife impressed me more than anything else at Bogus Lake. In addition to a dozen deer, I noted several otters, two or three foxes and beavers, a bear and a mountain lion. I found the unicorns especially interesting. Unlike the other animals, they wouldn't allow me to pet them.

That was not the case with the family of bigfeet living at the lake. And no, it's not true that bigfeet smell bad. Nor are they as secretive as I'd been led to believe. In fact, I couldn't shut them up. They nearly talked my ears off.

The father bigfoot, named Seybold, stood about 8 feet tall. Chestnut brown fur covered his hulking body from head to foot. His wife, Monica, tended more towards blonde while their three children displayed an array of hirsute shades. They shared a marvelous lunch with me, of cattail hearts, wild rice and wild onions sauted in butter. Or margarine. I really couldn't tell.

"Nice trail," I commented when we finished eating. Seybold, Monica and I sat in the grass, lobbing rocks into the lake and soaking up the gentle sunshine.

"You ain't seen nothin' yet," Seybold answered.

"Haven't seen anything yet," Monica corrected. "We wouldn't want this nice young man to think we're a bunch of illiterate apes, would we?"

Seybold hung his head in contrition.

That's when things started to get weird.

"What my husband is trying to say," Monica explained, "is that the trail doesn't end here."

She pointed to a droopy Brewer spruce cluster at the base of the cliff, on the lake's far side. Sure enough, I could just make out bits of the pathway among the trees and in the rocks overhead. I hadn't noticed it before.

A few minutes later, I trudged up the very spot where Monica had pointed. This time, not a single level pitch could be had. I gasped for air and dripped perspiration like a blown water main as I forced my body up the nearly vertical route. In the next mile, the path gained 2000 feet in elevation, placing me higher than any known peak in the region but still nowhere near the summit.

The trail wound to the top of the cliffs above Bogus Lake, where it crossed a wooded basin, then scaled yet another cliff. It then moved out onto a series of barren scree slopes, well above treeline. A white, tower-like pinnacle soared skyward from the center of the expanse. Smooth sided and unscalable, the tower stood 1000 foot higher than the surrounding rock desert.

The path apparently dead-ended at the tower's base. It was a stunning spot which I wouldn't have missed for anything. After Monica's build-up, however, I sensed that everything up to then was merely a prelude to the experience ahead.

I wandered around a few minutes, looking for a continuation of the trail. I tried saying "open sesame," a couple times, purely as an experiment, but it didn't work. Finally, I noticed a tiny notch in the rock wall where the path entered a narrow cave passage

Inside, an eerie yellow light permeated the tunnel, which was good because I didn't have a flashlight. After 1/4 mile of slithering on my stomach under low ceilings and through dank smelling mud, the cave opened to a huge chamber, filled with massive stalactites, stalagmites and columns. Green and purple swirls marbled most of the formations— the same colors as the sign back at the highway.

My stomach quivered as I paused at the edge of the room. This had to be the end. The scene easily exceeded any expectation I might have had, or any previous standard of beauty.

"Come in," said a gentle, barely audible voice. It came from behind the largest dripstone column in the chamber's center. Nearby, a constant water drip from the ceiling formed a small pool, encrusted around the edge with what appeared to be diamond crystals. Each drip echoed through the complex of caverns and side passages.

A tiny, wrinkled man, wearing Levi's, a flannel shirt and a beaded skull cap, crouched beside the pool. He looked like he'd recently shaved off a long beard, nicking himself several times in the process. After holding up a gnarled hand for me to shake, he bade me to sit beside him.

"Wow," I said, "you must be– dare I say your name? I sure am glad to meet you." I shook and shook his hand. For some reason, I didn't want to let go. He ended up forced to pry it away, which made me feel a little silly. The man handled the situation with graceful humor.

"Everyone around here calls me Boots," he said, after I sat down. "You may do likewise."

"Yes Sir, Your Highness, Mr. Boots, Sir."

"So tell me," said Boots, "how is life treating you down in 20th Century America?"

"Well, since you ask, I'm not exactly thrilled about the violence, greed and suffering. Still, it has its moments. I worry about having to die some day but I can live with that."

"Surely you must have questions. Now's your chance." He looked me in the eye, grinned and nudged my ribs with his elbow.

"Well, I do have one question."

"I'm all ears."

"It's like this: At this stage in my life, I have memories, glorious memories some people would kill for. Like the time I woke up at 3 AM while camping at Lake Louise, up in Canada, and found northern lights dancing the Cha-Cha-Cha across the sky. Or the day my daughter Sara took her first baby step. Or the time, at the Klamath Wildlife Refuge, when 10,000 snow geese suddenly rose up out of the marsh at sunset, just as a storm broke up in the background. Or my first date with the woman who was to become my wife."

"You're a lucky man. What's your point?"

"That's just it– what's the point? Someday, all these wonderful memories, which I worked so hard and long to accumulate, will simply cease to exist. It seems a terrible waste to just toss them all in a hole and cover them up like so much garbage."

"You sure are a worrier, aren't you?" Boots reached down to the floor, picked something up that looked like a soggy popcorn kernel, and popped it into his mouth. "Want one? It's manna. Harder than hen's teeth to get these days."

It sounded fascinating but I just wasn't hungry. "Can I save one for later?" I asked.

"Not likely. They get rotten after an hour or so." Boots stuffed another manna ball into his mouth. "Anyhow," he continued, "you were saying?"

"It's not just my own memories. So many beautiful minds with so many wonderful thoughts and ideas— Jefferson, Thoreau, Einstein. All rotting in the ground. What a cruel hoax to give them life, then snatch it away like a selfish child. And I haven't even mentioned all the people who live and die without ever experiencing joy or inspiration."

"They don't go to waste."

"What do you mean?"

"Just what I said. Your memories don't go to waste."

"Are you saying that my life force will get passed along to my children? Or that I'll live on through my writing? Forgive me, but I've never found metaphysical symbolism very comforting."

"You're making it far too complicated. Trust me— you needn't worry. The memories are never lost."

"So we really do live forever? And there really is a heaven? That's great. I can't wait to tell my wife."

"I didn't say that."

"Then we don't live forever?"

"I didn't say that either. You certainly like things spelled out, don't you?"

"Doesn't everybody?"

"I suppose. Except I never was a very good speller. I like to leave a little ambiguity. Makes life much more interesting."

"You can say that again. I've read the Bible."

"You have? Then I don't need to explain to you about faith. Or reassure you that God has too much invested in you to just abandon you when you die."

"I guess I always sort of suspected that. But it's good to hear."

"Straight from the horse's mouth, eh?"

We cracked up over that last remark. He was a pretty funny guy. After that, we talked for hours. Aside from my initial question, we mostly discussed U.S. politics. I learned all sorts of things but he made me promise not to repeat them. ·

I can reveal, however, that God is neither a Republican nor a Democrat. He loves both equally and gets equally exasperated with both.

Before departing, I was given a bagel and cream cheese to eat on the way back. I never could bring myself to try the manna. It looked too gross. As it turned out, I've never tasted anything as delicious as that bagel and cream cheese. But then, it always was my favorite food.

The main outcome of my journey was to confirm my theory that places of spectacular solitude and beauty are just a little closer to God. Or at least, a little freer from ungodly distractions. Especially places on or near mountaintops. That's the reason I became a wilderness fanatic in the first place.

We humans, alas, tend to get caught up the immediate and lose sight of the idealism which originally motivated us. It's good to be reminded of it once in a while. The Brigadoon Creek Trail rejuvenated my interest in hiking and I've been going at it hot and heavily ever since.

Salmon Mountain, Trinity Alps Wilderness.

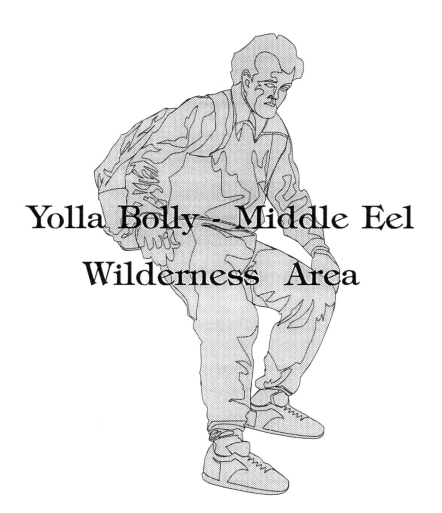

Yolla Bolly - Middle Eel
Wilderness Area

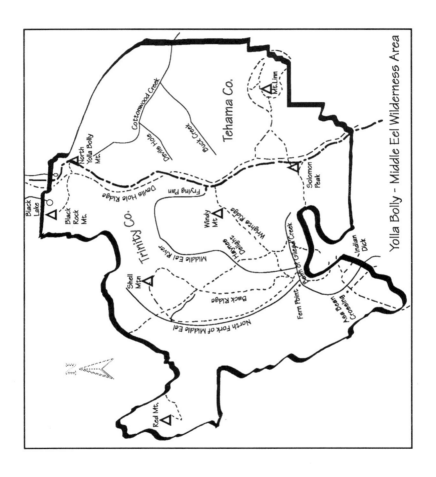

Yolla Bolly - Middle Eel Wilderness Area

NORTH YOLLA BOLLY/BLACK MOUNTAIN

Destinations: N. Yolla Bolly Mountain and Lake, Black Rock Mountain and Lake; N. Yolla Bolly Spring, Devil's Hole Ridge, Frying Pan Meadow.
Location: T27N-R10W-Sec.3
USGS 7.5" Topo: North Yolla Bolly, Solomon Peak, CA
Length: 3 miles to North Yolla Bolly Mountain; 14 miles to Frying Pan Meadow
Water: OK
Access: Excellent, mostly paved roads
Season: June through October
Difficulty: Moderate
Elevation: 5500 to 7863
Use: Non-motorized only
Ownership: Shasta Trinity NF
Phone: (916) 352-4211

Directions: Take Highway 36 from Red Bluff (off I-5), or from Fortuna, south of Eureka (off 101). West of Wildwood and the Hayfork Creek bridge, turn south onto road 30, the Wildwood-Mad River Road. Do not take the Stuart Gap Road (11), from the Harrison Gulch Ranger Station.

Follow road 30 for 10 miles to Pine Root Saddle. Turn left at the saddle to road 35 and continue 11 miles to Stuart Gap. All intersections are well signed. The pavement ends at Stuart Gap. Turn right at the gap, onto the gravel road, and proceed 2 miles to the very roomy trailhead.

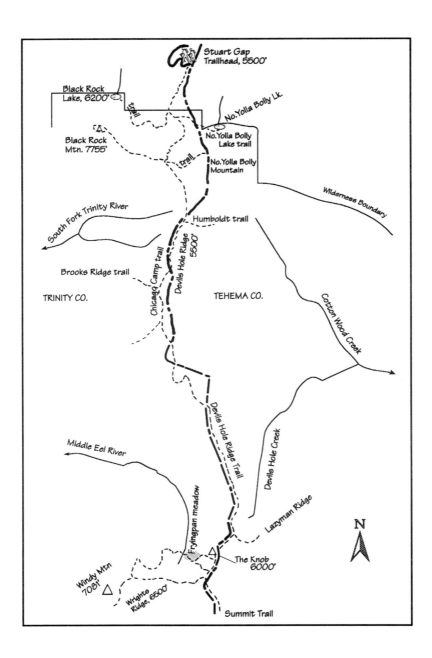

Stuart Gap
Trailhead, 5500'

Black Rock
Lake, 6200'

No.Yolla Bolly Lk.

trail

No.Yolla Bolly
Lake trail

Black Rock
Mtn. 7755'

trail

No.Yolla Bolly
Mountain

Wilderness Boundary

South Fork Trinity River

Humboldt trail

Brooks Ridge trail

Chicago Camp trail

Devils Hole Ridge
5500'

TRINITY CO.

TEHEMA CO.

Cotton Wood Creek

Devils Hole Ridge Trail

Middle Eel River

Devils Hole Creek

Lazyman Ridge

N

Fryingpan meadow

The Knob
6000'

Windy Mtn
7031'

Wrights
Ridge, 6500'

Summit Trail

192

This compact cluster of trails explores the North Yolla Bolly Mountains, a small but important formation in the Yolla Bolly-Middle Eel Wilderness. Most of the trails are within view of the paralleling South Yolla Bolly range, rising in the distance across a wide, forested basin. The Stuart Gap entry to the Wilderness offers the easiest road access and shortest trails.

The North and South Yolla Bolly ranges, while similarly named and only a few miles apart, couldn't be more different. The northern range is composed mainly of a crumbly, jagged, gray/green rock called greenstone. A very old, metamorphosed lava, greenstone is a major component of the Siskiyous, Marbles, western Trinity Alps and other ranges of the Klamath Mountains geological province.

The North Yolla Bollys are the southernmost range of the Klamath system. The unrelated South Yolla Bollys are much younger, belonging to the California Coast Range (Franciscan) province. Like much of the Franciscan formation, they're constructed of a wacky gray sandstone called graywacke.

From Highway 36, out of Red Bluff and Platina, the 20 mile route to the Stuart Gap trailhead is almost all blacktopped and almost all beautiful. After following a canyon of red serpentine rock, it climbs to Pine Root Saddle and cuts east through a vast, open pine forest.

Near Stuart Gap, the rock faces of the North Yolla Bollys come into view. The pavement ends at Stuart Gap, two miles from the trailhead. The forest here (5500 feet), consists mostly of white and grand fir; plus Shasta red fir, Western white pine and incense cedar.

The Stuart Gap trailhead lies in a huge field of bull thistle. There's plenty of parking, with shaded campsites 1/4 mile back.

It's a highly scenic, 2 mile walk from the trailhead to the high ridge, passing at least 5 side trails. The main path climbs through woods for a mile. Moderately steep at first, it soon levels off. Look for views of Black Rock Mountain immediately west. The 7755 foot peak, capped by a lookout tower, has a black north face which tumbles vertically into the Black Rock Lake glacial cirque.

Past a meadow, and side trails to Black Rock and North Yolla Bolly Lakes, the steep, well shaded route ascends to the ridge top. North Yolla Bolly Mountain eventually comes into view. The gray outcropping is as severe as Black Rock Mountain and the summit is 100 feet higher. Black Rock Mountain stands off by itself, however, while North Yolla Bolly is more integrated with the general line of peaks. That's probably why they put the lookout on Black Rock.

The trail from Stuart Gap crests at 7000 feet, on a magnificent hilltop prairie dotted with rock outcroppings, lupine and windswept whitebark pines. From there, one can follow the 1 1/2 mile trail to Black Rock Mountain lookout, on the right (offering views of Black Rock Lake and the entire wilderness area), scale North Yolla Bolly Mountain, or continue on to Chicago Camp and Devil's Hole Ridge.

To ascend North Yolla Bolly Mountain, second highest peak in the Wilderness (to the South Yolla Bollys' Mt. Linn, 200 feet higher at 8092 feet), follow an unmarked path left from the Black Rock Mountain junction. It descends for 1/3 of a mile through the woods and across a very steep slope, before entering a charming little cirque. There's no lake but it's a marvelous camping spot, with water and a meadow.

The trail climbs very steeply out of the cirque, becoming increasingly difficult to follow. Just before gaining the ridge top, I lost it altogether. On the map, it continues for a considerable distance.

After marking the spot with sticks and rock ducks where I lost the trail, I scrambled perhaps 200 feet to the ridge crest. From there, I headed left (east), along the ridge towards its highest point. This last 1/4 mile involved picking my way over loose scree and jagged rock but I finally reached the summit. It wasn't difficult. The views of Shasta, Lassen, the Sacramento Valley and the South Yolla Bollys, needless to say, were exquisite.

***

The 1 1/2 mile Black Rock Lake Trail and the one mile North Yolla Bolly Lake Trails offer short, easy side trips. The Black Rock Lake Trail holds a fairly even contour at first, swinging past a creek which turns out to be the East Fork of the South Fork of the Trinity in the Pettijohn Basin. It then climbs like mad before dropping into a rocky cirque.

Black Rock Lake is the Wilderness Area's largest. While it normally covers 2 to 3 acres, the current 6 year drought has reduced it to about 1 acre. A hard freeze in 1991, combined with reduced inflow due to the drought, created a severe fish mortality problem in 1992 at both Black Rock and North Yolla

Bolly Lakes. The lakes are stocked annually with Eastern brook trout.

The North Yolla Bolly Lake Trail is steeper than the Black Rock Lake Trail but only a mile long. The path crests after 3/4 mile, then circles into a tiny but very deeply gouged glacial cirque, with an extremely high headwall rising almost straight out of the lake. The last 1/4 mile down to the lake is quite steep.

I can't imagine flying an airplane close enough to North Yolla Bolly Lake to drop fish. While the drought reduced pool presently covers only 1/2 acre— down from 1 1/2 acres— the setting is lovely, with a view of the Sacramento Valley in the distance.

***

From the grassy, 7000 foot hilltop between Black Rock and North Yolla Bolly Mountains, one can continue straight ahead for another 11 miles, at least, tying into the far end of the Summit Trail (Chapter 28). The path's first leg drops through open meadows and hardwood glades, past several gurgling springs which form the headwaters of the Trinity River's South Fork.

Just before North Yolla Bolly Springs, the Pettijohn Trail, on which you've been traveling, dead ends at the Humboldt Trail. Bear left, then right immediately after, for the Chicago Camp Trail.

North Yolla Bolly Springs offers a fine campsite and good drinking water. It is the source of Cottonwood Creek, a major tributary of the Sacramento River. The creek meets the Sacramento at the town of Cottonwood, between Redding and Red Bluff.

From North Yolla Bolly Springs, the Chicago Camp Trail climbs to a grassy ridge top, which it follows for 2 miles, past Chicago Rock and Chicago Camp Spring. The spring tends to dry up after mid-summer.

Soon after Chicago Camp Spring, the Devil's Hole Trail— the route we've been looking for— comes in on the left. It climbs over two ridges in rapid succession, then drops into a forested pocket along Robinson Creek, with its cedar and white oak glades. The path fords Robinson Creek several times before making a sharp left and scooting straight up the mountainside for nearly a mile.

In its final 3 1/2 miles, the trail wanders back and forth along the ridge top, mostly to the east but crossing over to the west a couple times. Like most ridge tops in the Yolla Bolly, views border on the awesome. The route meanders in and out of forest, over grassy openings and up occasional rock outcroppings, holding a generally level contour. The highest elevations hit about 6400 feet.

Towards the end of this segment, Lazyman Ridge comes up hard on the left. Thirteen miles from the trailhead, atop a small knob, the path meets the Lazyman Ridge Trail. Several things happen in rapid succession soon after. First, the path makes a steep sidehill around the rocky slopes of a peak called The Knob. Then the Summit Trail cutoff breaks away to the left.

A right turn at the cutoff switches down into the tiny Frying Pan Meadow cirque, with its springs and campsites. The lush meadows mark the dead center of the Wilderness Area and the springs mark the very, very, very source of the Middle Eel River.

North Yolla Bolly Mountain.

SOUTH YOLLA BOLLY/IDES COVE

Destination: Square, Long Lakes; Harvey Peak; Burnt Camp; Ides
          Cove, Mount Linn.
Location: T25N-R9W-Sec. 11
USGS 7.5" Topo: South Yolla Bolly, Solomon Peak, CA
Length: 4 1/2 miles (10 mile loop)
Water: Lots
Access: Very long, dirt road
Season: June through October
Difficulty: Easy
Elevation: 6800 to 7500 feet
Use: Non-motorized only
Ownership: Mendocino NF
Phone: (916) 824-5196

Directions: *Leave I-5 at Corning and take road A-9 west to
Paskenta. At Paskenta, go straight (onto road M-2), where A-9 swings
left across a bridge. Follow M-2 to the Cold Springs Guard Station.
The pavement ends 19 miles after Paskenta. The last 6 miles to Cold
Springs are a little rough, with gravel and broken blacktop.*
    *At Cold Springs, turn right on road M-22 at the signed junction. Fol-
low M-22's dirt surface 8 miles, to a signed turnoff left. Continue 1
mile to another signed turnoff, to the right, indicating the backpacker's
trailhead. M-22 contains a few torn up spots at logging landings. The
last 1 mile spur to the trailhead contains a very steep, very tight
switchback but then levels off. The trailhead area is quite roomy.*

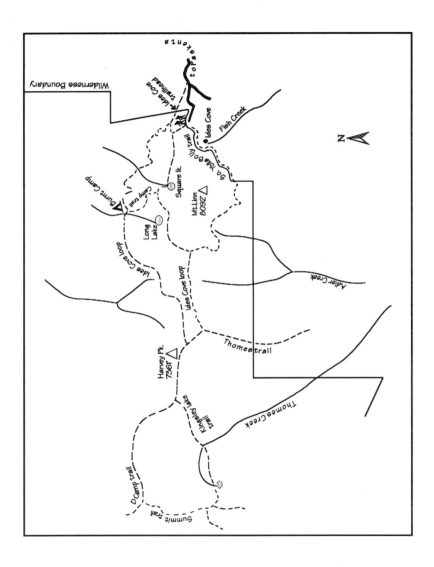

This National Recreation Trail –the Yolla Bolly-Middle Eel Wilderness Area's most popular path– explores the South Yolla Bolly Mountains, highest in the Wilderness. Unlike the North Yolla Bollys, however, no trail ascends the highest peak; 8092 foot Mt. Linn. Two paths skirt it's upper flank while the best view of the summit occurs back on the road.

Mt. Linn is, among other things, the highest summit in the California Coast Range geological province and the mountains known as the Mendocino Range. The latter is a huge, north-south ridge rising immediately west of the Sacramento Valley, between Mount Linn, the San Francisco Bay area and the coast.

Despite the altitude, the Ides Cove Trail is a beautiful, mostly level route which the Forest Service has laid out as a 10 mile loop. If that's too long, highlights at mile 1 1/2, 3 and 4 1/2 make natural turnaround spots while the Burnt Camp cutoff slices the loop in half. A recently opened pathway beginning at the same trailhead explores Ides Cove and the south side of Mt. Linn, converging with the Ides Cove Trail after 3 miles. It forms a 7 mile loop with the Ides Cove Trail.

Take particular note, near Paskenta on the way to the trailhead, of a long, grassy, hogback ridge topped with brown outcroppings. Called, appropriately, Rocky Ridge, it is the southernmost tail of the Klamath Mountains geological province; which includes the Siskiyous, Marbles, Trinity Alps and North Yolla Bollys.

Above Paskenta, the road climbs from grasslands, with cottonwood along the creeks, through a zone of scraggly digger pines and oak pockets, into open stands of ponderosa pine and Douglas-fir. Vistas of the Sacramento Valley are long and spectacular.

Roads in this highly convoluted region can be painfully slow, so allow plenty of driving time. Five or six miles past Cold Springs, look for a magnificent view of Mt. Linn (I passed the spot at sunrise, after camping out in the National Forest). Three-fourths mile before the trailhead, a steep curve took my little Toyota two runs to surmount. You'll find the trailhead atop a large, grassy, park-like knob, dotted with pines.

From the 6900 foot trailhead, highest in this book, the Ides Cove Trail (which does not go to Ides Cove– take the South Yolla Bolly Trail for that), climbs ever so slightly for its first 3 miles, with occasional steep (but short) ups and downs. After 1/2 mile, the loop trail's return end comes in on the right. It's about a mile along the main, high trail from this junction to Square Lake.

The route here, despite being relatively level, cuts across very steep slopes of loose scree. Forests are less dense than in the North Yolla Bollys, with middle elevation trees persisting to higher elevations. Ponderosa and Jeffrey pine predominate, even at 7000 feet, joined by an occasional Shasta red fir and Western white pine.

The North Yolla Bollys are easily observed from the trail. It's hard to believe they're 15 miles away since they seem much closer. Black Rock Mountain, with it's lookout tower, stands out. Mt. Shasta also looms in the distance, along with Thompson Peak, highest in the Trinity Alps.

As noted in the previous chapter, the South Yolla Bollys are geologically unrelated to the North Yolla Bollys. The latter, made of an ancient, metamorphic rock called greenstone, belong to the same mountain system as the Trinity Alps, Marbles and Siskiyous. The South Yolla Bollys are constructed of a fine grained, beige sandstone called graywacke, a thickly bedded beach sediment, which comprises the major bedrock of the Northern California Coast Ranges.

Square Lake, 1 1/2 miles from the trailhead, isn't much in terms of size. It is shallow, with a grassy shore, and covers only 1 acre. But it is stocked with brook trout and occupies a fairly large glacial cirque immediately below Mt. Linn's main summit. Barren cliffs and rocky slopes charge upward from the lake to well above treeline. Stunted whitebark and foxtail pines decorate the high ridges overhead. All in all, it's one of the prettier spots in the wilderness and a great day hike destination. The same sunrise I'd witnessed from the road was still going on when I arrived.

Should you continue on, 2 acre Long Lake lies a mile down the path, amid similar terrain. Its cirque is smaller, however, and the trail passes well above the lake, at a wet meadow. Look for a stand of foxtail pines in the vicinity.

Between Square and Long Lakes, the Burnt Camp Trail comes in on the right and offers a shortcut down to the return side of the Ides Cove Loop. Follow it for a 5 mile instead of a 10 mile outing.

Three miles from the trailhead, the route reaches its high point of 7500 feet, barely 700 feet higher than the trailhead.

There, it crosses the main ridge coming down from Mt. Linn, with vistas to the south for the first time. The far end of the new South Yolla Bolly Trail comes in here. The Ides Cove trail drops 500 feet in the next 1/2 mile; along a rocky slope dotted with windswept Jeffrey pines. It then continues along the ridge, threading in and out among several small crests and saddles, for another 1 1/2 miles.

Four miles from the trailhead, in a brief wooded pocket, the Thomes Trail takes off south along Thomes Pocket Ridge. A half mile further, the return loop of the Ides Cove Trail makes a hard switchback to the right while the faint D Camp Trail continues ahead.

Thomes Creek, after which the Thomes Trail and Ridge were named, passes under I-5 just north of Corning, on its way to the Sacramento River.

The Ides Cove and D Camp Trails meet on the southwest flank of 7361 foot Harvey Peak. To climb Harvey, continue up the D Camp Trail for 1/2 mile, to its highest point, then scramble uphill behind you to the right.

The Ides Cove Trail's return segment is longer, lower and more wooded than its outward portion, with fewer highlights and vistas. It passes a couple pleasant springs and corn lily meadows, especially at Cedar Basin and Burnt Camp.

Beyond the junction with the South Fork Cottonwood Trail, 5 miles from the D Camp junction, the path begins a steep, one mile climb past the horse trail, which breaks off to the left. It rejoins the upper trail 1/2 mile from the trailhead.

***

The new South Yolla Bolly Trail was completed in 1987. From the Ides Cove trailhead, it follows an old jeep road through the woods, gradually dropping into the vast, corn lily expanse of Ides Cove, at the head of Fish Creek, a mile from the trailhead. Look for views of Snow Mountain here, far to the south.

The jeep road veers south, and the actual trail begins, 1 1/2 miles from the trailhead, near the Wilderness boundary. From there, the path climbs a sparsely forested slope, crossing a narrow ridge at 7400 foot. The point where the trail tops the ridge and cuts sharply north (with views of Solomon and Harvey Peaks), struck me as the best spot from which to assault the Mount Linn summit (in theory– I didn't try it). It's 1/2 mile and a 700 foot rise to the top.

Beyond the ridge, the path descends gradually around the head of Alder Creek. It then climbs steeply up to a rocky crest, rounds it, and bumps into the Ides Cove Trail soon after. The Ides Cove, South Yolla Bolly junction also looked like a good spot from which to scale the mountain.

South Yolla Bolly, viewed from North Yolla Bolly.

SOLDIER RIDGE/SOLOMON PEAK

Destination: Soldier Ridge, Minnie Lake, Solomon Peak, Hammerhorn Mountain, Kinglsey Lake, Windy Mountain, Frying Pan Meadow, Summit Ridge.
Location: T25N-R10W-Sec. 19
USGS 7.5" Topo: Solomon Peak, CA
Length: Soldier Ridge - 5 miles (or 10 mi. loop); Summit Trail - 6 to 11 miles (or 12 mi. loop)
Water: OK
Access: Long dirt road
Season: June through October
Difficulty: Moderate
Elevation: 6050 to 7581
Use: Non-motorized only
Ownership: Mendocino NF
Phone: (707) 983-6118

Directions: *From Highway 101 at Longvale, take Rt. 162 to Covelo. Turn right at the Ranger Station and continue on 162 to Indian Dick Road (M-1), just past the Eel River Bridge. Proceed 28 miles to the Indian Dick Guard Station. Turn right, at the station, towards Soldier Ridge. It's 3 miles to the Soldier Ridge trailhead. Indian Dick Road is an excellent, gravel route. Soldier Ridge Road is wide and easily driveable but cut by numerous water bars to prevent erosion.*

For the Summit Ridge trail, leave M-1 at the Hammerhorn turnoff (M-21). Follow it 13 miles to road M-2. Turn left and continue 3 miles to the Green Springs trailhead. From I-5, follow the directions to the

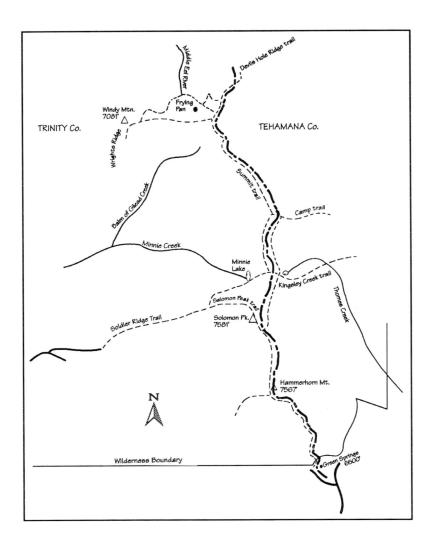

TRINITY Co.

TEHAMANA Co.

M.Middle Eel River

Devils Hole Ridge trail

Windy Mtn.
7081'

Frying
Pan

Wrights Ridge

Summit trail

Balm of Gilead Creek

Camp trail

Minnie Creek

Minnie
Lake

Kingsley Creek trail

Thomas Creek

Salomon Peak trail

Soldier Ridge Trail

Solomon Pk.
7581'

Hammerhorn Mt.
7567

N

Wilderness Boundary

Green Springs
6600'

Ides Cove trailhead, except continue on road M-2 at Cold Springs, foll-
wing the signs to Green Spings.

━━

Of all the trails into the Yolla Bolly-Middle Eel Wilderness, the Soldier Ridge/Solomon Peak Trail, to me, is the most scenic. In fact, Solomon Peak ranks among the loveliest mountains I've ever seen– and I've seen many. It's very different from the Trinity Alps, Cascades or Sierra Nevada, with a special Yolla Bolly charm all its own.

What's more, the hike into the area is remarkably easy, al-though it gets much more arduous if you elect to complete the loop around the mountain.

You have to really be a hard core scenery buff to seek out this place, however. It may be the most remote trailhead in this book (Unless you live in Ukiah or Willits). From Highway 101, north of Willits, it's 30 winding (and very scenic) miles up the Middle Eel River to the village of Covelo, seat of the Round Valley Indian Reservation. From there, it's 10 miles to the Eel River bridge and 31 more unpaved miles to the trail-head, 6000 feet above sea level.

I made the mistake of attempting a couple alternate driving routes to the Indian Dick area. Most disastrous was a "shortcut" from Highway 36 through the village of Ruth (Chapter 31). I averaged 20 MPH for 130 miles. The road from I-5, via Paskenta, includes 60 very slow, upaved miles over Mendocino Pass. It's a beautiful drive, although I'd hate to commute that way.

If you're coming from Eureka, 13 miles can be cut off the route to Covelo by taking the Dos Rios Road from Laytonville. It's unpaved, twisty and washbarded, however. The longer, paved road from Longvale is also pretty slow.

Getting back to Solomon Peak– at 7581 feet, it is the highest summit draining into the Middle Eel River and can be reached from both the Soldier Ridge and Green Springs trailheads. It can also be reached from any other trailhead in the Wilderness, since they all connect.

While the Green Springs trailhead is a slightly shorter drive from Indian Dick Road, the walk to Solomon Peak from there, via the Summit Trail, is a mile longer. It meets the Solomon Peak Trail after 3 miles and is discussed separately, at the end of the chapter. The Green Springs trailhead is much easier to reach than the Soldier Ridge trailhead, if you're coming from the Sacramento Valley. Either way, it's a long, tedious drive.

Presuming you opt for the Soldier Ridge route, begin by following the trail 2 1/4 miles from the trailhead, climbing 700 feet at a steady, easy-to-moderate grade, with a long, level stretch in the middle.

The route snakes along the top of a gorgeous ridge, decorated with outcroppings, grassy balds and occassional meadows. Artistically placed, open forest stands occupy the sheltered pockets while gnarled, windswept patriarchs (or matriarchs), dot the crest. Look for white fir and sugar pine near the trailhead (and a lovely juniper patch just before the trailhead); red fir, Western white pine and Jeffrey pine at the higher elevations.

You'll find a spring and corn lily meadow at Johnson Headquarters, 2 miles up. There used to be a cabin at the site, named for an old time rancher. It's gone now.

The Soldier Ridge Trail ends at a fork, 1/4 mile past Johnson HQ. There, the Minnie Lake Trail takes off left while the Solomon Peak Trail commences on the right. The Solomon Peak half of the sign was broken off when I visited. The latter path, most of which can be seen from the junction, reaches the high ridge just south of Solomon Peak in 1 3/4 miles. It contains some hefty grades over forested patches and bare rock, rising 800 feet in a mile at one point.

To climb Solomon Peak and/or make the loop around it, follow either the Solomon Peak or Minnie Lake Trail. Whichever you choose, first follow the Solomon Peak Trail a few hundred yards, to the high point on Soldier Ridge (just before it drops to the saddle from which it charges up Solomon's southwest flank).

The view of Solomon Peak from this vista point is commanding. It reveals the peak as a massive block of beige sandstone, uplifted by faulting and carved by erosion and long departed glaciers. The sandstone, called graywacke, is the primary rock of the California Coastal Ranges. Solomon Peak is the second highest mountain (after Mt. Linn, highest in the Yolla Bollys), made of this rock type.

Speaking of glaciers, note as you climb to the vista point, that Soldier Ridge's north side is cut with steep cliffs while the south side is much more gradual. That's because the north side was gouged out during the last ice age by several small, hanging glaciers.

The area's largest glacial basin, above Minnie Lake, boasts dramatic cliffs, which can be seen from the vista point. The lake itself, however, is barely more than a large puddle, surrounded by woods and extensive corn lily meadows, on a shelf high above Balm of Gilead Creek. You'll find a year round spring at the lake, and a couple of nice campsites. The 1/4 acre lake is unstocked.

The Minnie Lake Trail is similar to the Solomon Peak Trail, traversing open meadows, scattered forest clumps and exposed, rocky uplands. In two miles, it drops 600 feet to Minnie Creek, then ascends 650 feet to the high ridge.

Both the Minnie Lake and Solomon Peak Trails eventually connect with the Summit Trail. If you came up via Minnie Lake, turn right on reaching the Summit Trail to complete the loop. If you came by the Solomon Peak Trail, turn left. If you came in via the Summit Trail, go wherever you like.

The Summit Trail, the Yolla Bolly's main north-south thoroughfare, follows the crest of the Middle Eel divide. This is a spectacular route over open, subalpine country with long vistas in all directions. It skirts Solomon Peak to the east, missing the summit by a couple hundred feet. Early in the season, expect patches of snow on this and other area trails.

To scale Solomon Peak, follow the Solomon Peak Trail to a saddle, 1/2 mile before the path drops down to the slightly lower Summit Trail. The newly rerouted path passes within a hundred feet of the level mountaintop.

(Pointless aside: In all my trail writings, the most appropriate use of the word "scale," in conjunction with mountain climbing, pertained to Fish Mountain, in the Rogue-Umpqua Wilderness.)

From the Solomon summit, the peak immediately south is Hammerhorn Mountain, only about 30 feet lower than Solomon Peak. The line of gray outcroppings paralleling Soldier Ridge on the south is Hammerhorn Ridge, averaging about 6500 feet. Rattlesnake Creek separates Soldier and Hammerhorn Ridges.

The north side of Soldier Ridge looks down on Balm of Gilead Creek and across to Wright's Ridge (Chapter 28). The Middle Eel canyon lies to the north of Wright's Ridge. Look also for the North and South Yolla Bollys, Lassen, Shasta, the Sacramento Valley, the King Range, Leech Lake Mountain— and so on into infinity.

***

The Summit Trail from the Green Springs trailhead offers a route into the Solomon Peak area similar to— but slightly longer than— the Soldier Ridge route. As a bonus, it tosses in Hammerhorn Peak. Past the Solomon Peak area, the path continues to Frying Pan Meadow, in the dead center of the Wilderness, where it connects with the Devil's Hole Ridge Trail from the North Yolla Bollys (Chapter 25).

The short side road from M-2 to the roomy Green Springs trailhead is extremely steep. English Camp, just before the trailhead, rates high among area campgrounds. After leaving the trailhead, the path gains 1000 feet in its first 2 1/2 miles.

Since the spectacular ridge top walk past Solomon Peak has already been described, I'll add only that it runs mostly east of the crest, facing Mt. Shasta and the South Yolla Bollys (Chapter 26).

Last Camp, just past the Solomon Peak junction, entices hikers with expansive corn lily meadows, multiple springs and long, clear vistas.

The Kingsley Lake Trail takes off left just before the Minnie Lake Junction. The diminutive, unstocked pond lies 1/4 mile away.

From the Minnie Lake junction, it's 1 1/2 miles to the far end of the D Camp Trail and 4 miles to the Wright's Ridge Trail, over the tops of Sugarloaf Mountain and Vinegar Peak. The Wright's Ridge Trail ascends 7081 foot Windy Mountain, 1 1/2 miles from the junction.

After passing Wright's Ridge, the Summit Trail drops steeply for 1/4 mile to another junction. Go right to connect with the Devil's Hole Ridge Trail and avoid Frying Pan Meadows. A left turn winds down into the lush, wet meadows, with its springs and campsites. A short trail to the right, at the meadows' far end, loops back up to Devil's Hole Ridge.

HAYNE'S DELIGHT/WRIGHT'S RIDGE

Destination: Balm of Gilead Creek, Glade Springs, Hayne's Delight, Buck Ridge, River Trail loop, Wright's Valley, Wright's Ridge, Windy Mountain, Frying Pan Meadows.

Location: T25N-R11W-Sec. 23

USGS 7.5" Topo: Wrights Ridge, Solomon Peak, CA

Length: 4 1/2 miles to Wright's Valley; 6 miles to Hayne's Delight; 10 miles to Wright's Ridge/Frying Pan; 22 miles to River Trail loop.

Water: None in late season. Much early.

Access: Very long gravel roads

Season: May through November

Difficulty: Mostly moderate, some difficult

Elevation: 5000 feet at thetrailhead, 7081 feet at the top of Windy Mountain, 4100 feet at Wright's Valley

Ownership: Mendocino NF

Phone: (707) 983-6118

Directions: *Follow the directions in Chapters 27, 29 and 30 to Indian Dick Road. Just past the Indian Dick Guard Station, 28 miles from the Eel River Bridge, turn right, at the turnoff for the Soldier Ridge and Georges Valley trailheads. Turn left a mile later, following the Georges Valley sign. The trailhead is a mile down the road, at a sign saying "Hayne's Delight, Glade Springs." There's plenty of parking in a grassy flat just below the road.*

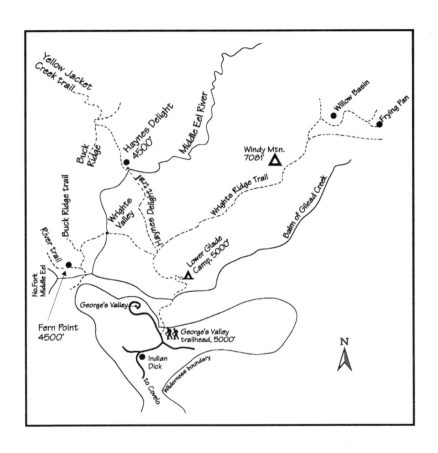

Yellow Jacket
Creek trail

Buck Ridge

Haynes Delight
4500'

Middle Eel River

Willow Basin

Frying Pan

Windy Mtn.
7081'

Buck Ridge trail

Wrights Valley

Haynes Delight trail

Wrights Ridge Trail

Balm of Gilead Creek

No.Fork
Middle Eel River

Fern Point
4500'

Lower Glade
Camp, 5000'

George's Valley

George's Valley
trailhead, 5000'

Indian
Dick

to Covelo

Wilderness boundary

N

I almost didn't include this chapter. From the map, the Hayne's Delight Trail, beginning at the Georges Valley trailhead, appeared to offer little. Certainly not enough to entice me to check it out. It visited no lakes or mountaintops and didn't follow any rivers. Instead, it climbed a couple low (and probably hot and brushy) ridges before crossing the Middle Eel and climbing yet another ridge.

I checked it out only after hearing that this was the most popular trail in the entire Yolla Bolly-Middle Eel Wilderness. As it turned out, that information was grossly in error. Also in error, however, was my conclusion that the path didn't richly deserve a spot in this book.

Hiking to Hayne's Delight on a balmy weekend during hunting season, I observed only one other car at the trailhead of this allegedly "most popular" trail. Which is actually pretty good, considering that of the 4 Indian Dick trailheads described herein (there are others not described), it was the first where I didn't have the place entirely to myself.

By contrast, a dozen cars festooned the Ides Cove trailhead (Chapter 26), during my 1988 visit. At the Canyon Creek trailhead, in the Trinity Alps (Chapter 20), I encountered more than 100 cars.

After deciding to include the Hayne's Delight Trail, I had the bright idea that Wright's Valley, from the same trailhead, might make a better day hike destination than Hayne's Delight. It crosses the Middle Eel after 4 1/2 miles, 1 1/2 miles sooner than Hayne's Delight.

Boy, was I mistaken. In its exhausting march to Wright's Valley, the path drops 700 feet in 1 1/2 miles to Balm of Gilead Creek, climbs 1100 feet in 1 1/2 miles to Wright's Ridge, then drops 1300 feet in 1 1/2 miles to the river.

To continue on from Wright's Valley to the Rock Cabin/River Trail (Chapter 29), you'd have to climb another 1100 feet in 1 mile, over Buck Ridge, before dropping 1000 feet in the next mile to the Rock Cabin Trail crossing. And that's assuming you locate the trail out of Wright's valley.

I'd been told that the Hayne's Delight Trail lacked long vistas and that it's main reason for existence was to tie into longer routes such as the River Trail loop or Wright's Ridge Trail. In fact, despite the ups and downs, I found it highly scenic and enjoyable.

Soon after departing the wooded trailhead, the path rounds a rocky point with a dazzling view of the Balm of Gilead canyon and Wright's Ridge. Across the canyon and halfway up the ridge, a grassy opening can be seen with a trail running up the middle. The opening is Glade Springs, 2 miles away.

The path from the trailhead circles through forest and brushy openings, over rockfalls and outcroppings and around steep walled ampitheaters. The forest includes Douglas-fir, incense cedar, sugar pine and ponderosa pine, with a few red firs higher up.

Stands are fairly open, with little underbrush, most likely due to frequent fires. Look for fire scars on the bigger trees. I noted some monstrous conifers on the north slope approach, including sugar pines 6 feet on the stump. Understory vegetation included prince's pine, hazel and hound's tongue. I did not observe these species on the south facing hillside across the creek. Understory vegetation there tended more towards squawcarpet, a sun loving ceanothus species.

Hardwoods– mostly black and white oak– abounded everywhere. Even meadows and brushfields were dotted with oak clusters. On the barest ground, brambles of scrub oak (and whitethorn ceanothus), clung to the rocks.

Balm of Gilead Creek runs through a steep walled gorge lined with slide scars and littered with house-sized boulders. A trickle of water flowed between stagnant pools on my late October visit.

I could not bring myself to drink the water, even after purification. Since every other spring and creek was dry, I would have been well advised to carry two canteens. After all that climbing and descending, I returned to the trailhead dry mouthed and miserable.

The south facing trail up Wright's Ridge from Balm of Gilead Creek is brushier and more open than its north side counterpart. A half mile past the crossing, it arrives at Lower Glade Spring Camp, a beautiful meadow with several seasonal creeks and springs (all dry, of course). The main path skirts to the west while a short side trail leads to the camp.

Above Lower Glade Springs, the path levels for a considerable distance, crossing several dry creeks. After 1/2 mile, it comes upon another meadow, then crests a rocky divide with a tremendous view of what I presumed to be the Middle Eel canyon.

At the time, I wondered why nothing in the vista matched the map. I later concluded that the view looked up the North Fork and that the Middle Eel proper lay far to the right, hidden by Wright's Ridge. It would not appear for a couple more miles.

Beyond the overlook, the path climbs along the ridge top, re-entering the woods and drifting back to the Balm of Gilead side a couple times. It's 1/2 mile from the overlook to the Wright's Valley turnoff, at a sign saying "Wright's Valley/Buck Rideg."

(According to the Forest Service, a large batch of signs, a few years back, arrived full of spelling errors. Because of the red tape and delays involved in replacing them, they used the readable ones.)

The Wright's Valley Trail was built by cattlemen impatient with such niceties as switchbacks. Since they were on horseback, a straight downhill shot got them to their destination most efficiently. For hikers, however, the path in the uphill direction is a killer. The Forest Service plans to reroute it eventually, but for now it's only minimally maintained.

Like much of the canyon, massive slide scars line the lower slopes around Wright's Valley. Where the trail hits bottom, a large, beautiful campsite sits on a bench above the river.

I found the river completely dry— except for a small, very stagnant pool at the base of what normally would be a waterfall. I'm told the Middle Eel often goes dry at this location. Since the riverbed here consists of massive gravel banks, the water runs mostly underground. There is water at Hayne's Delight, 2 1/2 miles upstream, and at the Rock Cabin crossing, 1 1/2 miles down.

The lack of water does not mean there are no fish upriver. It is illegal, however, to fish the Middle Eel below Uhl Creek, including Wright's Valley and Hayne's Delight. It's a good thing, too. Between the loss of spawning gravels from the 1964 flood and the recent 6 year drought, the famous Eel River summer steelhead have enough problems.

While the lack of water certainly doesn't help, the fish somehow manage to work around the situation. Summer steelhead can be found above Wright's Valley. They obviously will not head downstream until the rains come.

The biggest problem at Wright's Valley was my inability to locate the trail out the other side, up Buck Ridge. According to the Forest Service, the path from the other direction ends on the bluff top and hikers must bushwhack the last few hundred feet. Thus, if you plan on hiking through, start from the other end. The trail on the Wright's Ridge side is much easier to locate.

The Wright's Valley Trail is part of a loop running past Hayne's Delight, up and over Buck Ridge and down the Yellowjacket Trail (Chapter 31), to the North Fork/River Trail (Chapter 29). It then follows the River Trail past Fern Point to the beginning of the Buck Ridge Trail. The Wright's Valley Trail ends (or begins), 1/2 mile up the Buck Ridge Trail.

Don't try to make the loop in the opposite direction. You'll never get past Wright's Valley.

***

Back on Wright's Ridge, the Hayne's Delight and Wright's Ridge Trails part company 1/4 mile past the Wright's Valley turnoff. From there, it's 3 miles to Hayne's Delight.

The Hayne's Delight path, which drops 1000 feet in 3 miles, is infinitely more delightful than the Wright's Valley route. It hangs mostly in the woods, except for a rock outcropping 3/4 mile down with a great view of the Middle Eel.

The trail crosses the river at a rare wide spot, lacking the rock walls, slide scars and goats slopes common to most of the canyon. Rolling hills and dense forests dominate the area. An old landslide at the river softens the final approach but makes the path a little hard to follow.

After June, you should be able to boulder hop across the Middle Eel. In winter or early spring, high water may bar access to the campsites in the meadow just across the river.

I'm convinced, by the way, that the name Hayne's Delight is misspelled. On Forest Service maps, it's shown as "Hayne's Delight" while some references list it as "Haynes Delight." Presuming it was named after a Mr. (and/or Mrs.) Haynes, the correct spelling would be "Haynes' Delight."

***

The highest and best use of the Georges Valley trailhead is to access the Wright's Ridge Trail. While considerably longer than the paralleling Soldier Ridge Trail (Chapter 27), Wright's Ridge is similar but higher and more open, with better vistas. It tops out at Windy Mountain (7081 feet). Soldier Ridge reaches the Summit Trail after 4 1/2 miles (vs. 10 for Wright's Ridge), but provides no views of the Middle Eel canyon. Wright's Ridge offers the shortest route to Frying Pan Meadows, the geographic center of the wilderness and the Middle Eel's source.

The Wright's Ridge Trail leaves the Hayne's Delight Trail 3 miles from the trailhead, amid a lovely juniper grove. Follow the sign which says "Frying Pan."

The trail, while rising 1600 feet in 5 miles, doesn't reach the crest area for 2 1/2 miles. After that, it piles up scenic view upon scenic view, alternating between the Middle Eel side, with Shell Mountain in the distance, and Balm of Gilead Creek, with Solomon Peak and the South Yolla Bolly's in the distance.

The 3 humped Windy Peak, 8 1/2 miles from the trailhead, presents an easy, 1/4 mile side trip with vistas westward to the King Range and– on exceptionally clear days– the ocean.

Beyond Windy Peak, a 2 1/2 mile side trail (left), leads to Willow Basin and Frying Pan. It offers the only water since Balm of Gilead Creek. To connect with the Summit Trail, go right at the Willow Basin junction, towards Vinegar Peak. That direction also connects with the Devil's Hole Trail and the far end of the Willow Basin/Frying Pan Trail.

Hayne's Delight Trail above Balm of Gilead.

North Fork of Middle Eel from Hayne's Delight Trail.

ROCK CABIN TRAIL/FERN POINT

Destination: Middle Eel River, North Fork Middle Eel, Fern Point, Buck Ridge.
Location: T25N-R11W-Sec.22
USGS 7.5" Topo: Wrights Ridge, Four Corner Rock, CA
Length: 4 miles to Fern Point; 11 miles to Yellowjacket Creek
Water: Lots
Access: Good gravel and dirt roads
Season: May through November
Difficulty: Moderately difficult
Elevation: 4950 to 3750
Use: Non-motorized only
Ownership: Mendocino NF
Phone: (707) 983-6118

Directions: *From Highway 101 at Longvale, take Highway 162 to Covelo. Turn right at the Covelo Ranger Station and proceed on 162 to the Eel River Bridge. Just over the bridge, at the store, turn right onto Indian Dick Road (M-1). Continue for 30 miles. The roomy trailhead is located past the Indian Dick Guard Station, down a short, well marked spur to the left, just before Lucky Lake.*

This is easily the best river trail on the Middle Eel side of the Yolla Bolly-Middle Eel Wilderness Area. It is longer than the Foster Glades Trail (Chapter 30) and much easier than the Hayne's Delight Trail (Chapter 28), following a more forested route than either.

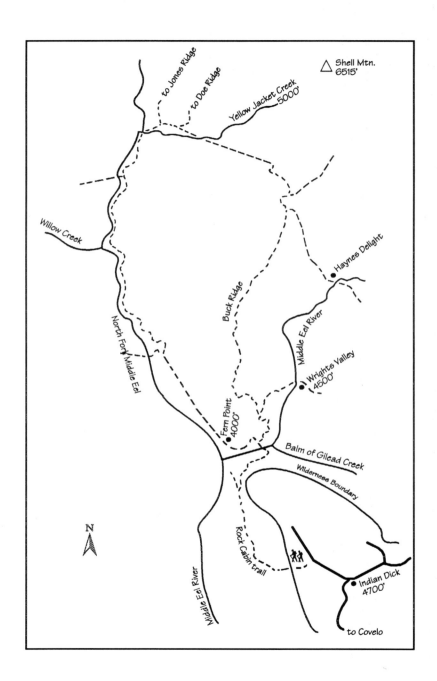

△ Shell Mtn.
6515'

to Jones Ridge

to Doe Ridge

Yellow Jacket Creek
5000'

Willow Creek

Haynes Delight

Buck Ridge

Middle Eel River

North Fork Middle Eel

Wrights Valley
4500'

Fern Point
4000'

Balm of Gilead Creek

Wilderness Boundary

N

Rock Cabin trail

Middle Eel River

Indian Dick
4700'

to Covelo

The path connects with a number of much longer routes exploring the west (and east) half of the wilderness. Its beginning segment, from the trailhead to the river and up to Fern Point, makes a marvelous, 4 mile day hike. The drive up Indian Dick Road to the trailhead, ranks among California's more surprisingly beautiful excursions.

From the trailhead area at Rock Cabin Camp, the path drops fairly steeply at first, then levels off for 1 1/2 miles before beginning its final plunge to the Middle Eel. Much of the route pushes through old growth Douglas-fir/ponderosa pine forest. As is typical of the area, however, there is no shortage of grass and brush openings, and hardwood glades.

This is gorgeous country, highlighted by Fern Point and the Middle Eel crossing. The ecosystem differs from other northwest California regions in being drier and gentler than the Klamath Mountains and much drier than the Avenue of the Giants area a few miles west. The juxtaposition of dense forest, park-like glades, spectacular canyons and grassy prairies with long vistas, is a scenic delight.

Be advised, however, that mid-summer heat in these canyons can be excruciating. I'd recommend a May or October visit. Earlier if you can make it to the 4950 foot trailhead.

From the forested trailhead, the path crosses Rock Cabin Creek and a small meadow before entering the woods. It drops steeply the first mile, then levels off. The next couple miles contour west and north, high above the river, past old jeep roads and side trails, and a couple maple lined creeks.

Two mile up, past the old Fern Point turnoff, the path swings sharply east. Soon after, it begins its rocky descent of the steep sided canyon. At the bottom, red alder, willow, Oregon ash and umbrella plants line the riverbanks.

Although the best campsite lies on the opposite bank, you may not be able to reach it before mid-June. Expect to get your feet wet whenever you cross.

The Buck Ridge Trail branches right, 1/4 mile past the crossing. This pleasant, hilltop route joins the Yellowjacket Trail in 7 miles and the Doe Ridge Trail in 9 miles (Chapter 30). The Yellowjacket Trail then meets the far end of the River Trail, which returns you to your starting point. It all adds up to a fine, highly varied, 20 mile loop.

Fern Point, a mile beyond the crossing (left, on the River Trail), is an outcropping 700 feet above the junction of the Middle Eel and the North Fork. The trail up from the crossing rises

400 feet in 1/2 mile, then levels off (the river drops). There used to be a bridge at Fern Point but it is long gone.

No trail follows the Middle Eel's main channel above the Fern Point crossing. It is forded, however, by the Wright's Valley, Hayne's Delight, Long Ridge and Cutfinger Trails. The Devil's Hole Ridge (Chapter 25), Wright's Ridge (Chapter 28) and Summit Trails (Chapter 27), all lead to Frying Pan Meadow, the river's headwaters.

Beyond Fern Point, the River Trail becomes considerably gentler as it continues up the North Fork for 8 more miles (although it does not approach the riverbank for 5 miles). At its far end, it turns up Yellowjacket Creek, emerging where the Waterspout, Yellowjacket and Doe Ridge Trails meet.

A word of caution to anglers— the Middle Eel is closed to fishing at the Fern Point crossing and the North Fork is closed below Willow Creek (the spot 5 miles up where the River Trail finally meets the river). While there are steelhead to be had above Willow Creek, the river frequently dries up by mid-summer.

HOWLING

In my 1991 visit to the Rock Cabin Trail, I spent the night at the lovely, shaded campsite at the trailhead. Driving there, I'd encountered only two or three Forest Service vehicles on Indian Dick Road —not a single other car. Except for me, all trailheads were deserted— which wasn't surprising since it was a weekday and the canyon gets extremely hot in summer. Use is highest in autumn, during hunting season, and in spring.

As I figured it, the nearest human was at least 15 miles away, at Hammerhorn Campground— and that, in all likelihood, was also deserted.

After pitching my tent, I cooked dinner, explored a little, then turned in for the night. It had been a long day and I slept better than I usually do on such trips.

At 3 in the morning, I was startled into consciousness by the howling of a dog, not far from my tent. And no, it wasn't a coyote and it definitely wasn't a dream.

I heard a single, long series of blood curdling yelps, then silence for the rest of the night. It took me nearly an hour to get back to sleep.

FOSTER GLADES/ASA BEAN CROSSING

Destinations: Foster Glades, Heron Lake, Asa Bean Crossing, Stick
       Creek Falls, Asa Bean Flat, Red Rock Mountain, Leech
       Lake Mountain, Leech Lake.
Location: T25N-R11W-Sec.27
USGS 7.5" Topo: Leech Lake Mountain, CA
Length: 3 1/2 miles (excluding Hotel Camp Trail)
Water: A little
Access: Excellent, long, gravel road
Season: May through November (earlier if snow free)
Difficulty: Moderate. Last 1/2 mile is very steep
Elevation: 3900 feet (low trailhead), 4500 feet (high trailhead), 3250
       feet at Asa Bean
Use: Non-motorized only
Ownership: Mendocino NF
Phone: (707) 983-6118

Directions: *Follow Highway 162, off US 101, from Longvale to
Covelo. Turn right at the Covelo Ranger Station and continue on 162
to the Eel River Bridge. Just over the bridge, at the store, turn left
onto Indian Dick Road (M-1). Continue 27 miles to the Foster Glades
trailhead, just past Rattlesnake Creek, where the road rounds the
point. Look for a grassy area and a wooden drift fence. The only sign
is a small hiker emblem.*

    *For the Asa Bean Trail, which intersects the Foster Glades Trail,
continue 1 1/2 miles up the road from the Foster Glades trailhead.
The sign is presently down (and has been since at least 1988), but*

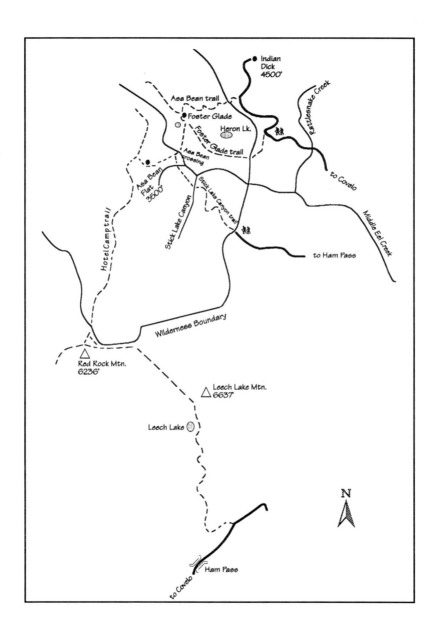

Indian
Dick
4500'

Rattlesnake Creek

Asa Bean trail

Foster Glade

Heron Lk.

Foster Glade trail

Asa Bean
crossing

to Covelo

Asa Bean
Flat
3500'

Stick Lake Canyon

Stick Lake Canyon trail

Middle Eel Creek

Hotel Camp trail

to Ham Pass

Wilderness Boundary

Red Rock Mtn.
6236'

Leech Lake Mtn.
6637'

Leech Lake

N

Ham Pass

to Covelo

222

there's a low post where it used to be. Parking is plentiful at both trail-heads. On some maps, the Asa Bean Trail is considered part of the Hotel Camp Trail.

Two trailheads access the Asa Bean area from the west side of the Middle Eel canyon. Just before the bridge and store at the Indian Dick turnoff, turn left onto road 24N21, the Ham Pass Road. Follow it to the unmarked Leech Lake Mountain trailhead (on the left, just over Ham Pass), or continue to the road end– also an unmarked trail-head– where a closed road/trail takes off to Stick Lake Canyon and Asa Bean Crossing.

In all my explorations, over hundreds of trails, I've been irrevo-cably lost twice. The Foster Glades Trail was one of them. For-tunately, while the trail vanished without a trace, my directional sense held up and I emerged exactly at the trailhead. I hiked cross country from the Eel River to Indian Dick Road, climbing 800 feet in about a mile.

The Foster Glades Trail is also memorable for having one of the lovelier trailheads. Twenty-seven miles up Indian Dick Road, with it's vistas of the Middle Eel and Leech Lake Moun-tain, the gravel route dips into Rattlesnake Creek Canyon, then climbs a beautiful grassy knob. Indian Dick Road ranks among California's most remote and scenic drives.

A mile past Rattlesnake Creek, the road rounds a beautifully landscaped point. A large, bouldery mound, crowned by a charming white oak grove, juts from the rolling, grassy expanse. The trailhead is marked by a split log drift fence and a hiker emblem.

From the trailhead, at a gap in the fence, the pathway dis-appears behind the mound, then swings left. This is the route on which I became lost, following cow paths through open meadows, oak glades and brush choked gullies, down to the river. Or at least to the top of the gray bluff above the river. The last 100 feet was a vertical drop.

The correct route is denoted by a pole in front of a large white oak, straight downhill and across the grass from the path which leaves the trailhead. Look for it just after the trailhead path cuts behind the mound.

From the pole, the trail crosses the gully, then bears slightly left around some bushes before crossing a little grassy opening.

A more well defined path begins at the edge of the trees on the far side of the opening.

After all my expended energy finding the trail, I should mention that the Forest Service prefers hikers to use the Asa Bean trailhead, 1 1/2 miles up the road, to reach Foster Glades and Asa Bean Crossing. The Foster Glades Trail, they correctly explain, is in need of maintenance and difficult (although far from impossible) to follow. It has been obliterated by slides and soil slumping in spots and is faint through grassy areas. Maintenance scheduled for 1990 did not take place, although I found it a little better defined in 1992 than in 1988.

This is unfortunate because the lovely path offers the easiest route to the Middle Eel inside the Wilderness Area. The alternative Asa Bean trailhead sits 600 feet higher in elevation. Its first mile is extremely steep as it tumbles towards the more level Foster Glades Trail.

If you have two vehicles, consider hiking in on Asa Bean and out via the Foster Glades Trail. It's impossible to get lost. Just remember that Road M-1 lies uphill and the river downhill. Remember, too, however you go, that the canyon can be excruciatingly hot in summer.

Once on the Foster Glades Trail, if you're brave enough to give it a shot (it's not that bad), the route contours to the right, through grassy openings, oak/pine forests and brushfields of manzanita, ceanothus and redbud.

Heron Lake is a one acre pond, 1000 feet above the trail, a mile along the path. A landslide near Heron Lake has obliterated a section of the path.

Two miles from the trailhead, Foster Glades presents a charming little opening, with a small pond in yet another grove of white oak trees. The trail to Asa Bean Crossing takes off downhill here while the Foster Glades Trail continues ahead. A right turn onto the Asa Bean/Hotel Camp Trail brings you to Asa Bean Crossing in 1/2 mile. The trek from Foster Glades to Asa Bean Crossing is quite steep but comprises the trail's highlight. Asa Bean is a wide, flat, easy river ford. Beyond the crossing, on the opposite bank, the Hotel Camp Trail climbs 3000 feet in 6 miles, connecting with the Leech Lake Mountain Trail. This west side pathway out of the canyon begins 1/8 mile downriver from Asa Bean Crossing.

After the effort negotiating the steep, dusty, brushy bluffs along the river, it's unfortunate that the beautiful Middle Eel is closed to fishing. Fish habitat was destroyed in the 1964 flood, which ripped out most streamside vegetation and swept away many pools and spawning gravels. The area had been slowly recovering until the recent extended drought significantly set back fish populations.

Once across the river, hikers face several options. If not quite up to climbing Red Rock and Leech Lake Mountains, the 3 miles Stick Lake Canyon Trail offers a superlative diversion. It breaks off to the left, above a series of steep switchbacks, 1/4 mile from the river, at an unsigned junction.

The path twists its way high above the Middle Eel, over a rock ledge and across Line Gulch Creek. After a mile, it drops into the spectacular gorge of Stick Lake Canyon, with its three tiered waterfall. This makes an outstanding turnaround spot. It's 2 more rather steep, winding miles– the last along a closed road– to the Stick Lake Canyon trailhead. Continuing on the Hotel Camp Trail, rather than the Stick Lake Canyon Trail, leads past Asa Bean Flat, a huge glade a mile up from the river. Look for several campsites, a creek crossing and a side trail taking off the the right.

Above Asa Bean Flat, the path become steep and brushy (or steeper and brushier), with a brief respite at Hotel Camp. Above Hotel Camp, things really begin to cook as the trail rises 2000 feet in 3 miles to Red Rock Mountain. It's two miles along the ridge top from Red Rock to Leech Lake Mountain.

***

I spent an enjoyable morning exploring Leech Lake and Red Rock Mountains. Being reasonably sane, however, I approached from the Leech Lake Mountain Trail, whose trailhead lies a scant 3 miles from its namesake peak's 6637 foot summit.

The path to Leech Lake is actually a gated– and quite driveable –road, which the Forest Service doesn't consider a developed trail. It's entirely outside the Wilderness Area, which begins north of the serpentine summit of Red Rock Mountain, one peak north of Leech Lake Mountain.

Leech Lake sits in a typical, if small, high mountain glacial cirque. The 2 acre, spring fed pool occupies a small terrace below a barren sandstone headwall. The actual summit is a jagged, ship-shaped outcropping poking abruptly from the whaleback ridge top.

The trail's high point is about 300 feet lower than the mountain's. To scale the summit, continue past the lake to the trail crest– a saddle overlooking the canyon. From there, scramble uphill to the right.

Not only can the canyon be seen from the top, so can most of the Wilderness, along with a goodly chunk of the Mendocino crest. To the west, beyond beautiful Round Valley– site of the Round Valley Indian Reservation– the landscape recedes in a series of lineal ridges. On the far western horizon, the King Range juts up from the Cape Mendocino peninsula, west of the Avenue of the Giants area, blocking the view of the ocean.

Cape Mendocino is California's westernmost point while 4300 foot Kings Peak, the height of the King Range, is the highest point on the West Coast rising directly from the Pacific. The hike up Kings Peak (take the Shelter Cove Road out of Redway from Highway 101), offers possibly the most astounding ocean view you'll ever see.

WATERSPOUT/DOE RIDGE TRAILS

Destination: North Fork Middle Eel River, Mud Lake, Shell Mountain,
          Ant Point, Red Mountain
Location: T25N-R11W-Sec.7
USGS 7.5" Topo: Wrights Ridge, Four Corner Rock, CA
Length: 6 1/2 miles
Water: Little drinkable.
Access: Narrow blacktop
Season: May through November
Difficulty: Moderate to Difficult
Elevation: 4800 down to 4400 to 6700 feet
Ownership: Mendocino NF (trailhead in Six Rivers NF)
Phones: Mendocino (707)-983-6118, Six Rivers (707) 574-6233

Directions: *Take Highway 36 from Red Bluff or Fortuna, to Ruth
Road, just east of Mad River. Proceed past Ruth Reservoir and the
town of Ruth. Beyond the air strip, cross the bridge and turn left. At
Three Forks, follow the right hand road (27N02). The trailhead is located just before MP 13. The sign says "trailhead," without naming
the trail. Three cars can park at the trailhead, many more across and
up the road.*

As a compulsive type, driven crazy when symmetry is lacking,
I felt it imperative that this book include at least one trail from the
Six Rivers corner of the Yolla Bolly-Middle Eel Wilderness. That,

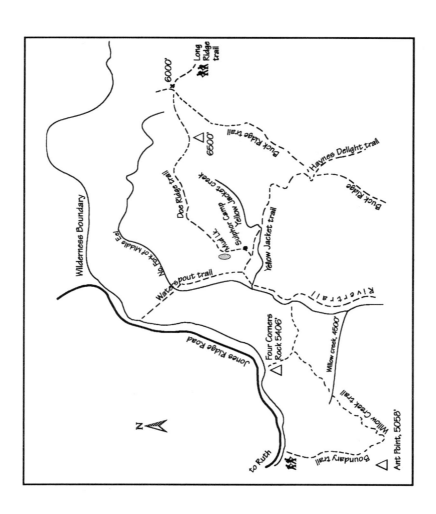

plus the hassle I went through to reach the trailhead, are the main reasons I didn't simply omit this path and try my best to forget it.

In fairness, the Waterspout/Doe Ridge Trails offer a lovely, challenging outing. Especially if you live in Red Bluff or Eureka. From my home, however, it's a 6 1/2 hour drive. You know you're in trouble when the shortest route someplace runs through the town of Hayfork.

Two things conspired to make this a miserable experience, despite much superlative and varied scenery. First was the 100 degree heat. You could steam a lobster in the Middle Eel canyon in mid-summer just by waving it around– and fry fish on the brushy, dusty ridges. Second –and worse– was the fact that I didn't see a single waterspout. I should sue for false advertising.

Since the season opens rather early, I'd suggest (or urge) a May or November trip, when the high lakes of the Trinity Alps are snowed over. This area receives a mid-winter snowpack but it doesn't linger very long.

I enjoyed the trailhead drive and loved Ruth Reservoir; wedged in the hatchet-cut Mad River Valley. Trees grow to the water's edge along the lake, with many hidden coves. You'll find a resort and motel at one end, a town (Ruth), on the other and several campgrounds in between.

Beyond the town and air strip, cross the bridge and follow the signs to Three Forks, where the road splits into two, not three. A sign on the right says, "Yolla Bolly-Middle Eel Wilderness Area– 13 miles." Because of its wordy name, signs for the Yolla Bolly are large and difficult to miss.

From Three Forks, the road climbs to the crest of Jones Ridge. I'd like to have tried the Red Mountain Trail, passed en route. I missed the trailhead, supposedly at mile 5 1/2 from Three Forks, but the path's first 1 1/2 miles are visible from the road. It swoops down, then up along the crest of a barren, 5 foot wide ridge, to a rocky, serpentine outcropping.

Despite the long vistas from Jones Ridge, most landmarks along the road, such as Four Corners Rock, are not obvious. Also, not all trailheads are clearly signed. The signed ones say only "trailhead," without naming the trail. I knew I'd located the Waterspout trailhead only because the pavement ended there, as indicated on the map.

The Waterspout Trail's first mile drops 400 feet to the Middle Eel's North Fork. Most of the plunge comes at the steep walled, densely wooded gorge just above the river. The first mile or so from the trailhead follows a gentle glade with a seasonal creek running down the middle and purple delphinium abounding along its banks.

The North Fork crossing features gray rock cliffs on either side, cut by frequent landslides. It did not feature much water when I visited (May 31). Like every other stream, I found the North Fork stagnant and rapidly drying up. After picking my way across a gravel bar, boulders and clumps of umbrella plants, I scrambled up the extremely steep far bank. This is a good turnaround spot, with an excellent campsite atop the bank.

The next two miles are rather boring. After leaving the river, the path pretty much stays in the woods, emerging only to negotiate a side creek or rocky gully every 1/4 mile or so.

This stretch offers a textbook example of forest succession, characterized by large ponderosa and sugar pines, younger and smaller Douglas-firs and still younger and smaller grand firs.

The slow growing, long lived grand firs are biding their time in the shade of the larger trees, waiting to replace the shorter lived, sun loving pines and Douglas-firs. While I saw no evidence of past logging or recent fires, the forest didn't strike me as particularly old.

Black oak, canyon live oak and brush (mostly ceanothus), choke the understory. Groves of valley oak bear testimony to the weather in these parts. Oregonians should not confuse this extremely sun loving species with the similar but larger Oregon white oak.

While I'm on the subject, grand fir is closely related to white fir, a dominant California species, and interbreeds with it where the two ranges overlap. White fir inhabits higher and more southern areas while grand fir tends more to the north, at lower elevations and closer to the coast. The grand fir I observed no doubt contained a few white fir genes.

Three miles from the trailhead, the River Trail branches off to the right. Stay left, on the Yellowjacket Trail towards Sulphur Glade. The River Trail joins the Rock Cabin Trail 10 miles down the North Fork, just beyond Fern Point (Chapter 29).

Past the River Trail junction, the path skirts a series of grassy openings, reminiscent of the Indian Dick area. These are not cool alpine meadows. Despite the nearly 5000 foot elevation, the heat can be intense.

At the edge of a grassy meadow, 1/4 mile past the River Trail turnoff, you'll come to a junction marked "Hayne's Delight/Doe Ridge." Go left for Shell Mountain and Doe Ridge.

Should you stay on the Yellowjacket Trail, you'll climb 1200 feet in 3 miles, following Yellowjacket Creek for a mile, then ascending to Buck Ridge. Views of Buck Ridge's bald summit dominates the Doe Ridge area. A 1 1/2 mile continuation of the Yellowjacket Trail drops past the Buck Ridge Trail into Hayne's Delight (Chapter 28), a popular destination on the Middle Eel's untrailed main fork above Fern Point.

After turning left at the Hayne's Delight/Doe Ridge junction (towards Doe Ridge), the path hits an immense, grassy expanse with corn lilies in the middle. This is Sulphur Camp, which supposedly boasts two tapped, drinkable springs. I couldn't find them and am told they dry up by early summer. The camp is in the woods, on the other side of the meadow.

The Doe Ridge Trail disappears at the corn lily patch. To continue, walk up the meadow's long axis towards a rock outcropping. Soon after, the aptly named Mud Lake appears, a 1/2 acre pond in the middle of yet another glade. While the lake is not without charm, I wouldn't say the same for its water.

Beyond Mud Lake, the path leaves glade and woods behind and begins a relentless charge up the brushy slopes of Doe Ridge. The presence of Western juniper here attests once again to the region's oppressive aridity.

Although these peaks, reaching 6700 feet at Shell Mountain, are as high as many in the Trinity Alps, most are round top balds capped by brush and scattered timber rather than jagged minarets and glacial cirques. Vegetational changes occur at higher elevations than in the Trinity Alps.

The first mile from Sulphur Camp, ascending to the ridge top, is steep, unyielding and exposed, especially in midsummer. Eventually, things level off and the trail finds scattered forest patches along the crest, even as the vistas improve and Shell Mountain finally emerges in the distance.

Three miles from Sulphur Camp, past several more steep pitches, the route hits a saddle, then skirts to the north (left) of Shell Mountain. It's an easy, off-trail scramble from the saddle, over rock and brush, skirting some north facing cliffs, to the mountaintop. From this pleasant summit, with its scattered shade trees, one can pick out the North and South Yolla Bollys to the east, Solomon Peak to the south and the King Range far to the west.

Shell Mountain —and the Doe Ridge Trail— connects to Buck Ridge and Dead Puppy Ridge to the east.

I tried to track down information on the name "Dead Puppy Ridge" but failed. I'm also curious about nearby Foot of Bull Ridge, Dead Horse Ridge and Opium Glade Ridge. Call me if you can shed any light on this.

Black Rock Mountain, Yolla Bolly Wilderness Area.

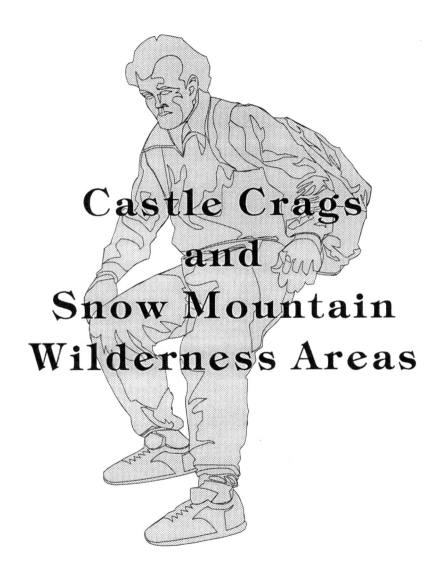

Castle Crags
and
Snow Mountain
Wilderness Areas

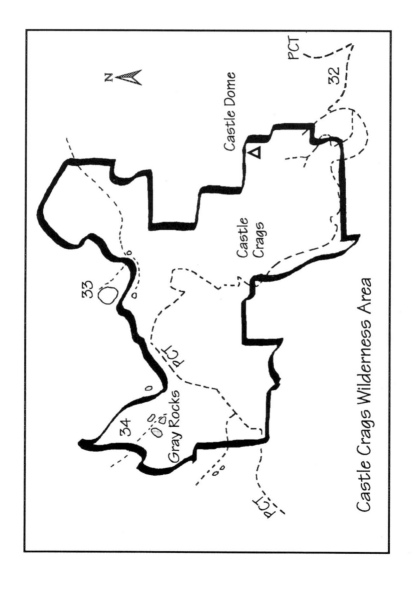

Castle Crags Wilderness Area

CRAGS TRAIL

Destination: Indian Springs, Castle Dome
Location: T38N-R4W-Sec. 15
USGS 7.5" Topo: Seven Lake Basin, CA
Length: 3 miles
Water: At Indian Springs
Access: Paved roads
Season: May through November
Difficulty: Very steep
Elevation: 2600 to 4800
Use: Hikers only. Horses on Pacific Crest Trail
Ownership: Castle Crags State Park, and Shasta-Trinity NF
Phone: (916) 235-2684 (State Park), (916) 926-4511 (NF)

Directions: Leave I-5 at the Castella/Castle Crags exit, south of Dunsmuir. The park entrance is about 1/4 mile from the freeway and a day use fee is charged in summer. Follow the signs to the trailhead and Vista Point.

Alternatively, leave I-5 one exit north, at Soda Creek, where the Pacific Crest Trail crosses the freeway. From the trailhead, head left and follow the PCT into the park.

While freeway travelers through the California far north expect to be awed by Mount Shasta, neighboring Castle Crags catches most people off guard. Rising above the dull, forested hills, the crags resemble an immense upwelling of melted candles. Or per-

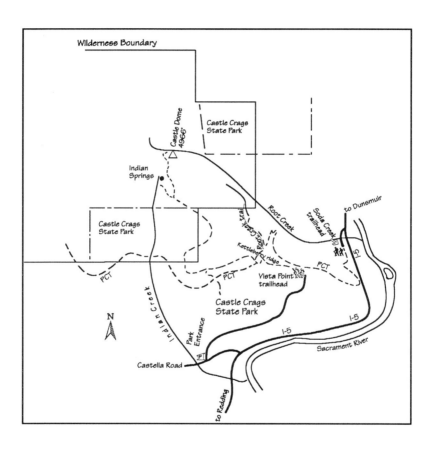

Wilderness Boundary

Castle Crags State Park

Castle Dome 4966'

Indian Springs

Castle Crags State Park

Root Creek

to Dunsmuir

Soda Creek trailhead

Root Creek Trail

I-5

Kettlebell ridge

PCT

PCT

PCT

Vista Point trailhead

Castle Crags State Park

N

Indian Creek

Park Entrance

I-5

I-5

Sacramento River

Castella Road

to Redding

haps upended surfboards eroded into grotesque spires. They are actually a small, fortress-like granite island whose glacially sculpted domes and minarets recall the southern Sierra.

I had much difficulty obtaining reliable information on this unusual and exquisite path. I encountered signs pointing the wrong way, a park brochure with an off-scale map where a 2 inch line took me an hour to walk while a 3 inch line took 10 minutes, and an ambiguous, misleading statement in the brochure that the Crags Trail leads to "the base of Castle Dome."

Since one side of the Dome's base sits at 3000 feet and lies outside the crags formation, while the other side is well inside the crags at 4800 feet, it is not sufficient to simply refer to "the base."

I've been assured the signs have been corrected and a more accurate brochure has been prepared.

Entering the park via the Pacific Crest Trail at Soda Creek adds an extra 3 miles to the Castle Dome hike, with an added elevation rise of 400 feet. The PCT here is fairly level, following an old railroad bed. Use it if unable to come up with the park's day use fee or if hiking up from the south.

Both the PCT and the Crags Trail from the Vista Point trailhead begin in middle elevation forests of Douglas-fir, pine, madrone and oak. The Crags Trail quickly climbs to higher elevation Shasta red fir and white fir forests. Jeffrey pine and incense cedar decorate the more open, upper slopes. Look for a few Brewer spruce near the upper end.

The Vista Point drive itself justifies the trip. The winding road ends at a spot on Kettlebelly Ridge with a commanding view of Castle Dome, the Crags and, immediately north, Mount Shasta. The trail ends at the brilliant green meadow, seen from the Vista Point between the Dome and the rest of the crags. The meadow is covered with manzanita, as it turns out, not grass.

The first 1 1/2 miles from the Vista Point climbs rigorously and boringly up Kettlebelly Ridge. There are few, if any, vistas. Note the sparse underbrush here, one of many indicators of frequent forest fires in this dry country.

Approaching Indian Springs, the Crags' southeast wall suddenly pops into view. Indian Springs sits at its base, at 3600 feet. While a lovely, wooded spot and a 3 minute walk, save Indian Springs for the return trip. You'll find its cold, sweet water the most delicious you ever tasted.

Shortly after Indian Springs, the park boundary is passed, with the remainder of the trail on National Forest land. Soon after, the trail breaks out of the woods and starts up the actual Crags. This final mile, while quite steep, is so exquisite you won't think much about the exertion.

On emerging from the woods, all you see at first is the Dome, plus a massive, gray wall you're somehow supposed to climb. After the path snakes around a series of zig-zags and spires and up seemingly impossible cliffs, the green meadow finally comes into view. If you look carefully, you can sometimes see climbers on the dome from here. If you listen carefully, you can hear them.

The trail ends at the far end of the manzanita meadow, under a huge pine tree. The route up the dome is fairly obvious. Take some time, however to explore the edges of the meadow. The gentle granite slopes immediately surrounding it plunge 1000 feet on the other side, in a nearly vertical drop.

The real challenge is the dome. While not very high, it's a long way down if you slip. You can feel perfectly secure one minute, then suddenly, the angle changes a couple degrees....

From the trail end, a faint way trail leads past a small notch, near a tremendous drop-off, onto the dome. Make your way up, bearing slightly left, to a little outcropping. This is the hardest part and presents some danger, so please be careful. From there, a slight draw can be followed to the summit. It's rather unnerving but you should make it.

(By "should," I mean if you don't chicken out, not if you don't fall. Let's keep a positive attitude here.)

HEART LAKE

Destination: Castle, Little Castle, Heart Lakes
Location: T39N-R5W-Sec.24
USGS 7.5" Topo: Seven Lakes Basin, Dunsmuir, CA
Length: 1 1/2 miles
Water: OK
Access: Excellent, paved road
Season: May through October
Difficulty: Moderate
Elevation: 5400 to 6050 feet
Use: Non-motorized only
Ownership: Shasta Trinity NF and private
Phone: (916) 926-4511

Directions: Leave I-5 at the Central Mount Shasta City exit. Head west, then south, towards Lake Siskiyou. Turn left on the 7 mile paved road to Castle Lake. The Trail to Little Castle Lake begins along the lake's south shore.

Although Castle Lake is mainly a driving destination, small lakes in the vicinity offer opportunities to get out on the trail. You may even have time left to check out Gray Rock and Cliff Lakes (Chapter 34), up the South Fork of the Sacramento (Road 26), beyond Lake Siskiyou.

At 42 acres, Castle Lake is the largest natural body of water in the Trinity Divide range (not the Trinity Alps), the string of

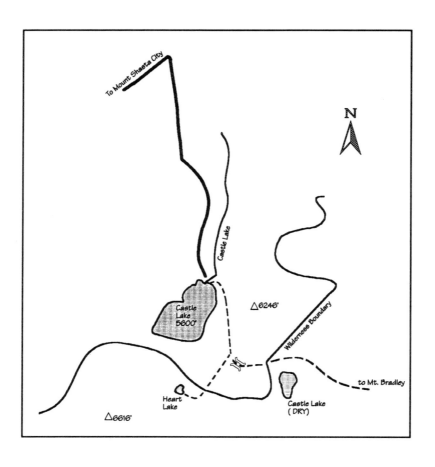

To Mount Shasta City

N

Castle Lake

△6246'

Wilderness Boundary

to Mt. Bradley

Castle
Lake
5600'

Heart
Lake

Castle Lake
(DRY)

△6616'

high peaks between the Sacramento and Trinity Rivers. Aside from Castle Crags, the range includes Mount Eddy, highest in the Klamath Mountains system at 9045 feet. Castle Lake offers easy road access, a nearby campground and superb fishing for brook and rainbow trout. It is set in a typical glacial cirque, with a sheer, gray rock headwall on the far side.

For many years, Castle Lake was the focus of fish stocking experiments conducted by the California Department of Fish and Game. They had a little booth where they measured every fish taken. The booth is no longer there but the University of California at Davis continues to conduct water quality studies at the lake.

Although Castle Lake tends to be crowded, the problem is easily alleviated since few people stray far from the parking area. If you need to get away from the chaos, the trail to the left, around the south shore, leads to Little Castle Lake and beyond.

Compared to it's neighbor, Little Castle Lake is a mere speck (and nearly dry in 1991), covering only 2 acres. Normally, it's about 8 feet deep with, they say, pretty good fishing.

The 3/4 mile walk up from Castle Lake rises 400 feet to a rocky crest, through woods of Shasta red fir and western white pine. It's quite steep but blessedly short. Little Castle Lake occupies an open, terrace-like bench framing a fine view of the upper Sacramento Valley. The trail continues east another 4 miles, over (to me) relatively featureless ridges, to the Mount Bradley Lookout.

Be aware that Little Castle Lake sits on private land. While public access is permitted, visitors should show appropriate respect. The Forest Service is attempting to acquire the property.

Nearby Heart Lake is about the same size as Little Castle Lake. A gorgeous pothole in a rocky pocket above Big Castle Lake, it is well worth a look. From the saddle between Castle and Little Castle Lake, a faint way trail ends up at Heart Lake in about 3/4 mile.

Actually, the area around the saddle is riddled with way trails and false paths. The best way to locate the Heart Lake Trail is to scramble up the rocks to the right (west) of the saddle above Little Castle Lake. After 100 feet or so, you'll find yourself looking down on a grassy flat, where two trails can be seen. Take the more obvious path (on the left). And don't worry too much about getting lost in this open highland dotted with green fields and clumps of phlox, pussy paws, delphinium and sedum.

The Heart Lake Trail, like the Little Castle Lake Trail, is rather steep but not very long. Pretty soon, you'll drop into the tiny Heart Lake cirque, with it's white headwall. The diminutive pool is clear and full of jumping fish. A large boulder juts into the middle of the lake from the shore, forming the heart shape. The view down from the stream outlet, 700 feet above Castle Lake, is spectacular.

Both Heart and Little Castle Lakes lie within the Castle Crags Wilderness Area. Castle Lake, with its paved access road, obviously does not.

Castle Crags

GRAY ROCKS LAKES

Destination: Gray Rock, U. Gray Rock, Timbered Lakes
Location: T39N-R5W-Sec. 31
USGS 7.5" Topo: Seven Lakes Basin, CA
Length: 1 1/2 miles
Water: Lots
Access: Good oil-top roads to terrible 4 wheel-drive road.
Season: June through October
Difficulty: Easy to slightly difficult
Elevation: 5600 to 6350
Use: Non-motorized in wilderness, any outside.
Ownership: Shasta-Trinity NF
Phone: (916) 926-4511

Directions: Leave I-5 at the central Mount Shasta City exit. Head west and south, around Lake Siskiyou, to Road 26; a wide, paved route up the Sacramento South Fork. For Gray Rock Lakes, turn left over a wooden bridge 6 miles beyond Lake Siskiyou. Park just over the bridge or drive as far as possible up the extremely poor, 2 mile road to the cramped trailhead. A small sign marks the path.

In the Mount Shasta City Park, a little spring bubbles into a stone impoundment. This enchanted spot is supposed to be the source of the Sacramento River, California's longest. From there, the waters flow through Lake Shasta into the Sacramento Valley and finally, past San Francisco Bay into the ocean.

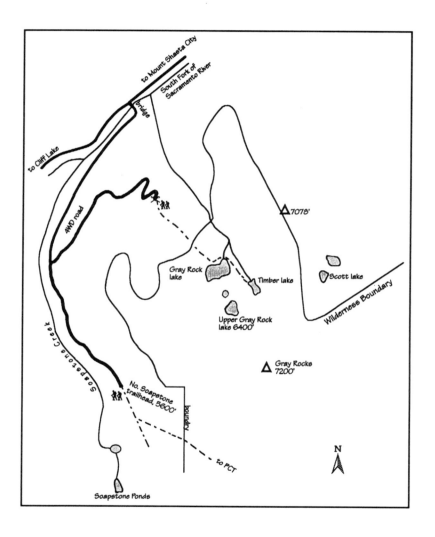

to Mount Shasta City

South Fork of Sacramento River

bridge

to Cliff Lake

4WD road

7078'

Gray Rock lake

Timber lake

Scott lake

Wilderness Boundary

Upper Gray Rock lake 6400'

Gray Rocks 7200'

Soapstone Creek

No. Soapstone trailhead, 5600'

boundary

to PCT

N

Soapstone Ponds

244

It's all very charming, except that it isn't the river's true source. The South Fork of the Sacramento, branching just south of Mount Shasta City, continues another 13 miles into the high peaks between the Sacramento and Trinity Rivers.

The South Forks' source is the far less poetic Gumboot Lake, an excellent fishing spot at the end of an easy, paved or oil topped road. Gumboot isn't as pretty as some other lakes. It's shore is brushy and it occupies the middle of a sparsely wooded field below a ridge.

A Gumboot, by the way, is a boot made of India rubber "gum," an old fashioned material for boots and waders. The lake, presumably, has eaten a few of them.

Aside from Gumboot, several extremely lovely lakes may be reached from Road 26. The turnoff to Castle Lake (Chapter 33), the largest natural lake in the Trinity Divide, is passed at Lake Siskiyou. Fifteen acre Cliff Lake lies between the Gray Rock Lakes and Gumboot Lake. At least one brochure claims Cliff Lake to be the area's prettiest.

Not likely. Personally, I bestow that honor on Timber lake, on the Gray Rock Lakes Trail. Cliff and Gumboot Lakes fall outside the Castle Crags Wilderness boundary.

Cliff, Timber and Gray Rock Lakes all occupy glacial cirques in a dark schist outcropping called the Gray Rocks. Easily seen on the left from Road 26, the Gray Rocks are unrelated to Castle Crags. The Gray Rock Lakes offers the only real hiking in the Wilderness Area from Road 26.

If you're wondering why I've described no 10 mile long backpacking trails in the Castle Crags Wilderness, only short day hikes, it's because the Wilderness is only 5 miles wide, covering some 12,000 acres. That's less than 1/10th the size of the Yolla Bolly-Middle Eel, which itself isn't very big. It's 1/50th the size of the Trinity Alps.

Just over the bridge to the Gray Rock Lakes' access road, a sign says "Gray Rock Lakes– 2 1/2 miles." Those miles cost me a muffler, an exhaust pipe and almost a radiator. A 4x4 with good clearance and power would have no problems, however. The road is extremely steep and bumpy, switching back and forth several times before attaining the trailhead a mile later.

Either park at the bridge or drive as far as you can. Parking and turnaround room is available at all switchbacks. For those opting to walk to the trailhead, a very steep trail cuts across the road's switchbacks. The road is better for walking up while this cutacross trail offers a quick route down.

From the tiny trailhead area, the narrow path heads into a huge, open glacial valley with a view of Shasta in the opposite direction and the Gray Rocks at the head. The path is moderately steep at first but it's only 1/2 mile to Lower Gray Rock Lake.

Lower Gray Rock Lake's 11 acre chunk of alpine splendor occupies a compact, wooded basin amid Western white pine, Shasta red fir and lodgepole pine. Above, the main cirque trends uphill to the left, where Upper Gray Rock and Timber Lake hold sway.

Both are smaller than Lower Gray Rock Lake but prettier, if possible. Especially Timber Lake, nestled against the main headwall near the summit, within view of Mount Shasta, only a few miles away. Both upper lakes lie a steep 1/2 mile above the lower pool.

Snow Mountain

Destination: High Rock Mountain., East Snow Mountain, West Snow Mountain, Milk Ranch.
Location: T17N-R8W-Sec. 10
USGS 7.5" Topo: Fouts Springs, John Muir Mountain, Crockett Peak, CA
Length: 4 miles
Water: No
Access: Very long, gravel and dirt roads
Season: June through October
Difficulty: Moderately difficult
Elevation: 5200 to 7056
Use: Non-motorized only
Ownership: Mendocino NF
Phone: (916) 963-3128

Directions: Leave I-5 at Maxwell and follow the signs to Stonyford and East Park Reservoir. At Stonyford, turn west up road M-10. Follow the signs to the Summit Springs trailhead.

M-10, though somewhat winding and steep, is wide and well maintained. It's paved at first, then gravel, then dirt. A well marked turnoff, 2 miles from the trailhead, leads up a narrow and steep, but driveable dirt road. The roomy trailhead lies 25 miles from Stonyford.

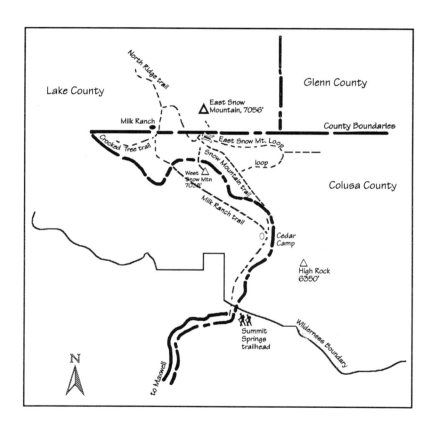

Lake County

Glenn County

North Ridge trail

East Snow
Mountain, 7056'

Milk Ranch

County Boundaries

Crooked Tree trail

East Snow Mt. Loop

Snow Mountain trail

loop

West
Snow Mtn
7056'

Colusa County

Milk Ranch trail

Cedar
Camp

High Rock
6350'

Summit
Springs
trailhead

Wilderness Boundary

N

to Maxwell

248

Snow Mountain is an impressive, 7056 foot summit rising from the west side of the Sacramento Valley's flat expanse (amid the "W" towns of Willows, Williams, Winters and Woodland). An astonishing number of people have never heard of it (although it's extremely popular among U.C. Davis students). Keystone of the 37,000 acre Snow Mountain Wilderness, the peak careens from sea level to 7000 feet in 25 miles, offering scenery, hiking and a spectrum of recreational opportunities. It may be the closest Federal Wilderness Area to San Francisco.

Snow Mountain is the second highest point in the Northern California Coast Ranges outside the Yolla Bolly-Middle Eel area (after the heavily roaded Black Butte, a few miles north). While neighboring peaks and lower ridges are composed of Franciscan formation sandstone, the Snow Mountain summit is an island of metamorphosed lava (mostly formed under the ocean), similar to that found in the Klamath Mountains.

South of Snow Mountain, the highest peaks of Coast Range system drops off rapidly. By Clear Lake and the Mayacmas, few top 4000 feet.

The inevitable serpentine rock outcroppings, so common in the Coast Ranges and Klamath Mountains, grace the flanks of Snow Mountain as well.

While Snow Mountain experienced minor glaciation during the Ice Age, there are presently no alpine lakes within the Wilderness. Many beautiful high meadows near the summit began as glacial lakes, however.

My personal bias in favor of alpine lakes and other clearly defined highlights is, I confess, the reason I saw fit to include only a single Snow Mountain trail. That is not to imply that the Wilderness does not contain other worthwhile and challenging paths. The Summit Springs route to Snow Mountain, however, towers above the others, both literally and in other ways.

The drive from the heat of the Sacramento Valley, beginning at the town of Maxwell, is as interesting and scenic— if not more so— than the hike itself. A few miles beyond Stonyford, road M-10 enters Fouts Springs Valley, a low elevation basin surrounded by steep, brushy slopes riddled with dirt bike trails. Snow Mountain's sheer east face rises grimly to the west, 5000 feet overhead. At least 4 Forest Service Campgrounds compliment the Fouts Springs area.

Beyond Fouts Springs, the road begins its relentless climb to the high ridge. Like most climbs up from the valley, the vegetation transitions from grass and brush, to digger pines and oaks, to ponderosa pine, Douglas-fir, madrone and grand firs. Sugar pine, Jeffrey pine and red fir (not Shasta red fir this far south), mark the middle elevations, with red fir the lone holdout on the highest flanks.

Past Letts Lake, the ever ascending road crosses the main crest of the range, then swings sharply north for a few miles. Look for a sign marking the Summit Springs turnoff. The last couple miles follow a narrow ridge top, with views east and west. The road here seems a little precarious but is not as bad as it looks. It soon ends at a roomy, open trailhead area with plenty of parking.

Virtually the entire south side of Snow Mountain burned in the fall of 1987. The aftermath can be seen all along the road and trail. This is a highly fire prone area, however, with plant species requiring an occasional burn to survive. The trail's first mile, for example, crosses fields of burned manzanita, black oak and white oak. All thrive on intense sunshine and cannot reproduce in shade. Their presence indicates recent fires prior to 1987.

When I visited in 1988, the oaks and many shrubs showed vigorous basal resprouting. Manzanita is less able to resprout but fire stimulates seed germination. Higher up, the blaze killed many Jeffrey and sugar pines. Near the summit, sadly, some lovely red fir stands were scorched. But again, this is dry country with vast acreage of grass and bare rock. Its sparse forests are largely confined to sheltered, upper elevation clusters.

The trail is steep at first, as it traverses a narrow ridge of burnt manzanita. Snow Mountain's main summit, composed of gentle domes covered with grass, gravel and scattered forest patches, can be seen from here, up a canyon in the distance, rising above a series of immense purple and gray scree slopes.

At the end of the first little ridge, the path climbs steeply towards High Rock, then levels off for a mile as it runs along the main front of the east facing crest. High Rock, a huge, barren dome, is easy to reach and worth a 15 minute side trip.

A few steps up to the ridge anywhere along this segment reveals outstanding views of the Sacramento Valley. Sutter Buttes, the world's smallest mountain range, rises out of the valley immediately opposite. The gray line of the Sierra Nevada marks the eastern horizon, with Shasta and Lassen dominating the northeast skyline.

At the Snow Mountain uplift's eastern base, the elongated, arrow straight valley containing Stony Gorge, East Park and Indian Valley Reservoirs, can be seen. The valley is shaped by the Stony Creek Fault, forming the boundary between the Coast Range and Central Valley geological provinces. The low foothills just east of the fault are unrelated to the Coast Ranges.

Beyond High Rock, the trail enters the woods and cuts to the west, into Cedar Camp basin, passing several side trails. The camp sits in a lovely sheltered bowl, beside a grassy flat. There's nary a cedar to be found there, however.

A junction at Cedar Camp directs hikers either straight ahead for Milk Ranch, or to the right, for the Snow Mountain summit, 2 miles away. The Milk Ranch route will take you to the summit in 4 miles. Milk Ranch offers splendid meadows and campsites and an approach to the summit from the north.

Past Cedar Camp, the trail winds steeply upward through woods, sheltered draws and grassy prairies. The East Snow Mountain Loop Trail comes in on the right, 1 1/2 miles above Cedar Camp. It also leads to the summit, via a route 1 1/2 miles longer than the one you're on.

For the last 1/2 mile before the summit, the trail follows a cedar lined draw for a ways, then ascends gravely slopes and open red fir stands, to the trail crest at a switchback in a small saddle. Look for ever improving views of East and West Snow Mountains, the area's twin towers. Located 1/2 mile apart on either side of the trail, East Snow (7056 feet), tops its western companion by 18 feet.

Two side paths take off from the 6850 foot saddle. For West Snow, take the left hand path. It's an easy, 1/4 mile hike to the summit. For East Snow, follow the East Snow Loop, which breaks off on the right. For Milk Ranch and the rest of the Wilderness, proceed straight ahead.

To reach the East Snow summit, follow the loop trail for 1/8 mile, over easy, open grades. You should come to a short spur on the left, which reaches the top in another 1/8 mile.

The summit view is similar to that from High Rock, except with added vistas north and west. Much of the trail looks west, on row after row of steep, rather low mountains covered with grass and pines. Goat Mountain (6100 feet) dominates to the south. The northward view reveals the full extent of the immense north/south ridge comprising the backbone of the Mendocino Range, culminating with the South Yolla Bolly.

INDEX

Listings include only trails and natural landmarks within Wilderness Areas. Trails named for landmarks are combined with the landmark. Only the first mention in each chapter is listed. Asterisk (*) means the page refers to the listing under "Destination" in the chapter head. Map listings are omitted.